Hearing the Hurt

Hearing the Hurt

Rhetoric, Aesthetics, and Politics of the New Negro Movement

ERIC KING WATTS

UNIVERSITY OF ALABAMA PRESS
Tuscaloosa

The University of Alabama Press
Tuscaloosa, Alabama 35487-0380

Manufactured in the United States of America

Typeface: Bembo

∞
The paper on which this book is printed meets the minimum requirements of American National Standard for Information Sciences—Permanence of Paper for Printed Library Materials, ANSI Z39.48-1984.

Library of Congress Cataloging-in-Publication Data

Watts, Eric King, 1963–
Hearing the hurt : rhetoric, aesthetics, and politics of the New Negro Movement / Eric King Watts.
p. cm. — (Rhetoric, culture, and social critique)
Includes bibliographical references and index.
ISBN 978-0-8173-1766-9 (trade cloth : alk. paper) — ISBN 978-0-8173-8616-0 (ebook)
1. African Americans—Intellectual life—20th century. 2. Harlem Renaissance. 3. African Americans—Race identity—History—20th century. 4. American literature—African American authors—History and criticism. 5. African Americans—Politics and government—20th century. I. Title.
E185.89.I56W37 2012
973′.0496073—dc23

2012000097

Cover: Winold Reiss, *Drawing in Two Colors (Interpretation of Harlem Hazz I),* ca. 1915–1920. Courtesy of the Library of Congress, Prints and Photographs Division.

For the energies responsible for my birth, growth, and sustenance—
my parents and my wife and children, Lynne, Tylen, and Tiana

Contents

Acknowledgments

The very idea of writing acknowledgments is both exhilarating and daunting. This sort of work arises out of spaces and times populated by folks who will be remembered here and by persons who will be sadly overlooked. I begin, therefore, by asking for your empathy as I approach a task that cannot be adequately accomplished. To all those unnamed, I thank you.

First, the lights shine on a group of persons who have sparked my imagination and set me off on productive paths. Michael J. Hyde has been generous beyond belief for opening up inspirational dwelling places and conversations. Earl Smith is a consistent and masterful mentor. Ever since we were classmates at Northwestern University, Kirt Wilson has been a great friend and even greater interlocutor. While on leave in 2004, I spent some extremely rewarding weeks visiting the University of Minnesota. I am very grateful to the faculty, staff, and graduate students of the Department of Communication Studies for a red-carpet welcome. In particular, I want to thank Karlyn Kohrs Campbell for her enduring generosity and Ronald Greene for reminding me of the power of the sublime. Speaking of helpful and timely prompts, many thanks to Christian Lundberg for bringing me back to the productive stresses of anxiety. My journey in scholarship has been aided in important ways by the influence of Martin Medhurst; his careful and insightful lessons regarding editing and writing over the years mark this writing.

My present academic home, the University of North Carolina at Chapel Hill, has been supportive and rewarding. On nearly every level and in nearly every way, the faculty, staff, and graduate students have made the completion of this book a joyful adventure, punctuated by numerous occasions to sharpen and challenge my thinking about how to pull it off. Similarly, my previous home at Wake Forest University allowed me to come into contact with several graduate students who graciously endured my wandering talks about the New Negro. I especially thank the students in a seminar in African

American rhetoric where we produced pertinent rhetorical biographies of folks like Nella Larsen and Aaron Douglas.

There are two chapters in this book that contain portions of works previously published elsewhere. I thank the University of Alabama Press for allowing the reproduction of parts of a chapter appearing in *Public Modalities: Rhetoric, Culture, Media, and the Shape of Public Life,* edited by Daniel C. Brouwer and Robert Asen. I also express appreciation to the University of South Carolina Press for granting the right to replicate in part a work appearing in *Queering Public Address,* edited by Charles Morris III. A book like this can be imagined as suddenly emerging in a flash of excitement, but in actuality it is manufactured out of the bits of words and documents housed in a number of archives and ordered by folks with seemingly endless patience. I am extremely grateful to the excellent staff at Howard University's Moorland-Spingarn Research Center, Beinecke Rare Book and Manuscript Library at Yale University, the Schomburg Center for Research in Black Culture of the New York Public Library; I am especially in debt to the Schomburg Center Scholar-in-Residence Program. I extend a hearty thank you to the archivists of the W. E. B. Du Bois Collection at the University of Massachusetts. And I offer a salute to the dedicated folks at the United States' Library of Congress.

Finally, I wish to acknowledge two former professors whose investments in me will forever push me toward whatever horizons I wish to bear my signature; I will always be thankful for the tutelage of Thomas B. Farrell and Michael C. Leff.

Introduction

Near the end of the final chapter of *Black Reconstruction in America*, his groundbreaking study of important sociological and cultural indices related to African American development following the American Civil War, W. E. B. Du Bois asked a question that reframed and clarified his motives for producing the work: "What is the object of writing the history of Reconstruction?"[1] The chapter, "The Propaganda of History," was dedicated to a searing critique of how writers, educational institutions, and publishers were aligned with an intense effort to produce an archive made up of new Southern histories; these educational resources, according to Du Bois, were meant to bear "authoritative" witness to the "harm" inflicted on the South by the North following the cessation of hostilities in 1865. These publications were circulated widely as documenting historical "truth," and they centered on creating a Negro "object" that could be immediately and unproblematically recognized as "ignorant," "lazy," "dishonest," and irresponsible. Du Bois clearly sensed a wide array of emotions backing the distribution of racist mythologies. The "object of writing the history" of the new South was not to distribute a putatively legitimate account of stories of human suffering and uplift; rather, Du Bois understood these histories as involved in the projection of fears and fantasies about blackness that triggered the articulation of fields of discourse promising a return to antebellum racial order, stories making "pleasant reading for Americans."[2]

The intersection of knowledge production and human emotions like pleasure and pain occupied Du Bois's imagination for much of his long life. As Toni Morrison has shown, the pleasure of writing and reading the American literary tradition is bound up with the "Africanist presence,"[3] understood by Du Bois to register the painful lived experiences of black folk. This conjuncture, then, sparked in him a conviction to manufacture African American artistic and aesthetic practices that could transform these affective sensibilities by telling alternate stories. Perhaps not surprisingly, many African

American scholars, journalists, poets, novelists, and painters have been similarly committed to projects designed to remake the "race." Indeed, at the writing of *Black Reconstruction,* Du Bois might have been reflecting on the apparent "demise" of an exciting art movement that brought together an assemblage of black and white creative agents that he helped launch two decades earlier. Popularly known as the Harlem Renaissance, this convergence of writers, intellectuals, entrepreneurs, editors, and graphic artists should be understood as choreographed through the self-consciously pious—but also sometimes "vulgar"—movements of the trope of the "New Negro."[4]

Among the volumes of works of history and literary studies on the "New Negro movement," we have seen emerge in recent years assessments that no longer focus on the "achievements" or "failures" of creative agents working to produce artistry in diverse forms for the advancement of civil rights, or the production of black national identity, or the promotion of radical Left politics, or the devotion to an emergent black modernist subjectivity in the form of the individual cosmopolitan.[5] Devotees of the New Negro movement will recognize an important change in regard to these studies: a sliding from judgments of "taste," often rendered through statements regarding black artistic propriety, durability, and sustainability, through preoccupations with intransigent aesthetic concepts like "originality" that structured coordinated efforts among intriguing New Negro characters seeking to dramatize the really "new," to explorations into the specific intellectual and ideological labor that was performed by opportunistic and creative configurations of artists and new media.[6]

Hearing the Hurt is motivated by an interest in assessing the pliability and mobility of the trope of the New Negro as it evoked the capacity to bring forth artistic and aesthetic practices and institutions. Tropes of the New Negro bonded together and dissolved social, cultural, and political commitments accompanying emerging forms of black subjectivity and heightened white interest in those subjects, practices, and institutions. In part, my project is consistent with the thinking of Henry Louis Gates Jr. as he understands the New Negro as a semiotic key in "a coded system of signs."[7] This work, however, is not neatly framed by an emphasis on semiotics; it recognizes but moves beyond the structural dynamics that are constitutive of investigations into the "mechanical" processes of signification. Rather than favor explicitly or implicitly dimensions of language at the heart of semiotics, this book foregrounds the rhetorical and aesthetic dynamics of discourse as a field of articulation and movement. Artistic and intellectual works of the New Negro, therefore, are treated as historically contingent "places" staging struggles amid competing interests regarding the very idea of a "New Negro."

Many scholars index the New Negro movement by bracketing it between the Great Migration and the Great Depression.[8] By these accounts the New Negro movement followed the flood of African Americans into Northern urban centers and was largely drained by the titanic collapse of Wall Street. There is good reason to think so. The New Negro movement required a population of black folk who saw themselves (more or less) as public agents, "free" to form clubs, newspapers, and magazines. This capacity to do public work on behalf of African America was forged on the killing fields of Europe during the First World War; it was also crystallized under the intense pressures of the Red Summer of 1919, when black folk fought through numerous race riots and were courted by radical Left politics promising an antiracist class-conscious activism.[9] And so, time *was* of the essence; clearly the New Negro movement was, in part, a product of a special kairos. David Levering Lewis, however, rightly points to concerted efforts to manufacture the movement.[10] Hence, it is wholly inadequate to attribute this "moment" in time to the vicissitudes of historical currents, as if the New Negro were suddenly washed ashore. We must treat the New Negro as a kind of "artifice." We must attend to the productive forces captured in black artistic practices, making emergent forms of black visibility and sensibility; we must trace how these tropes of blackness get set in motion through (and held hostage by) the complex and contradictory operations of and relations among aesthetic regimes invested in the production of the New Negro.

Since its emergence, the trope of the New Negro has shaped and animated diverse and divergent interpretive acts. As a metaphor, it refracted ways of seeing and knowing, encouraging alternative discursive and material associations and social configurations; it, thus, reveals itself to be an important and conflicted "time and place" to witness and explore ways of fusing together and pulling apart identifications. The New Negro drew into its gravitational field forms of discourse that could be reinvented and rearticulated as, in essence, not existing before, as the arrival of the unfamiliar that promised rebirth and renewal. The New Negro asserted blackness enveloped in an aura of possibility, sometimes of radical innovation; this was so because as a trope it was capable of performing the sort of masterful transfigurations one witnesses as metaphor morphs into metonymy, synecdoche, and irony.[11]

We should immediately recognize that the New Negro coordinated tropes of class, sex, gender, and geography. Alternative visions were at the same time new feelings, new soundings, and new sensations.[12] New Negro speech enticed folks with "black magic"—with the power to conjure, to wake the dead.[13] The very idea of the New Negro sparked serious disagreements regarding the social and political investments it enabled and the commitments it discouraged; the trope held forth great expectations for and intense sensations of social and political revitalization. *Hearing the Hurt* dramatizes the fluid and dynamic movements of the New Negro against a conceptual background that brings into relief the trope's resonance and its significance to the constitution of aesthetic experiences that turn a hearer toward the endowment of "voice." *Hearing the Hurt* conceptualizes "voice" as a unique means for making sense of the intersection of aesthetics, rhetoric, and the lived experiences of New Negro artists and activists working to manage intense political and cultural constraints. Voice refers to a phenomenon that is brought to life through artistic and aesthetic practices that move audiences into a sensual relationship with discourse, impelling a public acknowledgment of the affective and ethical dimensions of speech. As such, voice registers the specific historical predicament of speakers and writers, their forms of speech, and the conditions in which their speech was invented, performed, embraced, or denounced. Voice is our way of encountering diverse performances of the New Negro across time and space.

Hearing the Hurt contributes to the projects on the Harlem Renaissance in literature, American studies, and history by disclosing the manner in which rhetorical studies and aesthetics offer critical protocols for understanding how the attribution of "beauty" during this era was always already conditioned by the affective and ethical dimensions of tropes of "race." Chapter 1 anticipates these requirements by telling an "origins" tale of the New Negro starring W. E. B. Du Bois and Booker T. Washington. This chapter sets forth key theoretical concepts by coordinating affect, voice, and aesthetics. The chapter reframes the articulations of New Negro invented by Du Bois and Washington as counterparts meant to address virulent racist acts like lynching by animating different racial sentiments and memories. The chapter clarifies what is intended by artistic and aesthetic practices and the aesthetic regimes responsible for their (in)visibility and (in)audibility.

The New Negro movement was composed of a loosely organized and conflicting set of cultural institutions. There were some intensely competitive encounters among aesthetic practices and artistic activities organized by black nation building, literary commercialism, and white desires for a deeply penetrating make-over accomplished by consuming the raw flesh of the New Negro.[14] These competing resources, dreams, and fantasies fed the rhetorical invention, circulation, endowment, and suppression of voices. Hence, the New Negro was a hotly contested rhetorical and aesthetic "object," brokering complex and contradictory forms of discourse.

In chapter 2, "Of Beauty and Death," I treat Du Bois's collection of essays, *Darkwater: Voices from within the Veil,* as a potent intervention in the complex ways in which blackness and whiteness are productive of aesthetic values coordinated by attributions of beauty and ugliness. In this way, I read *Darkwater* as, in part, an aesthetic treatise concerned with exposing the manner in which the idea of beauty is racialized from within and how it is implicated in justifying social hierarchy. Appearing in 1920, *Darkwater* showcases the passion of Du Bois's rhetorical imagination as he lays bare the problems New Negro artists and their works encounter while negotiating the complex and contradictory features of Western aesthetics. This chapter explores the metabolism of tropes of "race" as they undergo energetic mobilization by the *Crisis* editor at the close of the First World War. *Darkwater* displays and enacts an artistic practice transfiguring returning black soldiers into New Negroes.

I am doing more than suggesting that Du Bois's project was caught up in producing the kind of political subjects "proper" to a postwar black national consciousness. Du Bois was keenly sensitive to the opportunity emerging in Harlem and elsewhere for the emergence of a politically viable and "autonomous" black public. Chapter 3, "The Last and Best Gift of Africa," examines Du Bois's attempt to bring a black public into being through the creative exercise of pragmatist aesthetics. Du Bois was introduced to the central tenets of pragmatism while studying under William James at Harvard. Resembling the pragmatist's experimentalism, Du Bois imagines and sutures African communal practices to diverse African American expressive forms by asserting their kinship with tropes of the New Negro; Du Bois's artistic practices allow me to figure a "conversation" between him and contemporary social theorists like John Dewey regarding the possibilities of shaping a less divisive American polity. In this sense, Du Bois argues that New Negroes offer ways of being and doing that should be seen as vital to an American public.

The power that a black public could muster seemed limitless because Harlem was brimming with racial optimism. The New Negro was alive, animated by some highly charged relations among folks caught up in presumably progressive social thought and inhabiting newly emergent spaces built for acting. The New Negro was an idealized character with tremendous value as an officer in the civil rights movement, as a member of the intelligentsia, as a comrade to the radical Left, and as a consumable body in Harlem's tourism trade. The New Negro movement, with its focus on the high-octane acceleration of the younger generation, was in part a celebration of youth culture. Chapter 4, "Negro Youth Speaks," explores the artistic and aesthetic practices productive of the monumentally influential anthology *The New Negro: An Interpretation,* edited by Alain LeRoy Locke. The chapter illuminates three interrelated movements: the significance of the emergence of Locke as an imprimatur of the New Negro, the unusual network of creative agents and aesthetic regimes made visible through the materiality of the anthology, and the ripple effect on artistic and aesthetic practices the work generated as it was widely circulated and consumed.

It is not improper to think that the New Negro, in part, was the occasion for a religious revival. New Negroes were expected to do the good work of a renaissance and were censured for blasphemy. Being reborn and rededicated to different causes, the New Negro, however, shared a commonplace: to give life. The New Negro sought social equality with whites and strove for equal work and pay; the trope bonded and set in motion discourses of self-determination and separatism, while painting a picture of a meritocracy where the only distinction that mattered was whether one would be anointed an artistic and intellectual genius, one of the artists and iconoclasts of a new generation.

As a mode of rhetorical practice, the movement of tropes of the New Negro can be mapped along fissures marking struggles among competing interests. As such, the New Negro went to the bone and marrow of Harlem's intelligentsia. The acid-dipped satire of the black journalist and novelist George Schuyler, for example, testified on behalf of the density and contested "authenticity" of the New Negro as an assemblage of tropes key to rhetorical invention and aesthetic practices impacting folks' work and play. Chapter 5, "Lampblacked Anglo-Saxon," focuses on how Schuyler's satire and criticism provoked the staging of the famous "debate" in the pages of the *Nation* with the budding poet Langston Hughes. The chapter offers a revised assessment of Schuyler's artistic practices as they were met with judgments rendered through the affective registers of New Negro jubilation.

As a trope dating to (at least) the late nineteenth century, the New Negro projected the dreams of elders. It came equipped with ideas in action. Hence, the New Negro was an exemplar of a peculiarly potent trope of "race"; it conditioned black folks' sentiments regarding the good life and how race, class, sex, and region contributed to or blocked its realization. The New Negro had body and motion and followed many ethics. The New Negro strutted the streets of Harlem. The New Negro spoke different "languages" and dialects; New Negroes spoke the truth and lied; some persons gleefully spoke *as a* New Negro,[15] and some dedicated tremendous energies railing against the very idea of a New Negro. The aesthetic and artistic practices of the New Negro were products of intersecting networks through which powerful impulses were captured and released in time with felt changes in the aesthetic values of dominant tropes of the New Negro. Chapter 6, "All Art Is Propaganda," takes up Du Bois's most acute critique of the politics of black aesthetics as he senses that the art movement had lost its civil rights bearings; the chapter confronts the dynamic interaction among the anxiety provoked by the increased publication opportunities provided by white aesthetic regimes, the disagreements among writers, editors, and activists regarding the impact these vigorous actions by aesthetic regimes might have on the visibility of blackness, and Du Bois's speech, "Criteria of Negro Art," delivered before an annual meeting of the NAACP in Chicago.

These flows of tropes, materials, and affects can be understood as action-reaction circuits that interrupted ongoing life and made spaces for a new awareness of the world, indeed, made new worlds emerge. They also provided robust feedback to the network of institutions and actors about which practices were favored by whom and why. And this feedback was narrated. It told stories of the experience of a momentarily short-circuited network and what folks did and did not do and why. Complicated emotions clustered in disturbing storm clouds about these transient ruptures, while other breaks gifted folks with games and fun. Chapter 7, "Paul's Committed Suicide," takes up the potent pleasures of transgression and subversion of stifling sexual mores and racial conventions in the domiciles of black bohemia. Wallace Thurman's roman à clef novel *Infants of the Spring* serves as a dramatis for sensing the pressures of New Negro orthodoxy as young artists sought the sort of "freedom" of expression promised, ironically, by the intense affects registered by the circulation of tropes of the New Negro. The chapter questions the impacts black middle-class propriety and civil rights marching orders have on an emerging black aesthetics.

Tropes of race coagulating within the metabolism of the New Negro did more than coordinate the movement of bodies in line with conflicting powerful interests; they rewarded preferred modes of identification and performance. In chapter 8, "You Mean You Don't Want Me 'Rene?," I explore the conjuncture of aesthetic and artistic practices producing Nella Larsen's second novel *Passing*. I argue that the context of Larsen's artistic work and life figure paradoxical understandings of the very notions of "race" and "sex" in the New Negro movement. The chapter ruminates on the impossible opening the novel eventuates as an ongoing challenge to operations of identification. I think it is altogether "fitting" for the final chapter in this project to dramatize the ridiculousness of "closure." It is in this manner that *Hearing the Hurt* reaches beyond the artificial boundaries of figuring out what the New Negro was *really* all about.

For now we should note that the New Negro could not be easily written out of existence no matter how hard some folks tried—and some folks tried very hard. This, then, is the story of the "life" and presumed "death" of the New Negro as a trope of race and an affective phenomenon endowing voice and imposing voicelessness, radiating in and through a variety of dwelling places. We shall witness the New Negro welcomed as guest and evicted as trespasser. In the end, what we shall see is the fascinating conduction and transduction of a trope of race that still emerges differentially in our voices. We will sense how tropes of race haunt our memories today and can still intermittently jolt us like a raw nerve.

1
"Hearing the Hurt"

In a lost essay entitled "The New Negro," submitted to *Century* magazine in 1887, W. E. B. Du Bois articulated the cultural mission that he believed was charged to him and his intellectual comrades at Fisk University—a time he later referred to as the "Age of Miracles"[1]—to make a new life for black folk by transforming America.[2] Thirteen years later, Booker T. Washington published *A New Negro for a New Century,* a book that accounts black patriotism in the Spanish-American War and asserts the moral and mental development of Southern "freedmen." Although more than a decade separates the production of these works, each idea was shaped by the dystopic racial relations choking black communities at the end of the nineteenth century. Each treatise offered education as the chief agency for black advancement for a "New Negro." Washington's New Negro contended that, "All education is good, but assuredly that [education] is the best which enables a man to *fit in* most readily with the conditions of life in which he finds himself."[3] One hears the echoes of the recommendation made five years earlier in his Atlanta Exposition Address that Southern black folk ought to "cast down your bucket" in order to raise a lifeworld out of the blood-stained soil cultivated by slaves.[4] Given their different lived experiences, these towering figures in African American history drew upon differing topics for inventing their versions of the New Negro; Du Bois's New Negro would be a person of letters, while Washington's creation would prosper through thrift and labor.[5] Both New Negroes, however, would be fiercely confident of their abilities to forge successful organizations for racial uplift. Washington's New Negro would eschew the Ivy League in favor of the agrarian life, turning black farming into agricultural industry. Meanwhile, Du Bois's New Negro would start "an institute of Negro Literature and Art," producing novels and plays constituting black communal values and beliefs.[6]

There are important lessons to learn here about the character of the New Negro as a peculiarly potent and pliable trope utilized in rhetorical, aesthetic, and artistic practices animating discourses of race and figuring notions of the social and the public. These lessons involve more than the conventional narrative of antagonism between the "wizard" of Tuskegee and the young man soon to emerge as the foremost black intellectual of the twentieth century. This book is concerned, in part, with achieving a better understanding of the compelling character of tropes of the New Negro, how they bonded together political and social commitments and how they dissolved others during the Harlem Renaissance, an era of emerging black collective subjectivity and heightened white interest in black creative expression. This work is also meant to disclose new ways of encountering the stubborn and complex nature of race, identification, and forms of subjectivity and their attendant ethical and affective dimensions. Thus, we would do well to appraise the material and discursive environments of Washington's articulations of a "new" black subjectivity and recognize their productive relation to Du Bois's rhetoric of a "new" black consciousness heralding in the New Negro movement. We should first consider the anxiety resonating in the Southern social imaginary due to a keen visibility and sensibility of black bodies following the end of slavery and Reconstruction. Frederick Douglass noted in 1889 "that when he was a slave, the Negro was largely outside of the nation's thought, but now his freedom made him discussed at every turn."[7] This is not to suggest that the institution of slavery failed to attract the nation's attention until it was on the verge of the American Civil War; rather, it is to note that, as "property" and "objects" of absolute white authority, black bodies as such were not imagined as posing a national dilemma.[8] It would take emancipation and Reconstruction for black people to enjoy the sort of "freedom" of movement and publicity that converted the Negro into a "problem."

The difficulty of black visibility is directly related to a question of the "proper" place for "blackness" in the American social imaginary. For Southern white "nationalists," the end of slavery let loose the black beast, driven by lust for white flesh and tainted with disease.[9] During the 1880s, the black body became grotesquely hyper-visible and contributed to rhetoric of the "Negro problem, a term used to encompass the whole issue of blacks' place in American life." Indeed, to many of Booker T. Washington's neighbors this "problem" called for the "total erasure of the black presence."[10] And as talk of emigration schemes—voluntary and forced—became louder and as terrorist acts butchering black bodies became more spectacular, blackness emerged in popular culture and media as a "new" aesthetic artifact made especially for white derision and destruction.[11] Racist cartoons, illustrations, advertisements, and short stories appeared in newspapers and magazines like *Century, Atlantic Monthly,* the *Atlanta Constitution,* and *Harper's Weekly:* "Editors typically depicted blacks as uncivilized animals and sexual fiends who hated whites and would attack them when least expected—a dangerous enemy in their midst. . . . The weeklies commonly disparaged blacks physically, referring to unpleasant smell, kinky hair, and thick skulls."[12] Blackness had always been experienced and "known" by white Southerners sensually—as an aesthetic product of the sensorium.[13] During the 1880s and 1890s, however, a vast array of cultural outlets were involved in the creation and distribution of blackness and the so-called Negro problem as aesthetic artifacts constitutive of an emerging white violent subjectivity.[14]

There is more to heed here, therefore, than a deterioration of the meager political power blacks had accrued during Reconstruction; we should sense a transformation in racial affection and sentiment. Uncle Tom grew fangs and became rabid: "Coon imagery was everywhere. . . . The distortion was so universal that it went essentially unquestioned among whites."[15] Race relations were gripped by a negative spiral that eventually threatened the very existence of the Tuskegee Institute since Washington's project relied upon the tolerance of Alabamans and their elected officials. Education was increasingly attacked as the chief corrupting influence among blacks, making them hostile to whites. But the South was also trying to emerge in this context as "new" and modern. The showcasing of industrial and economic maturity underwrote the Cotton States Exposition, and the need to portray a "New South" that worked peacefully alongside its black neighbors was felt by the planners. Washington was pegged to arrange a Negro exhibit and to deliver an opening day speech.[16] It is in this context that the Atlanta compromise was conceived and performed. Washington sought to stall the negative momentum of race relations by inventing a black subject agreeable to the social conditions of the present and necessary for the economy of tomorrow: "The Negro of the future would seek equality of industrial opportunity rather than waste time over questions of social equality. The rising Negro would become indispensable to the economy."[17]

Washington's New Negro emerged as an aesthetic artifact that encouraged if not careful handling, then regular maintenance. The sort of white Southern subjectivity to which this artifact appealed was steeped in affects of the past—throwback sentiments of paternalism and domestication.[18] Washington sought to stabilize a desperately deteriorating racial milieu. His speeches and writings mobilized tropes that animated sentiments and affects of a bygone era fondly recalled in Southern racial memory.[19] Washington's New Negro was progressive in the sense that it provided for the agencies of black collective economic development, but it was doggedly regressive in its orientation toward the "color line."[20] But this observation does not tell the whole story. Often juxtaposed as contra-Washington in contemporary narratives, we should note that Du Bois withheld criticism of Washington for six years following the Atlanta Exposition address in part because he engaged Washington's discourse from the point of view of a sociologist at a Northern black university—Wilberforce—and grasped the importance of Tuskegee.[21] It would be a mistake, therefore, to frame Du Bois's New Negro as strictly a counterstatement to Washington's creation, although some scholars have tended to do so.[22]

Du Bois's relationship with Washington was complicated. It negotiated strategic and ideological agreements and disagreements, struggles over limited financial resources, and differences in personalities. As the twentieth century dawned, Du Bois had come to believe that black folk possessed a racial endowment that made them capable of and responsible for perfecting the moral soul of America. His rhetoric about black subjectivity was racially dualistic and nationalistic—made up of distinct African and American characteristics.[23] Although Du Bois's sense of racial conservatism was at odds with Washington's materialistic Americanism, their discourses of a "new" black subject were largely complementary.[24] At the moment when Washington was dubbed *the* Negro leader, Du Bois could not have anticipated how Washington's New Negro, like the "bestial" black body it was meant to counter, would be subject to universalizing effects that would blot out alternative black aesthetic artifacts and marginalize different race alignments. His break from Washington would be better perceived as a gradual splintering; thus, his ensuing harsh criticism of Washington's words and deeds cannot be comprehended in terms of "pure" ideology.

Their eventual estrangement was in part constitutive of the allure of and contestation over the trope of the New Negro. For Du Bois, the New Negro was meant to do quite a bit more than "fit into the larger society."[25] The New Negro was made to transform America by producing black subjects who would generate the kind of aesthetic artifacts requiring "new" forms of perceptual care on the part of white folk. Each New Negro, however, should be perceived as capturing to itself the affective dimensions of a racial "crisis." Washington feared for the basic sustenance of Southern black life, thus, his version of the New Negro offered up triage for a hemorrhaging black social body. Endemic to such efforts were a series of calculated trade-offs in order to extend life. For Washington, the New Negro was largely a trope of stabilization and incremental economic improvement. To Du Bois, the "crisis" felt by black folk was a register of a national moral emergency. America's social body was in danger of death and decay. The key to assessing the capacity of tropes of the New Negro to be put in the service of complementary and contradictory usages—indeed, their capacity to produce those usages—can be found at the interstices of affect, voice, and aesthetics. This exploration of the New Negro will remain sensitive to the radical contingencies of the contexts out of which it emerged and in which it labored to reconfigure discursive forms and practices involved in the constitution of race, community, and nation during the New Negro movement. The lessons gleaned from our cursory view of Du Bois's and Washington's articulations were meant to highlight the fact that the New Negro was constitutive of powerful affects and sentiments sutured to specific political and cultural contexts and bodies.

The "Live Wire" of Voice

Tropes of race have the capacity to draw and transmit intense affects.[26] This observation leads to an explanation as to why we often feel like we are stunned by talk of race. It also opens up for us an accounting of the "failure" of poststructuralists to deconstruct race, to disable it and deliver it to a time and space where we may look back at it and wonder how we were ever that naïve and stupid about our humanity. Treating race like a social construction misses a crucial facet of its nature; the power of tropes of race emanates through a different order. The fact that tropes of race have form leads us to consider their effects as solely pertaining to their structure. We have been asking some of the right questions but seeking answers in the wrong way. Elsewhere I detail the troubles experienced by researchers of public address regarding the manner in which conceptions of race emerged.[27] Rhetorical studies have recently been marked by a general embrace of flesh and blood and the messiness of undecidability.[28] I am reminded of the scene in the film *The Matrix* where Neo gets advice about the nature of "things" from a young boy in the Oracle's living room; the young boy answers Neo's unasked question about how he can seemingly bend a spoon with his mind by commenting that "there is no spoon."[29] What is suggested here is not merely that the signifier "spoon" has no referent; rather, we are led to grasp that a "spoon" occupies a relation to us that cannot be understood as external to us. Put differently, the "spoon" may be said to have no "reality," but it does sustain actuality as an imagined "object" of our subjectivity. Similarly, the vitality of "race" cannot be disposed by asserting it as a "fiction"; its force to move us into relations corresponding to its "logic" resides *actually* elsewhere.

This vigor is, in a sense, always elsewhere. We can begin to trace its elusive character by contemplating the fact that our bodies respond physiologically to the sights and sounds of our environments. As organic beings, our environments move in and through us. If this movement ceases, *Dasein* moves toward demise.[30] From a phenomenological point of view, this movement is what we call experience. But it would be an uninhabitable world indeed if all of our experiences registered identically. The sheer monotony would drive us mad long before our bodies turned to dust.[31] Fortunately, the world offers differential experiences that are constitutive of affective energies we feel as changes in quality and intensity.[32] They mark us and we, in turn, punctuate them. We "locate" them in times, spaces, activities, and relations. I will return to these sensemaking practices below, but for now let us get better acquainted with the sensation of affective energy.

Affective intensity is a measure of the strength and duration of the impact of an experiential encounter.[33] At its climax, its most impressive register, it can be felt as terrifying and glorious, beautiful and horrendous, shocking and joyous, chaotic and erotic.[34] Affective intensity is constitutive of a coming apart at the seams, a short-circuiting of the whole being that begins on the "surface of the body" but triggers "depth reactions" throughout the body.[35] Intensity radiates and vibrates and can be imparted to inanimate objects, seemingly bringing them to "life." Consider striking a metal pole with the palm of your hand. The pole vibrates with intensity and at a frequency that can be heard. One might say the pole is *expressing* this intensity.[36] It would not do, however, to say that the pole itself was intense. We too can be "struck" in a way that sends chills down one's spine or causes one to gasp or giggle. When human beings express affective intensity, we often feel the need to articulate the sensation in an intelligible manner, to qualify it in emotional terms: "Emotion is qualified intensity, the conventional, consensual point of insertion of intensity into semantically and semiotically formed progressions, into narrativizable action-reaction circuits, into function and meaning."[37] Part of the elsewhere of affect, therefore, is generative of the logic of language and speech. We are driven by the capacities of language to try to envelop affect in words—what Richard Weaver called God and Devil terms[38]—to stitch many words together into stories radiating affective energies and, over time, to erect universes of discourse dedicated to the structures of intensity.

The signifier can transmit affective intensity, but the signifier does not precisely "make" it. Returning to the example of the pole: if the pole could somehow "think" its "thingness," it would experience the intensity of the slap as an unanticipated encounter with a hand slapping, a sudden and powerful emergence of a phenomenon into its "world." Affect does not reside in the hand proper nor in the pole; affect is emergent in the space *between* them. Affect names the experience of the virtual bursting through and becoming the actual. In the world of human being, we think and speak our thingness to the point of narcissism. In fact, narcissism can be thought of as a term describing the intensity of the sensation that is experienced in thinking our thingness. Thus, we experience affect as it registers emergence of an encounter across or through an opening in what we think we "know," as it keys a disconnection *in* form itself. Its intensity is directly proportional to the felt "violation" of the structure that "carried" it. The chaos and uncertainty of the world and our felt sensation of affect are managed by language and, in particular, the production of emotion. Signifiers, however, are always failing this "capture," and the "escape of affect" resonates "to the exact degree to which it is in excess of any normative line."[39] Speech tames affect, but at the same time it sets it off—launches affect into "flight"[40]—because signifiers are porous. The functionality of language can be thought of as "expectation" and the resonation can be called "suspense."[41] One last return to our actions toward that pole: the pole is functional (we have an "expectation" regarding what it's "doing" there), but its functionality undergoes change, is "suspended" by affect. We may convert it into a musical instrument by hammering out a tune. The pole makes a noise with qualities recording intensity and in surplus of its function.

It is vital not to equate affect with emotion,[42] but the emotions are crucial to an "affective theory" of trope and rhetoric.[43] Such a "theory" would need to lay the ground rules, so to speak, regarding the conditions of speech—not just this but, as Anatole Broyard has put it, "the conditional nature of the human condition."[44] The functionality and rationality of speech has earned it high value among scholars who regard symbolic exchange as the essence of modernity.[45] But the affect of speech, as I have been saying all along, lives "outside" of the phoneme, on a "live wire" disconnected from the semiotic code. The answer to the question, "What is this speech doing?," cannot be answered unless one understands speech as traversing spaces and times: "What is this speech doing here and now? What did it do then and there? And what might it do in places unknown and in times yet to be?" These notations do not "freeze" speech into any "original" context; they suggest that its labors are always transcontextual. The way into the affective dimensions of speech—to sense the resonance of energy—is to account for its discursive and material relations, the when, where, how, and among whom of its transmissions.[46] It is in this manner that we can perceive how affective energy does not automatically undue hegemony; intense affects can tighten or dissolve alignments and social configurations, depending on the discursive and material characteristics imbricated in the fluid ecology of the system. The emotions allow us to trace the wavelengths and circuits of affect, but we should not fool ourselves into thinking we will successfully hunt affect down. We can, however, become more sensitive to its vibrations and listen for its sounds.

Voice is the sound of affect. I am making a self-consciously humanistic assertion here. Although some scholars think of "voice" as capable of emanating from nonhuman beings or extrahuman sources,[47] I consider voice to be the most essential quality *of* being human. As the audible projection of persons, voice announces the felt experience of one's immediate relation to and inseparability from the world and others. Voice registers the "once occurrent concrete actuality" of being alive,[48] and it is "vibrationally experienced."[49] If affect is elusive, then so is voice; the difficulty of discussing voice is that "the vocabulary is inadequate. . . . It is not that our vocabulary is scanty and its deficiency should be remedied: faced with the voice, words structurally fail."[50] Affect makes its getaway due to this breakdown, and it does not occur in a vacuum. It is situated and up in the air. Voice carries being-in-the-event but refuses to make sense of the event. It "enables speech phenomena" but does not make a statement.[51] Louis Althusser thought of it as a "hail," Michael J. Hyde considers it a "call," and David Appelbaum a "cough."[52]

As with affect and the emotions, we cannot equate voice with speech. The audibleness of voice can be "conceived of . . . as coinciding with the very process of enunciation," the emergence of subjectivity desiring sensemaking.[53] Hence, voice does not occupy the private body for very long; it seeks a hearing and often "dies" before receiving one. A condition for voice, thus, is social. In a sense, voice "exists" without an Other to recognize its emanation; but this conception is poverty. The richness of voice is endowed as a function of the social body. This is so because when "I" speak, voice is situated between my "experience and representation of [my] experience."[54] It lives (momentarily) at the junction of my body's nature and our shared culture. The fact that "I" am writing these words refers to the instability of the emerging subject making sense and to the very opening through which affect takes off. The signifier "I" is in motion, always opening up; everything "I" say is at once a regimented signification—a placeholder for meaning—and a mobile morphology alive with alterity: "And even more: if the voice is the opening toward Being, the opening which extracts us from submersion in the existing things and disrupts the closed circle of self-presence and self-reflection, does it not follow that the voice ultimately coincides with Being itself?"[55] As with the relation of thunder and lightning, voice occurs at the precise point of the unleashing of the intense current of affect, yet it echoes along the limits of the subject's hermeneutical contexts. Its radiation, therefore, cannot satisfy the conditions for the rich actualization of voice; voice requires an acknowledgment of the affective and ethical dimensions of speech.[56]

Voice is a happening, an event made possible by human sociality. The "kernel" of speech is "planted" in voice, and speech implies an addressee. Voice is uncontrollable and signals the undecidability of affect's aliveness, it also announces a *statement-in-the-making.* As we go about our busy lives, we are "called" by many voices, tempting, singing, and threatening voices. To the extent that we resonate with a form of speech, we become attuned to the emotions vibrating along its edges. If we heed the sound and turn toward it and acknowledge it, opening ourselves up to the affective dimensions of speech, we endow the voice and convert its resonance into a "pure injunction," an ethical dilemma. Although a person's speech may be offering a series of premises about, for instance, the problems of living without adequate food or shelter, the endowment of voice suspends the statement, "and we have to supply the statement ourselves" in the form of "his our her moral decision, by the act."[57] It must be underscored that voice provokes evasions of responsibility as much as it might bring about acts of love and care. One does not necessarily embrace intensity.

Voice is an approach to publicity. I will elaborate in chapter 3 on notions of "the public," but for now let me associate the public with identification. In the uproariously impolite film, *Blazing Saddles,* Cleavon Little is harshly rebuffed as the first black sheriff in the all-white town of Rock Ridge.[58] As he strolls the town's streets trying to greet the citizens, an elderly woman shatters his fantasy of racial harmony by deflecting his salutation with her blunt reply: "Up yours, nigger!" But when the town is threatened by a giant outlaw called Mongol, the townsfolk plea for the sheriff's help. After the sheriff stymies Mongol's rampage, the old lady privately offers him a pie and apologizes for the earlier racial slur. One could argue that the peace offering was an acknowledgment of the affective and ethical dimensions of the sheriff's speech, endowing voice. This moment certainly holds the potential for an alteration in the form of the town's sociality. But as a private gesture, accompanied by a request that it remain private so as to avoid being identified with the black sheriff, it is not a mode of publicity. A public may emerge out of a social context only if the acknowledgment of voice is accompanied by recognition among members of a community of shared interests regarding the speech act. Voice is, thus, concurrent with *processes of identification* among persons and speakers bringing into existence a "public." The emergence of a public is not necessarily, nor even probably, innocent. US history alone tells us that lynch mobs and genocidal campaigns have spilled out from such occurrences. But this observation makes the work more urgent. Rhetoric is especially concerned with the relations among discourses, audiences, and publics, and so in this work voice integrates affect into rhetorical theory.

Bringing voice into alignment with forms of publicity and practices of identification energizes our exploration of tropes of race and the contexts of the New Negro. Let us return to the complementary images of the New Negro painted by Booker T. Washington and W. E. B. Du Bois. The social contexts confronting black folk in the South at the turn of the twentieth century were horrible. Outside the legal and economic structure of slavery, with its emphasis on the exchange and use values of "property," black folk descended into what could be termed a form of "bare life."[59] I am not suggesting that slavery was somehow "better" for black folk; indeed I am saying quite the opposite. During slavery, the loss of a slave registered as value negative. The sell-off, whipping, hobbling, or death of a slave, was often endured by the planter class as a *sacrifice* for the maintenance of the social order.[60] Following slavery and Reconstruction, the eradication of the black "beast" was transfigured into a heroic venture, accompanied by intense fear and hatred toward the "crime" of being black and deep enjoyment of the privilege of being white. Post-Reconstruction ushered in a racially polarized context wherein the affects of racial antagonism, violence, and dread congealed into a barrier against sensing the loss of blackness as regrettable to Southern sociality. Put this way, Washington's New Negro sought to generate enough intensity as to momentarily disconnect current emotional values, rituals, and practices, and to recall bygone sentiments of paternal affection suggesting that the disappearance of black folk would be forfeiture for the South once again. In some important ways, Washington succeeded too well. The relations among the New Negro, Tuskegee, white Southerners, and the general black population suffered sedimentation. This was the staging for Du Bois's New Negro and the affects resonating from its "body" and voice. No longer enduring the barely improved bare life, Du Bois's artifact sought to "shock" the system (again) and make emergent black political life. This was a tough grind because Jim Crow laws also resonated with intense gratification of white supremacy; thus, the voice of white nationalism was "structurally in the same position as sovereignty."[61] Life hanging in the balance, black folk who shared Du Bois's vision for an integrated social body became increasingly dedicated to a politics of agitation.

The Social Body in Crisis

The prospects for bringing about social equality were limited by the kinds of vehicles needed to spread the word and image of the New Negro. When in 1909 the NAACP was cofounded by Du Bois, he invented and took charge of the organization's official organ, the *Crisis.* New York City and Harlem, in particular, enabled the staging of a varied distribution of New Negro visibility and sensibility. Jacques Ranciere, in *The Politics of Aesthetics,* contends that "a distribution of the sensible . . . establishes at one and the same time something common that is shared and exclusive parts." Embedded in the production of objects and relations among subjects are modes of sense perception favorable to elite regimes that acquire the authority of propriety corresponding to the conditions of their emergence.[62] This perspective on aesthetics concentrates on the character of the materialization of subjects and bodily forms throughout the social. I maintain that these "emergencies" can be sensed as occurrences of affect and heard as voice. Hence, in this work aesthetics ranges beyond its traditional pet treasure—the domain of art; it refers to a way of thinking about the coordination and competition among institutions, groups, and persons as forms of life are produced and circulated. This distribution is not simply a diffusion of "objects" for admiration and contemplation; rather, it contains a "logic" of apportionment of times, spaces, and ways of being and making. Importantly, as Terry Eagleton remarks, aesthetics encourages sensitivity toward the conditions of possibility for configurations of the social and the political, where the aesthetic practices that seem to constitute a "law" of relationality produce the "very forms of subjecthood which will form the basis of political unity."[63] This sort of unity is fluid and dynamic and necessitates the formation of cherished rites and rituals to rearticulate pledges of allegiance. Roger Scruton, in *The Aesthetic Understanding,* considers these procedures and practices as essential to educating the senses and emotions regarding our experience of specific contents and contexts, rituals and spectacles. We do not merely "know" something to be "right" and "wrong," we *feel* it to be so.[64] The NAACP, then, marked a crucial change in the conditions for the distribution of black sensibility; as a regime announcing itself as a player in the New Negro art world, it helped to constitute and animate in the *Crisis* "new" aesthetic practices—innovative ways of making race and the New Negro.[65]

By the time the *Crisis* had wrapped up its first volume, Du Bois's incarnation of the New Negro coursed through the arteries of the NAACP's journal. In a sense, the *Crisis* was the first national periodical dedicated to bonding together the discursive and material resources for making up a New Negro world. In the April 1911 edition of the *Crisis,* Du Bois introduced his readers to an allegory that he would reinvent in his writing for years to come, prophesying a divine spirit and purpose for the souls of black folk. In the "Easter" editorial for the inaugural year of this influential journal, Du Bois portrayed the bodies of black folk as aesthetic artifacts designed by white supremacists for persecution, crucifixion, and burial: "Sweating and deep of breath the pale-faced murderers worked and delved, digging a cavernous grave and walling it with Oppression." The bloody deed was accomplished through an unholy alliance between Northern and Southern "brothers." Blackness was lynched "for the culture and supremacy of the White Race. . . . But suddenly the World was wings and the voice of the Angel of the Resurrection beat like a mighty wind athwart their ears, crying . . . 'He is risen.'" Black spirit was brought back to life through a moral force that Du Bois considered both a blessing and a curse. This power emerged from the duty toward and the bond that black folk have to the soul of America. This moral force was also made up of black folks' collective refusal to die. Thus, black spirit was reborn a savior. Having "new" life, the black spirit literally underwent a renaissance; it was "risen to a new literature and the faint glimmering of a new Art." For Du Bois, this black artistic revival was inherently political and ethical: "risen to a dawning determination to be free; risen to a newer and greater ideal of Humanity than the world has known."[66]

Du Bois's moral vision was piercing. He perceived the "faint glimmering" of an emergence of black political and social life. But Du Bois also believed that if a glimmer was ever to burn brightly it could not be left up to Providence or the dogged determination of black folk;[67] it required strategies, various modes of productive practices, and institutional resources. In other words, a renaissance can be made to *appear* to be immaculately conceived, but it obligated a special kind of human labor to create the conditions for its fulfillment. For example, in an adjacent editorial about the death of the black writer Francis Watkins Harper, Du Bois used the obituary to call "attention to the literature of American Negroes." Harper's life deserved distinctive acknowledgment, Du Bois said, because she wrote tirelessly on behalf of "the abolition cause" and due to "her attempts to forward literature among colored people."[68] Creative writing and activism were proffered as modes of doing and making a "new abolitionism (immediate winning of civil rights for African-Americans)."[69] Securing such rights meant that white Americans must come to appreciate the ethos of black folk and especially to see and hear the aspirations and desires of the "best" and brightest of black youth. To this end, Du Bois announced his plans to devote increased editorial space in the *Crisis* to the literary work of the newly risen black talent.[70] Let us not fail to note that Du Bois's aesthetic practice of calling out for would-be writers was engraved with an ethical imperative regarding working for the New Negro and was itself an early mechanism for lifting black talent onto a national stage and into New Negro networks.

During the first decade of the life of the NAACP, Du Bois forged the *Crisis* into his personal trumpet to blare a courageous and unrelenting call of conscience for his mostly black and educated readership.[71] As a materialization of his rhetorical imagination, the *Crisis* was at times a militant and hard-hitting "newspaper" determined to demonstrate "the unreasonableness of prejudice."[72] Hence, month after month Du Bois spat fire and poured molten lava onto its pages and into coffee shops and barbershops to cultivate and publicize an emerging black communal politics organized and mobilized by the New Negro. As I discussed above, both Du Bois and Washington seized the opportunity to use the New Negro to further each man's strategic goals. The *Crisis,* however, amplified Du Bois's capacity to remake black subjectivity and consciousness to ensure that the NAACP could be populated with political agents proper to its mission. He frequently spelled out to NAACP board members that his writings in the *Crisis* and elsewhere were responsible for making "the N.A.A.C.P. *possible.* To-day it is not possible [because] . . . the men who will fight in these ranks must be educated and *The Crisis* can train them: not simply in its words, but in its manner, its pictures, its conception of life, its subsidiary enterprises."[73] In this context, it is no longer so startling and perplexing to comprehend how Du Bois shifted from being friendly and tolerant of Washington's New Negro to harshly criticizing Washington and his legacy. Washington's "statesmanship," Du Bois wrote in the *Crisis,* was "ineffective in practice because under its aegis—under the silence, the absence of criticism, the kindly sentiments and wide-spread complacency, we have seen grow up in the South a caste system which threatens the foundations of democracy, and a lawlessness which threatens all government."[74] Orchestrated by a redistribution of black sensibility, the NAACP emerged in this time period as a regime of New Negro cultural expression capable of resisting and redirecting circulations of power. And so, the *Crisis* was no mere medium for the NAACP's judicial efforts; it was productive of aesthetic practices and aesthetic artifacts that encouraged new ways of being black in the world. Hence, Du Bois even refused to curb his condemnation of Washington's impact on the new generation of black thinkers and writers in the *Crisis* obituary marking Washington's death in 1915, saying that "we must lay on the soul of this man, a heavy responsibility for the consummation of Negro disfranchisement, the decline of the Negro college and public school and the firmer establishment of color caste in this land."[75] Hearing Du Bois, we might arrive at the troubling conclusion that black folk should also lay on the soul of Washington the responsibility for threatening the emergence of the New Negro movement. It is a convenient polemic for Du Bois to assert; it concealed the manner in which his New Negro did not mark a purely "post-Washington" turn. I want to suggest rather that Du Bois digested as nourishment Washington's tropes of the New Negro, passing some facets as excrement. Washington's autobiographies and editorial enterprises were stimulated by a moment of dire "crisis." It demonstrated a form of pragmatic action in tune with its times and places. Again, their New Negro artifacts cannot be summed up as simple antitheses; Du Bois's New Negro expressed the son rebuking the ways of the father—even as those ways made his living possible.

Booker T. Washington's political and rhetorical strategies were also instrumental in the provocation of Du Bois's politics of agitation. The dampening effects of Washingtonian leadership ignited in members of the Niagara Movement the strong desire to rage against the racist machine, rather than silently bend to put up with its intolerances.[76] Involving much more than an antiracist discourse, Du Bois and some of his comrades and competitors adapted arguments meant to convince other blacks that Tuskegee-styled compromise was inadequate to contemporary exigencies. The *Crisis,* Du Bois explained in his earliest editorial, "takes its name from the fact that the editors believe that this is a critical time in the history of the advancement of men."[77] Du Bois broadened the scene of the calamity facing humanity. In time, his sensitivities regarding the trouble confronting America—the problem of the color line—would lead him to split from the NAACP altogether due to its relatively narrow focus on the statutes of racial law. Meanwhile, the *Crisis* was launched expressing both a seriousness of purpose and a philosophy of social life that presupposed the moral imperative of bringing about social equality among the races.

Three years prior to the inaugural issue, Du Bois penned an essay entitled "The Value of Agitation" published in the short-lived Leftist journal the *Voice.*[78] In this work, Du Bois intellectualized "agitation" as an "unpleasant" action by sometimes "unreasonable" persons hoping to alert the world of some "evil" in need of redress. The essay set forth an argument about the flaws of being human and the necessity of the "agitator." In the first editorial in the *Crisis,* the editor again defended "agitation" as a "necessary evil," but this time he sounded more like he was screaming; the editorial was a short, forceful bark from a body in agony. In just a few short years, the prognosis, it would seem, had become dire. Even the title was clipped to one word: "Agitation." Both writings described agitation as something that has to be done, but in the *Crisis* this contention trembled with intensity: "The function of the Association is to tell this nation of the crying evil of race prejudice. It is a hard duty but a necessary one. It is Pain; Pain is not good but Pain is necessary. Pain does not aggravate disease—Disease causes Pain." We are not here reading a contemplative scholar, we are confronted with an agitator in need of acknowledgment: "Some good friends of the cause we represent fear agitation. They say: 'Do not agitate—do not make a noise: *work.*' They add, 'Agitation is destructive or at best negative—what is wanted is positive constructive work.'"[79] The silence urged by "friends" resembled and resounded the quandary Du Bois described in the opening passage of *The Souls of Black Folk,* where the "Negro problem" clung to the surface of the black body like scar tissue. Polite conversation substituted for the essential unasked question: "How does it feel to be a problem?"[80] If uttered, the question would function as an invitation to speak of one's experiences of racial injustice—to do more than have it marked on one's skin. The black body would announce its "racial" subjectivity, enunciating searing sensations and a readiness for political action. In *Souls,* Du Bois proceeded to speak *as if* the question had been asked. In the *Crisis,* we have run out of time. Impatient with politeness, the agitator takes up the perspective of Elaine Scarry's tortured subject in *The Body in Pain.* The experience of pain takes language away, but it also pushes the subject outward toward new images, new metaphors to remake the world.[81] Pain is productive: "A toothache is agitation. . . . It is supremely useful, for it tells the body of decay, dyspepsia and death. Without it the body would suffer unknowingly. . . . The same is true of the Social Body"[82]

Agitation involves movement and soundings. It excites and arouses attention and awareness. It demands a questioning. "How does it *feel* to be a problem?" The utterance of the query presents an opening for the acknowledgment of the ethical and emotional dimensions of speech. It also allows for the transfiguration of black objects into subjects, the spilling out of noise into the air, in search of a willing and daring sense maker. "Anything is better," Broyard writes plaintively, "than an awful silent suffering."[83] But Du Bois was also putting together the notion of how persons might develop habits of heightened sensitivity and courage when confronted with the sound of their own terrors, sounds amplified by the color line. If we bend an ear away from Du Bois and toward white supremacist bellowing, we can nearly detect the grunting agreement of the racist who "agitates" concerning the diseased black sore festering on the "hand," a wound so seemingly painful to behold that it does not matter that blackness and whiteness are separate as the fingers. The supremacist rallies the mob and unleashes the hounds—the black "cancer" must be cut out or terrorized into remission. Du Bois was well aware that the national social body fervently and violently rejected the very idea of social equality with black folk. This rejection marked the heart of the actual illness of America's body. Broyard observed that, "To be sick brings out all our prejudices and primitive feelings."[84] I sense a Du Boisian commonplace with Broyard that can be perceived through synecdoche. In the same way that Burke noted that a "cure contains the disease,"[85] we need only perform a modest alteration to reveal this sentiment: if *un*acknowledged, our prejudices and primitive feelings will make us sick.

The gulf yawning between white and black folk seemed immense, and its jagged slopes presented treacherous travel. Du Bois understood powerful affects radiating out of that chasm, the "strange fear" white folk have when sensing the pain of black folk: "Outside this physical shrinking which we have in common with children, comes the mental recoil—the disinclination to have our thoughts and ideas disarranged and upset. And still further on comes the moral dread of blame—of facing the man we have wronged and *hearing the hurt* from his own quivering lips."[86] This endowment of voice was itself a function of an ailing social body, a siren and a wail mortally situated and poetically resourced. As a metaphor, the social body discloses the relation our personal selves have to an imagined "us." Experiencing pain, we are flung out of ourselves toward the other; and when we hear the hurt of others, we are magnetized and repelled. Broyard discusses the paralyzing effect of the sound of his father's dying pain: "At that moment, by way of bidding the doctor good-bye, my father declared himself. We heard a cry that sounded as though it came from a creature that had just acquired a voice in the farthest reaches of pain, and was now exploring that pain and that voice simultaneously, intermittently confusing one with the other . . . an unearthly sound, unable to decide whether this was the most beautiful sound I'd ever heard or the most bloodcurdling."[87]

Once again we have arrived at the "imperative resonance" of voice.[88] What will you do? Will you flee or will you endure this sound and turn toward it because you hear a tonal quality of yourself in its "beauty"? Du Bois and other workers for social justice felt a strange emergence of black soul and dignity in creative expression. The New Negro was constitutive of a coordination of tropes to draw together the words, images, and deeds to produce and distribute an orchestration of sensibility regarding racial cooperation. But, I have been telling you from the beginning that voice is undecidable and uncontrollable. Du Bois would learn this painful lesson in due time; his grip on the production of the New Negro was illusory from the beginning. But we are getting ahead of ourselves; in the beginning the New Negro was "birthed" and reared through the fires of race hate and world conflagration. And the author of *The Souls of Black Folk* would soon unleash a passionate critique of the "souls" of white folk through a conjuncture of the habituation of racism and the very idea of "beauty."

2

"Of Beauty and Death"

W. E. B. Du Bois's *Darkwater*

When W. E. B. Du Bois returned to New York harbor in February 1919, after witnessing firsthand in Europe the world trying to destroy itself, he was haunted by the intuition that the First World War had somehow followed him back across the Atlantic. Resuming his responsibilities as editor of the *Crisis* (Jessie Fauset had ably managed the journal in his absence), Du Bois once again set his pen against racial injustice. But the splendid sight of "colored soldiers" in France could not be reconciled with the photographs of mutilated black bodies awaiting him on his desk at the *Crisis* headquarters on Fifth Avenue. Sifting through dozens of pictures of murderous rage exacted on black military personnel and their communities sent to him from brave NAACP operatives like Walter White, Du Bois's "already grim state of mind verged on apocalyptic bitterness."[1] His moral outrage at these sorts of atrocities had already been unfortunately invoked many times previously.

Years earlier, following the charring of a black man chained to a post in the center of Coatesville, Pennsylvania, Du Bois inked a ferociously sarcastic editorial called "Triumph," in which the spirit of "Anglo-Saxon civilization" was purified by the actions of a "howling mob of the best citizens . . . of the white race." Du Bois's editorial was noteworthy not just because he called national attention to this sort of terrorism; rather, the editorial bristled due to his insight into white racial psychosis. A black man was burned to death not due to any criminal act, real or imagined, Du Bois wrote: "The point is he was black. Blackness must be punished. Blackness is the crime of crimes. . . . Why is it a crime? Because it threatens white supremacy." This danger must be beaten back with all the might of white power. But Du Bois's penetrating vision went deeper: " 'The Churches were nearly deserted,' say the papers . . . Was it not fitting that Coatesville religion should lend its deacons and Sunday-school superintendents to the holy crusade . . . Ah, the splendor of that Sunday night dance. The flames beat and curled against the moonlit sky. The church bells chimed. The scorched and crooked thing, self-wounded and chained to his cot, crawled to the edge of the ash with a stifled groan, but the brave and sturdy farmers pricked him back with the bloody pitchforks until the deed was done."[2] The acidity of Du Bois's tongue and the anguish of his heart should not distract us from recognizing that he painted a picture of murder as a communal event and ritual.[3] Dislodging the church as the site of moral education, lynching teaches lessons about the "fitting" emotional and ethical response to black threats to white civilization: "people walked and drove out to the scene of the burning," Du Bois dourly reported. "Men and women poked the ashes and a shout of glee would signalize the finding of a blackened tooth or mere portions of unrecognizable bones." Prefiguring by eight years the militant stance of Claude McKay's poem, "If We Must Die,"[4] Du Bois closed the editorial with a call for black self-defense: "If we are to die, in God's name let us perish like men and not like bales of hay."[5]

Given this call to arms, it makes sense that Du Bois's grand editorial in the *Crisis,* "Returning Soldiers," signaled an effort to seize the enthusiasm of showcasing black military heroism during the First World War and magnetize it to another great cause: to save democracy at home: " 'Returning Soldiers' spoke to all of [the Talented Tenth] in their new, self-proclaimed, exhilarating incarnation: The New Negro." The manipulation of black patriotism in this manner illustrated, for David Levering Lewis, Du Bois's "militant petit bourgeois opportunism."[6] As I see it, Du Bois's "opportunism" was largely a function of his supreme ego coupled with his critical understanding of and sensitivity toward the manner in which diverse forms of public discourse and aesthetic practices marshaled the images and emotions responsible for making Coatesville possible. For example, in an editorial in the *Crisis* titled "The Manufacture of Prejudice: Three American Fairy Tales from the Associated Press," Du Bois accused the news agency of widely distributing an unsubstantiated story coming out of Mississippi regarding black thuggery. Du Bois and his staff could find no corroborating facts to support the story.[7] And, again, in "The Promotion of Prejudice," the editor asked how it could be that virtually identical stories could run in different newspapers around the country lamenting the rise in local crime committed by blacks. To Du Bois, such aesthetic practices by news agencies represented the operations of a coherent system of black sensibility promulgating race hate.[8]

Du Bois was incensed by and obsessed with this kind of deep hate as he watched the world plunge into war and as he waded in the blood in the streets and in the countryside of America during the Red Summer of 1919. These two sorts of bloodletting were conjoined and made explicable, in part, by the "crime" of blackness. Thus, Du Bois would beat his head against the cold wall of racist pseudoscience and fill the pages of the *Crisis* with antiracist propaganda. What varying forms of American public discourse had in common, Du Bois noted in the *Crisis* and elsewhere time and time again, was an unreasonable commitment—an intense devotion—to conveying blackness as an ugly thing—indeed, as a thing to be destroyed. By 1918, Du Bois may have felt as though he were drowning, but given his faith in his own power of speech, he turned those murky depths into a baptism, a life-giving gift of dark water. Although Du Bois continued to revise essays for his sixth book, *Darkwater: Voices from within the Veil,* for another eighteen months, he considered it structurally sound on the occasion of his fiftieth birthday. When the manuscript reached the offices of Harcourt, Brace, and Howe in the fall of 1919, *Darkwater* had been pressed into a form that would cement Du Bois's status as an "avatar of a race whose troubled fate he was predestined to interpret and to direct."[9] As black America's leading intellectual, Du Bois also sought with *Darkwater* to showcase New Negro dramatic genius and to lead by example a generation of "race men."[10] Hearing the hurt of black folk required the cultivation of a new form of perceptual care—a way of being that opened one to the embrace and the acknowledgment of black beauty. The faces and the voices from within the veil were hidden and muffled by a refusal to appreciate black life, a denial of black magnificence.

In this chapter, I explore *Darkwater* as an illustration and as an interpretation of beauty that posited a sophisticated way of imagining poetics and black aesthetics as potentially transfiguring the social and the political contexts of African American life. *Darkwater* blurred a popular distinction between aesthetics and ethics by dramatizing how our capacity (or incapacity) to recognize the beauty of things is cultivated through our everyday living with others. *Darkwater* performed an artistic practice that disrupted the aesthetic practices of emergence and circulation of contemporary racist propaganda regarding blackness; *Darkwater,* thus, suspended—held in tension—conventional aesthetic judgments of blackness. *Darkwater* represented moments of "truth" where persons sense that they might have been wrong, agonizing moments when previously neglected or despised beings were perceived as participating in the beautiful. Du Bois insisted throughout *Darkwater* that these moments were always affective and invoked ethical imperatives. *Darkwater's* moments of "truth" call to us, and our appreciation of our error in aesthetic judgment alerts us to new forms of beauty; our attention to the summons of beauty also acknowledges the ethical and affective dimensions of Du Bois's speech in *Darkwater,* actualizing his voice. Endowing Du Bois's voice allows us a more robust and intimate encounter with the commonplace shared by the sedimentation or disorientation of aesthetic judgment, the attribution of beauty or ugliness, and their impact on what stands as social justice. Du Bois's aesthetic "theory" was not presented didactically, it infused every crevice of *Darkwater;* thus, my reading of this text resembles the form of his theory—I sample its delicate leaves in no predetermined order, knowing each bite contains the flavor of the whole. This is not to say that there is no "method" at work here: Du Bois's writing violated the metaphysics of time and space by holding together past and future and by imagining the moment when time might stand still; thus, to be released toward the beauty of *Darkwater*—its moments of "truth"—we must first contemplate being wrong, we must explore the taken for granted aesthetic practices that reify aesthetic judgments and that habituate ugly emotions. Du Bois's grief and bitterness are palpable in this writing about race hatred.

The Senses of Aesthetic Practices: Of Beauty and Death

At the risk of committing heresy regarding the prescience and poignancy of *The Souls of Black Folk,* I think it reasonable to presume that by 1916 Du Bois may have sensed that his highly acclaimed work had failed in an important way. With *Souls,* Du Bois had "resolved to write of the genius, humanity, and enviable destiny of his race with such passion, eloquence, and penetration that claims of African American inferiority would be sent reeling, never to recover full legitimacy and vitality, despite their enormous resiliency."[11] Although he would never admit it, at the time of the writing of *Souls* Du Bois had underestimated and misunderstood the irrepressibility of racism. He could not then have fully appreciated how America's culture of racial violence was not simply the product of race hatred but was constitutive of aesthetic practices that birthed anew values, beliefs, and habits made sensible, affordable, and pleasurable in our bodies and minds through our active participation in them.

Like *Souls, Darkwater* was autobiographic, poetic, and analytic. Unlike *Souls, Darkwater* furnished the vigorous heat of an evangelist caught up in the rapture of witnessing sinners in the hands of an angry God. Rather than principally seeking to disclose the humanity of black folk, *Darkwater* contained humanity's primal screams; it shouted, cursed, and offered itself as a nearly silent supplicant. Beginning with Du Bois's personal narrative and ending with a hymn for us to sing to salvage our collective souls, *Darkwater* seems incomplete, as if it were in the middle of asking a question as one turns the final page. But this is its basic aesthetic, artistic, and rhetorical character; it ends incompletely. In the essay, "Of Beauty and Death," Du Bois suggested why this was so. Trained in aesthetics by George Santayana at Harvard, Du Bois appropriated his teacher's aesthetic conceptions and reinterpreted the important relation between aesthetics and ethics. As a philosophical concept, beauty was related to death, wrote Du Bois following Santayana, because beauty was a form of perfection, of completion. Beauty demanded an end that yielded pleasure. Aesthetics, however, as Du Bois understood, was about more than beauty; it concerned the messiness of social life that always already impinged on the sense of beauty.

In his seminal work, *The Sense of Beauty: Being the Outline of Aesthetic Theory,* a collection of lectures delivered while Du Bois matriculated to Harvard, Santayana set out to explore "the nature and elements of our aesthetic judgments" so as to supply a philosophical justification for "more diversified aesthetic enjoyment." To Santayana, the relation between perception and emotion was the key to comprehending one's aesthetic experiences because one's appreciation of beauty cannot be understood by referencing an object's or our own "divine attributes." Santayana lamented the impoverished status of aesthetic theories that explained beauty by gesturing toward a realm beyond human experience. Replacing metaphysics, *The Sense of Beauty* focused on "human sensibility itself." Santayana maintained that beauty was a value that got objectified in objects and internalized as a complex set of ideations and emotions. Santayana's prime example was God: beauty became a "manifestation of God to the senses, since, in the region of sense, the perception of beauty exemplifies the adequacy and perfection which in general we objectify in an idea of God." In other words, when one attributed beauty, one actualized an ideal form. But an explanation of how that aesthetic judgment was rendered cannot be found in Platonic idealism because all one found there was an expression of Plato's feelings while he beheld the "truth." Against this sort of idealism, Santayana sought to "increase our knowledge rather than to cultivate our sensibilities."[12]

Santayana's thinking both liberated and constrained Du Bois. To clarify how beauty was an aesthetic value and how we may appreciate it properly, Santayana engaged in a series of dissociations, most notably the distinction between the aesthetic and ethical realms. "Values spring from the immediate and inexplicable reaction of vital impulse," wrote Santayana, "and from the irrational part of our nature." This reaction "furnishes the data with which" our rationality worked. Values, then, were "irrational," but they got rationalized. This process "leads us from data to conclusions, or from parts to wholes," and yet, in and of itself, it was "as arbitrary, as much dependent on the needs of a finite organization, as any other ideal . . . what makes it a good and indispensable thing and gives it all its authority, is not its own nature, but our need of it both in safe and economical action and in the pleasures of comprehension." There were two forms of judgment being implicated here: We may assess the logic of the rationalization, the relation among parts and wholes. We may also attempt to consider the "inexplicable reaction" itself—what I am in this work calling an effect of affect. Santayana posited the former as an "intellectual judgment" that was concerned with evaluating facts; the latter was a judgment of value. Santayana excluded intellectual judgments from this work based on the idea that, "If we approach a work of art or nature scientifically, for the sake of its historical connexions or proper classification, we do not approach it aesthetically." The danger in confusing the two judgments lies in the capacity for reason to assume authority over our senses and require "truth" in the form of "correctness. . . . The implication is that to be correctly copied from a model is the prerequisite of all beauty." While verisimilitude may be a facet of aesthetic judgment, beauty cannot be reduced to it; indeed, when one presumed that beauty follows laws already laid down, "the scientific habit in [the artist] inhibits the artistic."[13]

Having separated questions of fact from questions of value, Santayana devoted himself to elucidating the difference between moral and aesthetic judgments, each of which was a judgment of value: "One factor of this distinction is that while aesthetic judgments are mainly positive . . . perceptions of good, moral judgments are mainly and fundamentally negative, or perceptions of evil." Moral judgments, then, were handed down in order to prevent suffering, while aesthetic judgments were constitutive of maximizing pleasure. This distinction also implied that moral judgments were rendered as the result of conscious deliberation, and aesthetic judgments occurred at the immediate point of contact with the beautiful: "The appreciation of beauty and its embodiment in the arts," wrote Santayana, "are activities which belong to our holiday life, when we are redeemed for the moment from the shadow of evil and the slavery to fear, and are following the bent of our nature where it chooses to lead us."[14]

The notion that we were only thrust toward beauty during moments of "holiday life" was a popular one. In "Of Beauty and Death," Du Bois recounted the time when he first appreciated the beauty of the Maine coastline while on vacation. He expressed gratitude for the sight so "that in the tired days of life men should come and worship here and renew their spirit." The beautiful coastline, however, provoked a question: "Why do not those who are scarred in the world's battle and hurt by its hardness travel to these places of beauty and drown themselves in the utter joy of life?"[15] Santayana placed such a query in the realm of ethics because it involved the contemplation of class inequities and marginalization, negative values. The ugly, to Santayana, was only an aesthetic concern inasmuch as it produced "amusement," an aesthetic pleasure. Once ugliness became "vitally repulsive, its presence becomes a real evil towards which we assume a practical and moral attitude."[16] Thus, to contemplate the character of social injustice, one must depart the realm of aesthetics.

Respecting Santayana's ideas about the affective implications of accounting for beauty, Du Bois, however, eroded his professor's distinction between moral and aesthetic judgments by drawing a different kind of distinction—one between sacred beauty, "the beauty of Love and Friendship," and secular beauty, "the glory of physical nature; this, though the least of beauties, is divine!" Having separated high beauty from low beauty, Du Bois asked: "But may we not compare the least of the world's beauty . . . the sea and sky and city, with the little hatefulness and thoughtlessness of race prejudice, that out of such juxtaposition we may, perhaps, deduce some *rule of beauty* and life—or death?"[17] Du Bois's association of beauty with ugly was made in order to do what Santayana claimed his book was all about: to increase our knowledge of beauty. If "low" beauty can be corresponded with "little hatefulness," then we might learn about what happens in us when thinking these experiences and forming values constitutive of them. Santayana posited that the understanding of aesthetic value was immediate and intrinsic to the perception of beauty itself. Usually pleasure was understood as an effect of perception because "pleasure is separated in time from the perception, or it is localized in a different organ, and consequently is at once recognized as an effect and not as a quality of the object." Santayana, however, offered a crucial caveat:

> But when the process of perception itself is pleasant, as it may easily be, when the intellectual operation, by which the elements of sense are associated and projected, and the concept of the form and substance of the thing produced, is naturally delightful, then we have a pleasure intimately bound up in the thing, inseparable from its character and constitution, the seat of which in us is the same as the seat of the perception. We naturally fail . . . to separate the pleasure from the other objectified feelings. It becomes . . . a quality of the object, which we distinguish from pleasures not so incorporated in the perception of things, by giving it the name of beauty.[18]

This was an important statement because it offered Du Bois a way of conceiving how feelings generative of perceiving a thing can be imbedded in the thing as if they "naturally" belonged there. And although Santayana recognized the fact that such a conclusion resulted from a kind of failure, the end was a good thing since it yielded beauty. Rather than localize an appreciation for beauty in the "seat of the perception," Du Bois derived *interpretive rules* for beauty from the ethical realm. Du Bois's reinterpretation of Santayana points out for us that there is another kind of failure at work here. Positive pleasures are not the only emotions that can be bound up in objects of perception. Being neither objects of aesthetic "amusements" nor properly belonging exclusively to the ethical realm, *Darkwater* illuminated how the massive circulation and consumption of monstrous images and narratives of black life impacted the ordinary attribution of beauty.

The answer to Du Bois's earlier question about why battle-weary black folk did not flock to places like the Maine shore and could not appreciate its beauty was because such beauty was prohibited by segregation: "There is not in the world a more disgraceful denial of human brotherhood than the 'Jim Crow' car of the Southern United States." Du Bois suggested that if artists were to really appreciate "the sunset and moonlight on Montego Bay in far Jamaica," they must also apprehend the aesthetic qualities of the Jim Crow car because "both things are true and both belong to this world, and neither can be denied."[19] The reluctance to paint the ugliness of Jim Crow America stemmed from the belief that beauty evoked pleasure and was a positive value. But such a contention shielded white folks from the pain of racial segregation as an aesthetic experience. To be fair, Santayana admitted that "aesthetic sensitiveness is . . . properly enough called moral, because it is the effect of conscientious training and is more powerful for good in society than laborious virtue, because it is much more constant and catching."[20] But Du Bois was not just commenting on the character of aesthetic sensitivity—one's readiness to behold beauty—he was suggesting that the *very idea of beauty,* which Santayana conceived in terms of an emotional experience, was "corrupted" at the outset by the basic character of racism.[21] And this depravity remained concealed by Santayana's theorizing. To illuminate this point, let us turn to Du Bois's critique of the aesthetic value of whiteness.

"The Souls of White Folk," first published in the *Nation* in 1910, is a fascinating dissertation on the ethos of whiteness. Revised and extended for *Darkwater,* the essay described how, in the subjectivity and sensibility of white folk, whiteness achieved the status of the highest aesthetic value. Beginning with the conventional false claim "that whiteness is the ownership of the world forever and ever, Amen!," Du Bois theorized that behind such a fantastic lie lurked an aesthetic judgment: whiteness was the ultimate beauty.[22] Santayana's theories helped him here. When we begin to contemplate why we feel that a certain class of things was beautiful, Santayana explained, we naturally (and dangerously) represent our perceptions in terms of general principles that over time may cease to properly represent a community's feelings, "but which still obtain the idolatrous veneration of mankind. . . . It arises wherever an abstract good is substituted for its concrete equivalent."[23] Du Bois described this substitution in terms of a "sudden, emotional conversion" of folks who recognized in their own faces the putative ideal form, the abstract good of (white) beauty. "Now what is the effect on a man or a nation," Du Bois asked, "when it comes passionately to believe such an extraordinary dictum as this?" Well, one also may cultivate a passionate faith in one's ethical obligation to remake the world in one's own image—after all, such an aesthetic practice serves the universal good, does it not? Here, Du Bois's critique tapered to a stiletto: "Neither Roman nor Arab, Greek nor Egyptian, Persian nor Mongol ever took himself and his own perfectness with such disconcerting seriousness as the modern white man."[24] Santayana also lamented the impact that a belief in one's perfection had on one's critical understanding of truth: "The unreflective conscience, forgetting the vicarious source of its own excellence, then assumes a solemn and incomprehensible immediacy, as if its decrees were absolute and intrinsically authoritative, not of to-day or yesterday, and no one could tell whence they had arisen."[25]

What emerged in "The Souls of White Folk" was Du Bois's understanding of how the ontology of whiteness had transmuted into an aesthetic value that could not be altered through force of reason alone—it was held in place as a "vicious habit of mind," and it made "the statement 'I am white,' the one fundamental tenet of our practical morality." The term "habit" was significant, for Du Bois showed throughout *Darkwater* how the sense of white beauty was constitutive of aesthetic practices steeped in intense emotions regarding whiteness and its Other. For example, in the chapter called "The Hands of Ethiopia," Du Bois presented a stunning analysis of how racism structured the global economy that helped drive the world into the First World War. In this chapter, Du Bois burned and simmered and nearly called for a race war: "If the attitude of the European and American worlds is in the future going to be based essentially upon the same policies as in the past, then there is but one thing for the trained man of darker blood to do and that is definitely and as openly as possible to organize his world for war against Europe. . . . To surrender would be far worse than physical death."[26]

More than displaying Du Bois's Pan-African vision, *Darkwater* made aesthetic experiences and practices the subject of moral deliberation. Speaking broadly, Santayana conceived of aesthetic practices as the making of cultural phenomena and artifacts that shaped our understanding of the world. I am accentuating another matching function: aesthetic practices are productive of values, beliefs, and emotions that make emergent the very political subjects who are "proper" to that understanding.[27] Du Bois recognized that aesthetic practices that confirmed the value of white beauty included "supporting arguments [that] grow and twist themselves in the mouths of merchant, scientist, soldier, traveler, writer, and missionary: Darker peoples are dark in mind as well as in body; of dark, uncertain, and imperfect descent."[28] Here, Du Bois's revision of Santayana packed interpretive punch. To Santayana, white beauty was a proper object of aesthetic contemplation; but the hateful literatures painting black imperfection were merely "amusing" or "annoying" aesthetic objects. If they were "evil," they became subject to ethical, not aesthetic, inquiry.

For the *Crisis* editor, this dichotomy was troubling for two related reasons. First, it helped suppress black voices by discouraging white folk from encountering the words and images of black suffering as aesthetic experiences. The opening of "Of Beauty and Death" enacted a conversation between Du Bois and "my friend, who is pale and positive" who accused him of being "too sensitive." The dialogue reflected real life at the NAACP; it animated numerous discussions held face to face and in letters with friends Joel Spingarn and Mary White Ovington in which Du Bois's tender sensibilities were the topic.[29] It also dramatized an acknowledgment of the affective and ethical character of black speech as the white "friend" was made to hear and feel Du Bois's pain. Indeed, the dialogue was reminiscent of a fascinating exchange Du Bois had with Ovington where he vehemently defended his autonomy as editor and as an executive officer of the civil rights organization.[30] In *Darkwater,* Du Bois's "pale friend" asked: "'Why don't you stop all this [agitation]?'" To which he replied, "'You will not let us.' 'There you go, again. You know that I—.'" Du Bois cut her off: "'Wait! I answer. Wait!'" Following this curt suspension, Du Bois offered a litany of racial insults rightly eventuating moral outrage: "I arise at seven. The milkman has neglected me. He pays little attention to colored districts. My white neighbor glares elaborately. I walk softly, lest I disturb him. The children jeer as I pass to work. The women in the street car withdraw their skirts or prefer to stand. The policeman is truculent. The elevator man hates to serve Negroes. My job is insecure because the white union wants it and does not want me. I try to lunch, but no place near will serve me."[31] As Du Bois's voice is actualized by the reader's acknowledgment of the ethical and affective dimensions of his speech, one is also opened up to experiencing Du Bois's dramatization of these racial insults as constitutive of aesthetic value. From this vantage point, we can see the reinterpretation of Santayana come into sharp relief; these incidents were not "amusing," and yet they were not presented as quite "evil." They sit at the junction between Santayana's moral and aesthetic worlds, transfusing an abstract pleasure with the resonance of actual pain. Like in a lengthy letter to Joel Spingarn in October 1914 that sought to explain Du Bois's icy editorial "temperament," the conversation linked his sensitivity to white insensitivity:

> "Do all eating places discriminate?"
> No, but how shall I know which do not—except—I hurry home through crowds. They mutter or get angry. I go to a mass meeting. They stare. I go to a church. "We don't admit niggers!" . . . I enter the free field of science. Every laboratory door is closed and no endowments are available. I seek the universal mistress, Art; the studio door is locked. I write literature. "We cannot publish stories of colored folk of that type." It's the only type I know. This is my life. It makes me idiotic. It gives me artificial problems. I hesitate, I rush, I waver. In fine,—I am sensitive![32]

Du Bois told of the way that black folk must be highly aware of the multifarious modes through which the color line shaped the social and cultural landscape; such insight, however, made one touchy and vulnerable precisely because it cannot be adequately rationalized. Its affects escape logical explanation. The reader was also shown that white folk do not readily recognize this predicament:

> My pale friend looks at me with disbelief and curling tongue.
> "Do you mean to sit there and tell me that this is what happens to you each day?"
> Certainly not, I answer low.
> "Then you only fear it will happen?"
> I fear!
> "Well, haven't you the courage to rise above a—almost a craven fear?"
> Quite—quite craven is my fear, I admit; but the terrible thing is—these things do happen!
> "But you just said—"
> They do happen. Not all each day,—surely not. But now and then—now seldom, now, sudden; now after a week; now in a chain of awful minutes; not everywhere, but anywhere—in Boston, in Atlanta. That's the hell of it. Imagine spending your life looking for insults or hiding places from them—shrinking (instinctively and despite bolstering of courage) from blows that are not always but ever.[33]

Such a conversation, real or imagined, was stunning. Du Bois related how racial insults conditioned one's sensitivity to affect, "now sudden . . . now in a chain of awful minutes"; such occurrences were made sense of as intense emotions like a "craven fear." As he delved into the character of the conditions in which black folk were subjected to degradation, he showed that acts of racism cannot be simply understood as impacting an individual body nor can they be isolated to the South and lynching; as a phenomenon, racism can materialize "anywhere" and at anytime. It cannot be fully perceived through an intellectual gaze, it dragged one into its fires of "hell." Du Bois asked the reader to "imagine" a life where one was "not always but ever" easily hurt by it. In short, he requested that the reader be *more* sensitive; his discourse moves us to a place where we can be receptive to his point of view and responsive to the ethical obligations incumbent upon this new sense and perception. After describing the indignity of being sent to the "smoking gallery" rather than be seated near the orchestra, we are called to do more than be empathetic; we are asked to help him beat back the fear by joining him in a form of violence: "Then the great fear surges in your soul, the real fear—the fear beside which other fears are vain imaginings; the fear lest right there and then you are losing your own soul; that you are losing your own soul and the soul of a people; that millions of unborn children, black and gold and mauve, are being there and then despoiled by you because you are a coward and dare not fight!"[34] Du Bois sounded an alarm meant to alert the reader about the ever-present threat to the soul of humanity; if we are not "cowards" his anxiety becomes ours and the resonance of suffering behind the veil can no longer be contained in dark bodies that one can look upon with "amused contempt and pity."[35] If one's perception is attuned to Du Bois's nightmare, one experiences his dread and endures this resonance as one examines the hateful contexts out of which it emerges. It does not seem quite right to call this evaluation an ascription of beauty, and yet one cannot deny that *Darkwater* evokes a concentrated sensation. It is the sort of experience often leading to a thing being called beautiful and can be appreciated in terms of Eros and Thanatos—in terms of love and death. I shall return to this notion shortly, but let us get to the other reason to resist a neat distinction between the moral and the aesthetic.

The separation of moral and aesthetic values also buttressed the dismissal of Du Bois as a stalwart propagandist as he attempted through literature to interrogate the ideologies imbricated in attributions of beauty. Related to this sacking, a notable Harlem writer would later refer to Du Bois as a "potentially great writer gone wrong."[36] Moreover, the distinction hid the manner in which ideas of beauty were part of aesthetic practices like colonialism where in Africa and elsewhere there was "no voice or law or custom to protect labor, no trade union, no eight-hour laws, no factory legislation. . . . All the industrial deviltry, which civilization has been driving to the slums and the backwaters, will have a voiceless continent to conceal it. If the slave cannot be taken from Africa, slavery can be taken to Africa." Du Bois linked the contemporary colonial effort in Africa and Asia to an ongoing "world campaign beginning with the slave-trade and ending with the refusal to capitalize the word 'Negro,' leading through a passionate defense of slavery by attributing every bestiality to blacks and finally culminating in the evident modern profit which lies in degrading blacks,—all this has unconsciously trained millions of honest, modern men into the belief that black folk are sub-human.... After this," Du Bois sighed heavily, "the descent to Hell is easy ... I see again and again, often and still more often, *a writing of human hatred, a deep and passionate hatred.*"[37]

Du Bois had seen such hateful writing before, but on February 8, 1915, he encountered a new kind of hate speech imprinted on celluloid. D. W. Griffith's racist epic *The Birth of a Nation* premiered at the Clune Auditorium in Los Angeles to enthusiastic crowds. David Levering Lewis reported that President Woodrow Wilson praised its apparently poignant realism saying that it was "all so terribly true."[38] Based on the novel *The Clansmen* by Thomas Dixon, the film pits the "heroism" of the Ku Klux Klan against rapacious sexual appetites of black men for white women. The film promoted the idea and the feeling that it was right and just to hunt down and destroy this black sexual carnivore. After viewing the film with other NAACP board members, Du Bois and the civil rights organization put their full weight against every new screening of the film. In fact, there was some discussion among civil rights activists of financing a cinematic rebuttal. A play by Angelina Grimké, "Rachel," was considered for the project, but Du Bois was unenthusiastic; he was immersed in the Washington and Philadelphia productions of his grand open-air spectacle about the development of African kings and queens. Lewis notes that the *Star of Ethiopia* "which played to large crowds over several nights ... was to be the most thoughtful, ambitious theatrical response to Dixon and Griffith's racist epic."[39] *The Birth of a Nation* was not only "the worst public libel ever perpetrated,"[40] wrote Du Bois in the *Crisis* more than a year after the film debuted, the film's revisionist national narrative, cultivated fierce anger over white beauty defiled by black beasts: "The benefits our Republic will be likely to reap in future generations from the degrading spectacle ... can perhaps be inferred from the remark of a young boy, who, after seeing the play in New York, said to a friend: 'I'd like to kill every nigger I know.'"[41] Keeping in mind that Du Bois often fabricated such scenes for rhetorical effect, *Darkwater* contemplated how intensely affective aesthetic practices could provoke grown men to "curse a little child, who had wandered into the wrong waiting-room, searching for its mother: 'Here, you damned black—' He was white." The emotional conversion that accompanied the passionate belief in the ultimate aesthetic value of whiteness and the worthlessness of blackness, argued Du Bois, was itself transformed during the Red Summer of 1919 into an "orgy [of] cruelty, barbarism, and murder done to men and women of Negro descent." And no one should be surprised. "Say to men, earnestly and repeatedly: 'Honesty is best, knowledge is power; do unto others as you would be done by.' Say this and *act it* and the nation must move toward it, if not to it." But if our dominant aesthetic practices make and distribute blackness as a crime and say that the " 'one virtue is to be white,' [then] the people rush to the inevitable conclusion, 'Kill the nigger!' "[42] Such killing was rampant during the years that most of *Darkwater* came to be. Du Bois defended his decision to publish gruesome pictures of burned and twisted corpses in the *Crisis* by asking his shocked readers how "could the tale have been told otherwise?"[43]

This deep and passionate hatred was forever on the verge of boiling over into blind rage. A. C. Grayling, in a thought-provoking little book about the emotions and the good life, has this to say about the ethics of anger: "The angry man's desire is to vent his heat, to appease himself by doing harm, not pausing to consider whether the greatest harm will eventually accrue to himself rather than his opponent. And when anger drives, such is the usual outcome."[44] The pause to which Grayling refers might be similar to the quiet peace of Santayana's "holiday life." Silent spaces offer freedom, reflection, and, in the words of E. M. Cioran in *The Trouble with Being Born,* "true contact between beings . . . by mute presence, by apparent non-communication, by that mysterious and wordless exchange which resembles inward prayer."[45] To an inflamed Du Bois, the problem with being born white can be summed up by Kenneth Burke's famous epigram: one is rotten with perfection.[46] This rottenness can be seen at work as it tries to achieve its putative perfection: "How easy, then, by emphasis and omission to make children believe that every great soul the world ever saw was a white man's soul; that every great thought the world ever knew was a white man's thought."[47]

Darkwater suspended the functionality of these aesthetic practices of "emphasis and omission" in part by performing Ralph Waldo Emerson's observation that, "Sometimes a scream is better than a thesis."[48] According to Du Bois, "If I cry amid this roar of elemental forces, must my cry be in vain? . . . I hear his cry reverberating through the world, 'I am white!' Well and good, divine thief! . . . Why, then, devour your own vitals if I answer even as proudly, 'I am black!' "[49] Du Bois often felt that his cries were in vain because they were muffled and their affects dampened by the roar of those elemental forces manufacturing the earth in the imperialist's self-image. But, at the heart of *Darkwater* lurked Du Bois's nearly unbreakable faith in the human spirit. This is why it ends incompletely; as long as there is life, the nearly "perfect" presence of white power will be forced to be on the move, always trying to reclaim its ground, as that ground rattles and rolls. Du Bois's revision of Santayana pushed him to the point of suggesting that the ultimate beauty is not God but death—the peace that cradles the weary after life-long labors without vacations: "At last to us all comes happiness, there in the Court of Peace, where the dead lie so still and calm and good. If we were not dead we would lie and listen to the flowers grow. . . . But we know that being dead, our Happiness is a fine and finished thing and that ten, a hundred, and a thousand years, we shall lie at rest, unhurt in the Court of Peace."[50]

And so *Darkwater* lives on as a reminder that there is no such thing as perfection among the living, only human perseverance. Du Bois's faith was severely tested in the chapter "Of Work and Wealth," where he recounted a moment when the "truth" would not do. While teaching at Atlanta University a student asked the young Du Bois: " 'Do you trust white people?' You do not and you know that you do not, much as you want to; yet you rise and lie and say you do; you must say it for her salvation and the world's; you repeat that she must trust them, that most white folks are honest, and all the while you are lying, and miserably you sit and lie on."[51] Coming from an activist whose dictum was "dare to tell the truth," this tale was ironic; but the moral of the story was not that, depending on the circumstance, Du Bois would say whatever it took to achieve his goals; rather, we learn that his students understood the motives for his lie; they sensed the lie as his painful sacrifice for them so that they may be in touch with his faith in their futures. Should Du Bois's lie be called a beautiful thing? Perhaps, but this is not the first question to pursue. We should not get hung up on whether the lie was "really" beautiful. Its affect was actual, resonating through the classroom as a transmission from beyond and above the color line. It is this sort of indeterminacy that keeps *Darkwater* from ending completely and that shows us how aesthetic judgments are always ethical and subject to being "wrong." And as we shall see next, acknowledging that one can always be erroneous about beauty is itself a beautiful thing.

Of Beauty and Error: Experiencing the Passion of the "Truth"

In the chapter, "The Call," first published in the *Crisis* in 1911 under the title "The Woman,"[52] Du Bois transported the reader to the mythical "land of the Heavy Laden," where a great war was waging; the King called to his servants, numbering 144,000 strong,[53] to meet the mounting threat gathering on a far off hill, but "their ears were thick with the dust of the enemy," and they hid. And the Lord called again and again but without reply; finally a black maid answered, but protested that she was not worthy to fight for the Lord, to protect truth and justice because she was a woman and was black: "The

King spake not, but swept the veiling of his face aside and lifted up the light of his countenance upon her and lo!," to the maid's wondrous shock, "It was black."[54] Not only did Du Bois associate the "lowly" with moral righteousness in keeping with the spirit of radical Christian love, he dramatized a moment when commonplace assumptions of divine (white) beauty were shown to be flawed. In a beautifully shaped work called *On Beauty and Being Just,* Elaine Scarry discussed the moment when one realizes that one has made an error in the attribution of beauty as a profoundly powerful aesthetic experience and as an ethical call of conscience. Scarry described two forms of "error": first, we can discover that an object we once held as beautiful has lost its sheen; but, to Scarry the second form is much more provocative because it occurs when something that we did not behold suddenly has its beauty unconcealed to us. In such a moment, it is as if the thing appears to us for the very first time.[55]

Scarry considered how "cultural difference" contributes to this kind of mistake while relating to us how the beauty of a palm tree dancing in the breeze off the edge of her hotel balcony unexpectedly pressed against her: "It is the case that if I were surrounded every day by hundreds of palms, one of them would have sooner called upon me to correct my error. Beauty always takes place in the particular, and if there are no particulars, the chances of seeing it go down. In this sense, cultural difference, by diminishing the number of times you are on the same ground with a particular vegetation or animal or art work, gives rise to problems of perception." Problems of perception, Scarry continued, are aggravated by Western culture's tendency to populate the landscape not with particulars but with stereotypes, "syntheses in which there is not a single atom [of] happiness and beauty." But once one acknowledges the "error," "beauty is lifesaving. . . . It makes the heart beat faster. It makes life more vivid, animated, living, worth living." This is why beauty is a life-giving gift; beauty is the name we often give to the intense sensation of being pulled toward the animating force of living. Its nearly unprecedented character also "incites deliberation." Scarry argued that the structure of the perception of beauty requires us "to move chronologically back in the search for precedents and parallels, to move forward into new acts of creation, to move conceptually over, to bring things into relation, and does all this with a kind of urgency as though one's life depended on it." During this act of remembrance, we are both certain about the beauty before us and reminded that we had been wrong. Beauty suspends belief in the character of *a* thing as it seals devotion to things-in-the-event of emergence. We at once rejoice in our newfound "perceptual care" and agonize over our previous carelessness. Not only, then, is "beauty a starting place for education," as we learn how to act more carefully, but Scarry explained its ethical imperative through an appeal to antiquity: "Plato's requirement that we move from 'eros,' in which we are seized by the beauty of one person, to 'caritas,' in which our care is extended to all people, has parallels in many early aesthetic treatises."[56]

Reading *Darkwater* as, in part, an aesthetic treatise warrants that special perceptual care is taken with Du Bois's appropriation and reinterpretation of the passion of Christ. Du Bois's allegory unfolded in two short stories, punctuated by the dramatization of a sinner's anguished and redemptive prayer. We have already seen how, in "The Call," a black woman's moral courage brought her to the proper place to recognize herself in the face of God—an acknowledgment that both lifted her up and brought her to her knees. Scarry was just as penitent in the presence of beauty. The palm tree spreading its wings outside of her hotel room reached toward her and lifted her as the room swirled and the ground spun away. This disorientation was provoked by the notice that one had been wrong, perhaps about everything; Scarry described the feeling as exhilarating.[57] Du Bois did not. The short story "The Second Coming" began in three different locations where three bishops ponder a mysterious communiqué calling them to Valdosta, Georgia, to witness a "prophet" being welcomed back into the world. A white bishop from New York, a black bishop from New Orleans, and a Japanese bishop visiting San Francisco met in Georgia "the day before Christmas." The governor of the state had been getting increasingly nervous about Valdosta's black bottom, and when he greeted the white bishop, he expressed this anxiety as sutured to blackness: "I never saw niggers get so. They're leaving by the hundreds and those who stay are getting impudent! They seem to be expecting something." The governor greeted the other bishops coolly and absentmindedly; then the four of them made their way toward an odd light in the distance. They soon arrived at a "hut" where "a shaft of glorious light fell full upon the child." The white bishop inched forward for a look at the child: "It was black! He stepped back with a gesture of disgust, hardly listening to and yet hearing the black bishop, who spoke almost as if in apology: 'She's not really white; I know Lucy—you see, her mother worked for the Governor—.'"[58] Although these references and relations may sound perfectly clear to our twenty-first-century ears, to Du Bois's audience, even more sensitive to the sexual predicament of black women in the service of powerful white men, his implication that miscegenation—and maybe rape—was responsible for a black baby Jesus would have been felt by some folks as blasphemous.

In "The Second Coming," Jesus was begotten through the seed of raced lust and crime; rather than appeal exclusively to Immaculate Conception, an idea that Santayana called one of life's most powerful "abstract goods,"[59]

Du Bois offered divinity also born of America's "practical morality," its struggle with the color line. Shamoon Zamir, in *Dark Voices,* rightly noted that Du Bois's refusal to transcend history or synthesize the particularities of life within reason undermined the philosophies of both Hegel and Santayana. Furthermore, Du Bois's critical reinterpretations draw our attention to the fact that he conceptualized the "development of black American self-consciousness [as] always a political history scarred from the very start by the experience of rejection and subjection."[60] Jesus's beauty was both heavenly and earthbound; like the sorrow songs that Du Bois loved dearly, Jesus's beauty was healing and expressed our obligation to be careful with others. America's aesthetic practices, however, constituted black ugliness and veiled from the white bishop this "truth" as he recoiled in "disgust"; but the Japanese bishop "knelt with bowed head" in reverence.[61] "The Second Coming" ended with this staging of how cultural difference did not necessarily lead to "errors" in attributions of beauty; that aesthetic judgments about black beauty were also vivified by a deep and passionate hatred.

"Jesus Christ in Texas" reintroduced the reader to a now grown prophet dedicated to a drifter's life, taking part in folks' lives on behalf of his "Father." As a sequel to "The Second Coming," the reader was fully prepared to take in the spectacle of folks struggling to come to terms with their monumental errors. Du Bois paced the story methodically; Jesus was a ghostly figure in a small Texas town. He exuded a quiet warmth in the twilight that stalled questions about his origins; people felt as though they somehow already knew him but knew not from where. He received invitations to talk and to dine, and he did so while seated in shadows. But while having a "curious conversation" with an important man referred to as the "Colonel," and his wife, Jesus's face was revealed by a servant preparing for a dinner party by turning up the lights: "With one accord they all looked at the stranger, for they had hardly seen him well in the glooming twilight. The woman started in amazement and the Colonel half rose in anger. Why, the man was a mulatto, surely."[62] The dinner guests began to arrive and the Colonel's wife fretted over how they will respond to the presence of a Negro in her home. The servant dropped his serving tray; recognition of his savior provoked trembling prayers. The Colonel's daughter had already welcomed this stranger into her heart and bounced down the stairs to leap into his arms again before going to bed. Jesus left the Colonel's house with the dinner guests feeling somehow dreadful and disoriented.

Jesus then befriended an escaped black convict who repented and sought shelter and work at a nearby farmhouse. Jesus engaged in quiet conversation with the farmer's wife on her darkened porch; he asked her if she loved her neighbors as she loved herself and gestured toward a dilapidated farm in the distance. She could not love them, she stammered, because " 'They are niggers!' " Turning on the porch light abruptly to better see this curious stranger, "she shrieked in angry terror and rushed down the path" in search of her husband but was accidentally knocked down by the black convict. Just then, the prison guard and an armed mob approached looking for the escaped man who the farmer turned over for assaulting his wife. They seized the man, and finding the nearest tree, they lynched him. For a moment, we are unsure of Jesus's plight for the mob's spirit climbed to ecstatic heights during this orgy of cruelty. But then we see him offering a prayer to the still writhing soul in knots. The farmer's wife teetered on the verge of a kind of insanity as she was held in place by this awe-full sight:

> She saw the dead man writhe. He stretched his arms out like a cross, looking upward. She gasped and clung to the window sill. Behind the swaying body, and down where the little, half-ruined cabin lay, a single flame flashed up amid the far-off shout and cry of the mob. A fierce joy sobbed up through the terror in her soul and then sank abashed as she watched the flame rise. Suddenly whirling into one great crimson column it shot to the top of the sky . . . and behind the roped and swaying form hung quivering and burning a great crimson cross. She hid her dizzy, aching head in an agony of tears, and dared not look for she knew . . . and the very horror of it lifted her dull and shrinking eyelids. . . . She stretched her arms and shrieked.[63]

Du Bois depicted the powerful unveiling as a painful and awe-full moment of "truth." Trembling at the bedroom window, the farmer's wife beheld the once ugly black thing slowly dying on his murderer's vine. Her complicity in a racist and brutal murder in the presence of a black Jesus Christ brought on a sublime experience. Once again, Santayana was appropriated and revised. In *The Sense of Beauty,* Santayana's Catholicism helped to shape his understanding of the sublime. As a tremendous emotional experience, the sublime was typically understood as an extreme pleasure that derived from one's will to power while confronting an overwhelming horror, "the glorious joy of self-assertion in the face of an uncontrollable world." But Santayana was not content with this definition because it led to "confusion" in classical conceptions of the sublime; that the sublime necessarily depended on the presence of "evil." Awesome sights make "us withdraw into ourselves . . . and we have that emotion of detachment and liberation in which the sublime really consists." Unlike perceiving beauty, where we sense identification with the object, the sublime was achieved through a "separation from our world" because the thing that has grasped our attention is utterly inconceivable and alien; in such a moment we can only "stiffen ourselves against it." Santayana acknowledged the role that "evil" plays in inducing the sublime but argued that "the immense is sublime as well as the terrible." Santayana reasoned that exposure to infinity, the capacious character of existence, displays, all at once, every possible desire or dream. And since we cannot possibly contemplate every desire, every love, or every dream, we become indifferent and unmoved by them. We are, thus, independent and detached. Santayana referred to this experience as the "Stoic sublime" and called the experience of emancipating the self in the face of terror the "Epicurean sublime." In each case, however, the "sublime is essentially mystical: it is the transcending of distinct perception in favour of a feeling of unity and volume." Importantly, Santayana's definition of beauty required him to conceive of the sublime as possible in the absence of "evil," because if he failed to do so he would be admitting that there were aesthetic experiences that were necessarily "negative." Hence, he confidently proclaimed that "the sublime is not the ugly, as some descriptions of it might lead us to suppose; it is the supremely, the intoxicatingly beautiful. It is the pleasure of contemplation reaching such an intensity that it begins to lose its objectivity, and to declare itself . . . [as] an inward passion of the soul." While denying identification with objects in the material world, the sublime impels one to "identify ourselves with the abstractest essence"; the Stoic sublime, then, allows us to commune with God.[64]

In *Darkwater,* the sublime was both Stoic and Epicurean. The presence of God confirmed that the sublime could be evoked by the vastness and fullness of Christ. But, the farmer's wife was also stricken with the incommensurability of identification with that immensity because she could not love "niggers." She could not fully release the object of her hate even while being torn away from her world by tremendous affects. She did not experience the "pure" pleasure of contemplation here; she endured acute pain. She was bonded to a sensation of blackness from which she could only be freed by the destruction of the aesthetic value of whiteness. Her terror deepened as her confinement crystallized. Du Bois suggested that through her joyful agony she sensed not liberation but entrapment and that was her actual horror. Rather than rising above the world, she descended into misery for being complicit in the killing of an untold number of beautiful souls; her punishment was eternal regret. But Du Bois also suggested that the sublime, although philosophically attractive, has little pragmatic value. The farmer's wife was tied to her terror and grief in such a way as to forever forestall a full acknowledgment of her error; she could not dedicate her life to a search for similar mistakes and be redeemed. And so, it is easy to imagine that she is somewhere and somehow still screaming, caught in a closed short-circuiting loop. For a release from this shocking rapture and an acknowledgment of voice, we must turn finally to Du Bois's enactment of the conditions for a more careful reply.

"The Prayers of God" was a poignant poem that included a startling conversation with God and captured the experience of two sorts of aesthetic errors:

Red murder reigns;
All hell is loose;
On golden Autumnal air
Walk grinning devils, barbed and hoofed;[65]

The poem's apocalyptic scenery was a pastiche of all the riots of the Red Summer, casting their mobsters as minions of the underworld, finally spewed forth; the prayer accused God of being motionless and perhaps uncaring, "Thou sittest, dumb,":

Father Almighty!
This Earth is mad!
Rotten, palsied,
Our cunning hands
Stink with the entrails
Of our souls,
And Thou art dumb.[66]

Hell on earth was a form of spiritual and bodily decay; a sinner's plague upon all of humanity festered at the center of the poem, transfiguring it into a vigil awaiting the end of ends; the horror of world war loomed here as well as the earth prepared for its final abortion:

Death is here!
Dead are the living; deep-dead the dead
Dying are earth's unborn . . .
Poems and prayers, sun-glows and earth-songs;[67]

All the beautiful things were dying and in the face of such finality, the prayer heaved upward a final call:

Have mercy!
Have mercy upon us, miserable sinners! . . .
Hear!
Speak!
In Christ's Great Name—[68]

And as the prayer seemed to resign to its pitiful end, God acknowledged the affective and ethical character of the offering, actualizing the prayer's voice and alerting us to two significant shortcomings in aesthetic judgment:

I hear!
Forgive me, God!
Above the thunder I hearkened;
Beneath the silence, now,—
I hear![69]

God questioned the worshiper:

This gold?
I took it . . . Blood?
It flowed for Thee, O Lord.
War? . . .
Dominion, Lord, and over black, not white;
Black, brown, and fawn,
And not Thy Chosen Brood, O God,
We murdered.
To Build Thy Kingdom[70]

Du Bois's poetry revealed a calculus; the reader had been led to hear the poem as a plea to God from the voices from behind the veil. Initially one sensed a black prayer to a distant God in a world gone crazy. But now we know that we were foreclosing other possibilities; and the pathos constitutive of the prior assumption was mediated by the deep and passionate hatred evident in the prayer of an imperialist suffering with the loss of certainty regarding the permanency of white supremacy. And of course this was Du Bois's plan—to undermine our sense of conviction in our own judgments even as we acknowledge the aesthetic character of the "truth" of what was now before us. It is this sort of calculative thinking that literary theorists have criticized in *Darkwater* and throughout Du Bois's literary life.[71] Elaine Scarry was more generous with aesthetic practices such as this, saying that calculation evoked an important aesthetic response; we must "figure out the right answer [for this moment of revelation] because this is not an occasion for carelessness or for leaving your own postures wholly to chance."[72] In order to figure out the "right answer" we must read on with even greater perceptual care as the white supremacist sought to justify white supremacy through an appeal to its highest aesthetic value:

> To drape our wives and little ones,
> And set their souls a-glitter—
> For this we killed these lesser breeds . . .
> For this, too, once and in Thy Name,
> I lynched a Nigger—[73]

But the sheen of white glitter could not shield the Imperialist from seeing the awful truth of his shocking crimes:

> *Thou?*
> *Thee?*
> *I lynched Thee?*
> Awake me, God! I sleep!
> That black and riven thing—was it Thee?
> That gasp—was it Thine? . . .
> Have all the wars of all the world,
> Down all dim time, drawn blood from Thee?[74]

The horror of this "truth" momentarily threatened to incapacitate this worshiper in the sublime like we saw with the farmer's wife. But it was the voice of God itself that mobilized and "saved" this person. The world's darker folks were no longer felt as despicable beings that should be happily sacrificed for white beauty and the "greater glory of God." The aesthetic value of whiteness as an ideal form collapsed under the strain of this "truth" and it was a wonder that the roar from this demolition did not make the worshiper deaf and dumb; in the place of white perfection, Du Bois substituted his own faith in the human spirit finally confronting the possibility of the end of all ends:

> I sense that low and awful cry—
> Who cries? Who weeps?
> With silent sob that rends and tears—
> Can God sob? . . .
> Who prays?

I hear strong prayers throng by, . . .
Can God pray?[75]

God prays, suggested Du Bois, in and through the anguish, the suffering of humanity; every life utters a prayer, a call, and every life must reply. This call was the undercurrent of *Darkwater,* spilling out of Du Bois's personal narrative and rushing through every word of the book; it coursed through "The Damnation of Women," where it asked for the acknowledgment of the desperate need for female reproductive rights; it spouted from the chamber of the "King" in "The Call," where a sole black woman stepped forward among the chosen servants; it poured softly over the beautiful face of a black baby Jesus, and it rained down upon a weak and weeping farmer's wife. People turned away, hid, and fell back in "disgust." But here, standing at the end of time, the prayers of God were answered:

Thou needest me?
Thou *needest* me?
Thou needest *me*?
Poor wounded soul!
Of this I never dreamed. I thought—
Courage, God,
I come![76]

Du Bois did not exactly offer prayers to God, for his "God" was "the potential nobility of man."[77] What he did give us in *Darkwater* was a passion resembling the faithful; a devotion that shaped his ongoing efforts at conjuring black aesthetics corresponding to the kind of black subjectivity required for the making of a black public, an artistic practice that would enact a "direct confrontation with the other's freedom."[78] Thus, *Darkwater* met head on the fears of racist works like Lothrop Stoddard's influential screed *The Rising Tide of Color Against White World Supremacy.*[79] *Darkwater* confirmed some of the deepest fears and dramatized how such worries arose out of aesthetic practices that habituated ugly emotions. There was a moment in Elaine Scarry's book where she was not so optimistic about our willingness to accept our errors; the denial of newfound beauty cemented a false conviction in the perfection of our sense perceptions. Through a delicious interpretation of the *Iliad,* where Odysseus, drawn by Nausicaa's beauty on the beach, emerged out of the ocean that threatened to take him down, Scarry represented beauty as a life preserver that brought us ashore; but carelessness or neglect of beauty left one vulnerable to being flung back into the murky depths.[80]

This was why *Darkwater* offered both beauty and death. In the face of a deep and passionate hatred, *Darkwater* constituted the defiance of a community and the determination to drown out the voices of those who deny the "truth" of human worth and dignity. And as a work that approached beauty, which demanded that the reader search among its pages for beautiful things, it constituted the conditions for the endowment of Du Bois's voice. *Darkwater* still ends incompletely because Du Bois did not want to finish a statement, he desired to begin a conversation. At this, he succeeded. Many white critics grilled it as a work of bitterness and hate, even while recognizing Du Bois's unparalleled power as a writer. More importantly, tropes of the New Negro orchestrated black intellectual attitudes and politics for and against its substance and its form; it was clear that many black intellectuals wanted the *Crisis* editor to tread more lightly around white sensitivity and to provide a clearer demarcation between the "poetic" and the "scientific." Lewis noted that "the culture of criticism of the New Negro, then, was becoming more robust, with Du Bois serving both as its preeminent model and victim."[81] The predicament was appropriate and was an enduring sign of the aesthetic value of *Darkwater.* Unlike *The Souls of Black Folk,* which, despite its controversial assault on Booker T. Washington, is remembered as having critics lined up behind it in near-uniform praise, *Darkwater* may be forever thought of as a work that pushed mightily against the fault lines of America. And if we apply an unusual amount of perceptual care to our America, we may yet sense its intensity. But *Darkwater*'s more immediate impact was on the emerging New Negro movement; as the younger generation clamored and squawked about artistic freedom, the elder intellectual was in no mood to grant such literary license. His writing about deep race hate sparked intense discussion and debate regarding the sort of aesthetic and artistic practices that would best seize and channel new energies circulating in urban settings about race and society. Whether New Negroes wished for it or not, *Darkwater* splashed about in the streets of Harlem and elsewhere, whetting the appetites of impressionable youth while threatening to turn black aesthetics into a "purely" political movement. The voices from behind the veil blared forth in cacophonous discord.

3

"The Last and Best Gift of Africa"

Du Bois, Dewey, and a Black Public

W. E. B. Du Bois may have been seated comfortably in his high-back leather chair in the offices of the *Crisis* as he perused the morning mail in August 1925, a day that was sure to be a muggy one in New York City; but he almost certainly felt like the captain of a ship trying to put down a full-scale mutiny. After enjoying the rank of "prime mover" of the New Negro movement and navigating the NAACP's journal onto uncharted racial waters,[1] Du Bois was hit full in the face by an insurgency from within his organization and was being outmaneuvered by rival imprimaturs of the budding black arts. A year earlier, Mary White Ovington and Joel Spingarn, long-time NAACP board members, produced a study of the editorial and financial strength of the *Crisis.* The motive and timing of the study rankled the editor greatly, for Ovington and Spingarn had been trying to get their prickly friend to be more responsive to the views of the trustees with little success. Now, however, they were armed with evidence that the state of the *Crisis* was weakening. Their report was scathing: subscriptions were down by nearly 50 percent from all-time highs, the editorial direction seemed muddled, and much of the reporting was redundant. But the real dagger thrust at Du Bois was the opinion that the National Urban League's upstart journal, the *Opportunity,* had offered to date the finest intellectual assessment of black artistry of any "colored magazine."[2]

The morning of August 3rd promised no relief for the beleaguered editor; a letter from one of the more prominent black judges of the literature contest sponsored by the *Crisis,* the respected novelist Charles W. Chesnutt, raised the hotly contested issue of how and when blackness should be a topic in African American literature. After dutifully spelling out for Du Bois the key elements in good storytelling—theme, plot, language, style, and reader impact—Chesnutt stressed that "the most important of all is the effect upon the reader." Since a good story must "ring true," must exhibit fidelity to the reader, the submission entitled "Three Dogs and a Rabbit" failed to persuade the late-Victorian writer of its sincerity due to the revelation of a "race motive" that violated "dramatic necessity." Chesnutt's critique sharpened its focus: "The story would have been, from any standpoint *but that of a colored reader,* equally dramatic and effective without that disclosure. So the story is not convincing." Du Bois would have surely bristled at the core presumption underlying this opinion; that the standpoint of the "colored" reader should not be used to shape New Negro artistic and aesthetic practices; that the "colored" standpoint signals distortion of and deviation from the "truth." The question of when and where blackness enters was answered, according to Chesnutt, by appealing to objectivity—a universal audience. For everyone knows, Chesnutt continued to lecture Du Bois, that Negro dialect, for example, while wonderfully funny and popular, was "merely mispronunciation . . . a local corruption of good English."[3]

Chesnutt's opinion was hardly peculiar. William Stanley Braithwaite, a black educator and critic and a frequent contributor to the *Crisis,* "refused to write political propaganda and generally avoided the theme of race."[4] It was not from the "colored" reader that these black intellectuals sought approval. From their perspective, the "colored" reader needed to be taught how to transcend "racial motives" even when, as Chesnutt himself demonstrated in one of his most widely read books, *Conjure Woman,* the black writer writes about "colored" characters. The key to understanding Chesnutt's remonstration lies in the commonplace perspective on "dramatic necessity." The phrase invokes the logic of analytic aesthetics, which seeks to uncover the a priori conditions regarding the achievement of beauty. Reflecting the grasp of Kantian aesthetics, the reader must experience pleasure from the storytelling by being a disinterested reader—by attaining a state of mind where the cognitive faculties can enjoy free play, can be released from any particular use, value, or moral purpose while contemplating the aesthetic object.[5] To Chesnutt, then, the necessary conditions for the free play of the reader's imagination were deferred by the introduction of a "racial motive"—a motive that constrained rather than liberated.

Du Bois had long ago dedicated himself to promoting just this kind of racial motive. To him, the "colored reader" was not merely an audience, a group of subscribers to the *Crisis;* the colored reader stood for the "problem" of the color line as well as the project necessary for its remedy. The colored reader made up the "thinking Negro," the black folk who could be pulled together to spearhead the fight for civil rights and social justice. The colored reader was neither passive nor disinterested; her or his standpoint was situated in time and space where vague memories of African genius can be cultivated and ushered through to the present and to Harlem. The colored reader, therefore, could be moved from sharing common feelings about racial oppression to sharing common specific interests about social change through collective action. The dustup between Du Bois and Chesnutt signaled the instability of the project of bringing into liveliness a black aesthetic reflecting any sort of consensus about black art. Du Bois saw such fragmentation as a threat to the production of an African American public. Du Bois believed he could not count on folks like Chesnutt or Braithwaite to perform this sort of race labor. In this chapter, I examine Du Bois's attempt to produce a black public by imagining pragmatist aesthetics as a conceptual schema for New Negro artistic works. Du Bois appropriated and altered American pragmatic philosophy in order to theorize black aesthetic experiences and practices. To Du Bois, the value of black art lies in its capacity to transform the basic character of black life and American civic culture. In order to bring about such a transformation, Du Bois sought to grasp, shape, and channel the artistic and aesthetic practices of the New Negro movement as modes of producing a public for the constitution of black voice.

In so doing, Du Bois anticipated the problems of publicity that occupied his contemporaries like John Dewey. American pragmatism displays a nostalgic imagination regarding the Great Community, a vibrant organism capable of democratic governance of just relations among diverse people and groups. By reading Du Bois beside Dewey, I intend to address the American pragmatic "evasion" of African American intellectualism. As Du Bois's rhetoric generated black publicity, we may better apprehend how he positioned black aesthetic practices as constitutive of the artful communication for which Dewey longed to reanimate the Great Community. Also, by putting Du Bois in dialogue with Dewey, we may appreciate another echo of Du Bois's voice—the endowment that is achieved when we mediate across time and space Dewey's acknowledgment of Du Bois. First, I provide a discussion of pragmatist aesthetics, paying particular attention to the relations among aesthetic experience, aesthetic practice, and the potential for publicity. Pragmatism asserts that aesthetic experiences stimulate one's senses toward one's environment, provoking new forms of understanding one's relations with others. Aesthetic experiences may also inspire novel aesthetic practices that accompany new forms of black audibility and visibility; the affects animated through these practices may move folks into fresh social alignments where they may realize shared interests, constituting publics. I will demonstrate how Du Bois argued that New Negro artistry should be generative of black aesthetic experiences of racial strife and African cultural memory. Du Bois exploited the pragmatist's yearning for forms of naturalism by reinterpreting primitivism as a modern and ancient source of aesthetic experiences and practices. Black pragmatist aesthetics imagines "savagery" as a public agency. In closing, I contemplate the constraints on black voice and publicity introduced and modified by Du Bois's rhetoric.

Toward a Pragmatist Aesthetics

John Dewey, in *Art as Experience,* responded to a form of bodily suffering brought about by existing in the machine age. The rise of the factory as the engine of the Industrial Revolution helped to create wealth and leisure for the owners of capital while dominating the everyday work life of labor. It is easy to see why Dewey would be concerned about how mechanical reproduction would affect the working body; one goes about one's day regimented by the tempo of automatic processes. The muscles in the arms, legs, and back stretch and strain in time with the cadence of the making of things seen only in fragments; the assembly line nearly perfected the orchestration of human collective movement. The worker is trained to do the same series of behaviors over and over as fast or as slow as automation and productivity dictated. Dewey lamented three forms of separation produced, along with all those commercial objects, in the machine age: the imagination from the body, the worker from the overall means of production, and everyday life from aesthetic experience.[6] Although this description of self-alienation is of the laborer's life, we shall see that virtually everyone in the modern era endured "esthetic hunger."[7]

At the heart of pragmatism is naturalism, it "is dedicated to rooting aesthetics in the natural needs, constitution, and activities of the human organism."[8] The human body requires interaction with its environment and with other creatures to survive and thrive. As living beings, our bodies mediate our surroundings; we process nourishments, we encounter heat and cold and adjust to each, we measure the distance between objects with our eyes and hands, we hear the buzz of bees and the song of birds, and we flee in fear of beasts and delight at the sight of children playing. Human life itself is made up of these encounters with our times and spaces, and death marks our departure from them: "Here in germ are balance and harmony attained through rhythm. Equilibrium comes about not mechanically and inertly but out of, and because of, tension." Communion and confrontation define the porous membrane between us and everything else, and the mediation that occurs (always already occurring) is constitutive of change that comes momentarily to rest and then changes again. This transaction, this passage between states of being, marks our experience of our humanity. Essential to this experience are the affects that are stirred, intensified, and coordinated by the subject's construal of these movements and rationalized as emotions. Dewey explained the relational character of feelings in this manner: "But, in fact, an emotion is *to* or *from* or *about* something objective, whether in fact or in idea. An emotion is implicated in a situation, the issue of which is in suspense and in which the self that is moved in the emotion is vitally concerned." What we sometimes obliquely refer to as "normal" life *is* experience. But this reference occludes an important insight. Dewey bemoaned the fact that the "normal" in the machine age was regimented and routinized; the "normal" was the same as always and, thus, experience risked becoming a programmed joylessness.[9]

In Weberian terms, this over-rationalization of social life was accompanied by various forms of segmentation that deceived us into feeling that it was "normal" to be unhappy—shunted away from the sources of livelier living. In this apportionment, religion lost spirituality, education misplaced imagination, and government forgot the people. Artists, too, were victimized. Once an integrated person in the social life of the community, artists now were separated—pushed aside by mass production of fetishized objects; they produced art for the sake of personal expression. Moreover, in order to be noticed, artists "often feel obliged to exaggerate their separateness to the point of eccentricity." These individualistic works of art became identified with prized personal possessions of art collectors and museum curators, further discoloring "normal" life. Once fooled into believing that it takes high-minded leisure to appreciate artworks in order to be brought back to life, we accept the premise that the ordinary citizen should not expect to enjoy aesthetic experiences—that one's mundane state of affairs was inevitable, perhaps even right. But we crave stimulation and seek it nevertheless; so we turn to "the cheap and the vulgar."[10] It was in this fashion, Dewey asserted, that high art was believed to foster aesthetic experiences, while popular culture was considered to be mere entertainment. Importantly, this misunderstanding about the nature of aesthetic experience dampened the capacity of so-called low art to be transformative: "The idea of art and the aesthetic as a separate realm distinguished by its freedom, imagination, and pleasure has as its underlying correlative the dismissal assumption that ordinary life is necessarily one of joyless, unimaginative coercion." We have arrived at Dewey's central concern: to make aesthetic experiences more readily available to "normal" people. If "art would be richer and more satisfying to more people,"[11] aesthetic experiences might provide the "impulsion" for folks to dream otherwise.[12] But what does a pragmatist really mean by aesthetic experience?

When we speak of aesthetics broadly, we refer to a philosophy of sense-making that occurs through our organic experience of our surroundings. Alan Goldman calls the resultant understanding "sensuous knowledge."[13] The intellect is critically engaged here as well. We ask ourselves what does it mean to have this feeling? How is it different from previous affects? And what should I do now? These questions, however, do not fully amount to inquiries into aesthetic experience as a special kind of experience because they characterize our daily, unavoidable negotiations with our living. As noted before, we must ask them in order to survive, to get along with others. There is a notable difference between asking these sorts of questions robotically—like we may do at large gatherings when we are met with a faceless crowd with which we must interact—and doing so with enthusiasm. The former is unenergetic and, perhaps, insincere; it may be performed through the instigation of previous manners and mechanisms; we pay attention, but it is a dull sort of consideration. We learn from it too, thus it has value. But it is not aesthetic value because it does not awaken us to the possibilities for living and being outside of the scope of behaviors and attitudes routinely recalled by the faceless crowd. It does not pull us intellectually, spiritually, and emotionally toward new ground. What is required is a unified response that literally changes our perception of the faceless crowd into a sparkling vision of fascinating faces. In a sense, we must (for a short time) surrender our balance: "The live being recurrently loses and reestablishes equilibrium with his surroundings. The moment of passage from disturbance into harmony is that of intensest life."[14] Richard Shusterman describes an aesthetic experience as a temporary disjuncture in time and space that "invigorates and vitalizes us, thus aiding our achievement of whatever further ends we pursue." American pragmatism owes much to the historicism and holism of Hegelian dialectics, a debt implicated in Shusterman's continued account: "Aesthetic experience is differentiated not by its unique possession of a particular element but by its consummate and zestful integration of all the elements of ordinary experience."[15] Standing idly in the midst of the faceless crowd, what happens to bring about such an intense interest in faces?

Aesthetic experiences can be provoked from within and from without. A raspy voice when one expects velvet; a soft kiss on the cheek when a firm handshake is the norm; a strong guttural laugh that breaks through the white noise of hushed conversations. Or, the shade on an idea recedes to reveal cognition more clearly as one looks upon a political campaign button worn on a colleague's lapel. In any event, Dewey asserted that this happening "stirs up a store of attitudes and meanings derived from prior experience. As they are aroused into activity they become conscious thoughts and emotions, emotionalized images. To be set on fire by a thought or scene is to be inspired." Inspiration, like heat applied to any object, excites the being through and through. Once inspired one cannot sit still: "Yet what is evoked is not just quantitative, or just more energy, but is qualitative, a transformation of energy into thoughtful action, through assimilation of meanings from the background of past experiences." In skillful hands, an aesthetic experience can become an aesthetic practice that "reaches out tentacles for that which is cognate, for things that feed it and carry it to completion."[16] Indeed, pragmatist aesthetics insists that aesthetic experiences find meaningful expression; inspiration sets them off, but aesthetic experiences themselves are achieved "because they are shared." A personal transformation can become a collective one under the right circumstances and with the right expression. This is, of course, why Plato feared poetics and disparaged rhetoric. And since pragmatism seeks to level the kind of distinctions erected by Platonism, "art's role (like philosophy) is not to criticize reality but to change it; and little change can be effected if art remains a cloistered domain."[17] Far from sequestering art, Dewey sought for aesthetic experiences to inhabit everyday life so as to revitalize the psychical and material conditions obliged for a Public.

In *The Public and its Problems,* Dewey set an idealized Great Community against the Leviathan he called the Great Society. There are competing senses of "Great" working here; the former indexed the civic good while the latter indicated immense complexity. They also arose and were sustained by distinct "theories of the state." Dewey contended that prominent conceptualizations of government started from a false premise; that is, they assumed that there was an inherent and immutable "instinct" in humanity to formulate specific forms of political systems. Theorists beginning with this instinct in mind, rationalized current state formations as "natural" reflections of the idea of the state with which we were born. This thinking also led to the tendency to make corrections in state policy to better yield the a priori instinct. Great men, who are presumably wiser than the hoi polloi, shaped the growth and maturation of society "in terms of authorship." But men have special interests in mind (not an a priori instinct), Dewey averred; we enter into transactions and exchanges with interested others to promote our well being. And when those exchanges and contracts produce consequences that ripple (or flood) outward, away from the private citizens directly involved and toward others who are indirectly impacted by them, we have the making of a public: "The characteristic of the public as a state springs from the fact that all modes of associated behavior may have extensive and enduring consequences which involve others beyond those directly engaged in them." Dewey contended that if we wished to constitute better government, we must dispense with the notion of authorship, principally determined by a collection of individuals, and reclaim the notion of authority granted by citizens: "Those indirectly and seriously affected for good or for evil form a group distinct enough to require recognition and a name. The name selected is The Public."[18] How is such a group formed? What process secures acknowledgment of shared interest?

The problem with the public is precisely the gathering force required to allow persons to perceive clearly how they are impacted by the associated behaviors of others and act collectively to have those consequences regulated and controlled. Persons must be sensitive to their shared plight as something to be addressed as a public; they must be awakened from slumber. Here, Dewey took what we have come to call a "linguistic turn." While critiquing social theory for presupposing a preindividuated subject who must then be reconciled with society, Dewey claimed that "the essential need . . . is the improvement of the methods and conditions of debate, discussion and persuasion" for persons to more fully recognize the power that resides in coordinated action. Individuals, Dewey said, were not striving for freedom *from* the domination of society; rather, persons were desiring new forms of social relations: "They may think they are clamoring for a purely personal liberty, but what they are doing is to bring into being a greater liberty to share in other associations, so that more of their individual potentialities will be released and their personal experiences enriched." Such enrichment is constitutive of aesthetic experiences that serve as the inspiration for artistic and aesthetic practices in the form of communication arts.[19] What I have just described is *the process of publicity.* The public is not waiting for us "out there," it must be born through aesthetic experiences mobilizing specific affective registers making up and bonding together the shared interests of a group.

Dewey was at once realistic regarding the innumerable ways that the Great Society structures nonaesthetic experiences and hopeful about the reanimation of aesthetic experiences. Rapid technological advancement accelerated the transformation of the city-state into the nation-state by establishing political economic connections among localities through the telegraph, telephone, railways, and highways. Given the racially diverse make up of these localities, Dewey marveled at how successfully a form of "unity" was manufactured. He also saw the shadow of an "eclipse" of the public: "In many respects, the consolidation has occurred so rapidly and ruthlessly that much of value has been lost which different peoples might have contributed."[20] We need to keep in mind that at the time Dewey was fashioning his critique of the public, American rhetoric of race conceived Eastern and Southern European immigrants as having distinctive "racial" characteristics from Anglo-Americans; these racial differences needed to be "ruthlessly" subjected to forms of "consolidation" to yield "unity." My point here is to note two competing implications of such ruthless consolidation: first, processes of Americanization, made popular and inexorable by Theodore Roosevelt, worked arduously through carefully crafted aesthetic practices to homogenize cultures, contributing to everyday nonaesthetic experiences. Early twentieth-century immigrants from Europe were compelled to adopt as many Americanisms as possible, changing their names, religions, and languages. But second, David Roediger contends that new arrivals to New York harbor learned from the start a rhetoric of race that located their bodies in relation to other "raced" persons and the political economy of the nation. One may be a "wop," a "greaser," or a "guinea"; each term pregnant with meanings and values that constrain and promote specific bodily and collective movements. Folks subjected to this rhetoric of Americanization quickly learned how to negotiate it, to make the terms fluid or coherent so as to constitute shared interests. In short, this American racial rhetoric shaped aesthetic experiences through aesthetic practices of "race" constitutive of segregation, discrimination, and violence.[21]

Even though mechanisms of Americanization dulled experience in keeping with the logic of the machine age, the rhetoric of race animated aesthetic experiences due to the associated demand to navigate tense racial demarcations and occasionally enter into sensitive "interracial" exchange. To Dewey, these competing forces were responsible for the "eclipse" of the public and might also serve as the source of its manufacture. Recall the remarkable technological network responsible for producing even a tenuous "unity" among diverse groups. Dewey outlined a complex political economic system required to regulate and order exchange relations: the party system, the big business lobby, and the operations of caucuses. How can a public be constituted through the perception of shared interests regarding the consequences of actions by political agents if we only vaguely sense the agents and cannot fully understand the consequences? In response to such complexity, the circumference of shared interests shrinks. "It is not that there is no public," Dewey lamented, "There is too much public, a public too diffused and scattered and too intricate in composition. And there are too many publics . . . with little to hold these different publics together in an integrated whole." This problem was fascinating, and its resolution was in the interest of a healthy democracy and the operations that constitute it. Dewey warned against a fragmentation of the Public into distinct and uncommon publics, and I share his concern. But we must be wary of the mechanisms for consolidation, for they can squeeze the life out of us, and we rightfully regenerate ourselves in enclaves where we can specify and ritualize norms and customs, values and beliefs made of a common interest in the "same" political "object." Dewey comprehended this too; sources of aesthetic experience were available in art: "Artists have always been the real purveyors of news, for it is not the outward happening in itself which is new, but the kindling by it of emotion, perception and appreciation."[22]

The chief problem with "too many publics," for Dewey, was the fact that they were mainly derived from complicated governmental agencies that may lose touch with democratic daily life; political democracy was the result of technology altering the manner in which persons, groups, and institutions associated with one another. Once established, however, forms of political democracy were treated as sacred symbols of democracy and, thus, resisted being changed. But the conditions of everyday life were dynamic and vital; the agencies and bureaucracies ostensibly set up to serve our daily needs fell out of observance of us. They must be revised and such reform must be humanistic, not mechanistic: rehabilitation must be guided by public interest. Somehow publics must be able to identify themselves with a Public that hears and responds to their differing needs and desires without melting them into one, and this sort of identification has to *precede* political reform so that the transformed relations among the Public and its publics may structure it: "The highest and most difficult kind of inquiry and a subtle, delicate, vivid and responsive art of communication must take possession of the machinery of transmission and circulation and breathe life into it." But Dewey's work gestured unconsciously toward the practical problem of the "color line." The Great Community only has a chance for life if it is generative of a "close neighborhood experience. . . . How well do we understand our neighbors? . . . Democracy must begin at home, and home is the neighborly community."[23]

New Negro movement leaders resided in Dewey's intellectual neighborhood—and he knew it.[24] *The Public and its Problems* emerged out of a series of lectures delivered in January 1926, at the height of the New Negro movement. Dewey drew from the critical thinking of an impressive array of minds—from Aristotle to Walt Whitman. And yet, the work is disquieting because it sought "the reconstruction of face-to-face communities" without acknowledging any black face or black community. I am not merely pointing out the raced presupposition that black intellectualism was nonexistent. Dewey's project was doomed if it could not, from the beginning, be sensitized to the aesthetic experiences of race. At the heart of Du Bois's rhetorical activity, before, during, and after the production of *The Public and its Problems,* was a critical inquiry into how aesthetic experiences of blackness may open up ways of making emergent forms of publics through the constitution of black voice.

Pragmatist Aesthetics, Voice, and Publicity in the New Negro Movement

It is no exaggeration to assert that the audience gathered at New York's Civic Club on the evening of March 21, 1924, entered into a covenant goaded on by aesthetic experiences of what would soon be referred to as a Negro Renaissance.[25] Organized by Charles S. Johnson, editor of *Opportunity,* the affair was advertised as a celebration of Jessie Fauset's novel *There Is Confusion.* The promotion of the evening's events as recognition of the accomplishment by the literary editor for the *Crisis* could easily be considered as bait and switch. Fauset received kind applause as she was introduced, but the master of ceremonies Alain LeRoy Locke, of Howard University, had no intention of dwelling on her for very long. There were many distinguished black writers to be presented, some in absentia. Langston Hughes, the handsome young poet from many parts of the world, was traveling abroad while his name was uttered with great enthusiasm. Also present in spirit only were Claude McKay and Jean Toomer. Countee Cullen, Harlem's very own favorite poetic son, was in attendance and there was already anticipation of a future book of verse. Fauset would sit stewing while Georgia Douglas Johnson, Rudolph Fisher, Gwendolyn Bennett, and Eric Walrond were thrust into her spotlight.

Du Bois undoubtedly felt a little uneasy about the rapid displacement of his compatriot from the center ring but sensed something grander percolating among the participants. There was a heightened awareness of the convergence of diverse and intense affects around the bodies of these young black hopefuls. New York City had rarely before seen such an array of interracial power brokers seated elbow to elbow, standing together in ovation of black nascent stars. There was an impressive array of black intelligentsia not only from Harlem but also railed in from Philadelphia and Washington, D.C.; moreover, the playwright Eugene O'Neill, the satirist H. L. Mencken, the editor Carl Van Doren, and Freda Kirchwey, the first female editor of the *Nation,* were only a few of the white illuminati contributing to the vigor and verve of the evening's proceedings. Everyone at the "coming out party" seemed electrified by the awesome spectacle of wealth and race made strangely palpable by the rupture the event exhibited of class and racial convention. If this was an aesthetic experience of the New Negro, it did not occur accidentally. Charles S. Johnson, a well-respected and Chicago-trained sociologist, arrived in New York in 1922 with the express intention of joining the fight for civil rights. After becoming editor and after watching the *Crisis* become the key forum for black artistic expression, *Opportunity* "switched . . . from being a forum for the cutting-edge articles of distinguished social scientists and educators to become the premiere review for the literary and artistic effusions of the so-called New Negro." Du Bois was already enacting a tactic that could perhaps transform the racial landscape by producing "exemplary racial images in collaboration with liberal white philanthropy, the culture industry centered in Manhattan, and artists from white bohemia."[26]

The Civic Club affair was a kiln that fired these persons and groups into a magnificent illusion of a unified community dedicated to cultivating keener and more powerful New Negro aesthetic experiences and practices. Indeed, we might be tempted with perfectly good reason to say that the shared interests in New Negro art—in directing its thematic structure, its editorial oversight, and the terms for its publication and distribution—amount to the emergence of a New Negro public; that the Civic Club hosted a strategic discursive act, "the first act of the Harlem Renaissance," and an important aesthetic practice constituting New Negro publicity. As black and white folks rose to pay tribute to this public and movement, persons testified to two complementary and competing conceptions of aesthetic understanding. Du Bois, Locke, Charles Johnson, and James Weldon Johnson had been waiting for many years to have a high-level acknowledgment of the affective and ethical dimensions of black speech—to be endowed with voice. Each wasted no time proclaiming that the New Negro heralded a "generation-skipping" force of nature; black folk had leapt forward in time, talent, industry, and temperament, and were now ready for social equality. Others took the podium and expressed a quiet angst regarding the modern human condition and revealed that their aesthetic experience of the evening was, in part, sparked by a craving for relief from the mechanics of society. For example, Carl Van Doren argued that the American literary scene had become monotonous, bland, and listless. These New Negroes brought gifts like the ancients to the modern world; the New Negro ushered in " 'color, music, gusto, the free expression of gay or desperate moods.' "[27] It is easy to imagine thunderstorm clouds gathering in Du Bois's mind upon hearing a prescription for black cultural performance written on checks and publishing contracts. But on this night, he joined in the applause for Van Doren while planning to appropriate the desire for a vibrant blackness as a topic for rhetorical invention and as a schema for New Negro aesthetic practices.

There were several problems facing any definition of black art: black cultural performance was already being thought of as imitative, or as primitive, or as needing to rise above the theme of race. As Sterling Brown argued in 1933, black writers had to contend with a long legacy of racist Southern literature that sought to heal a psychic trauma in the minds of white supremacists regarding a loss of prestige.[28] To some observers, the very idea of serious black writing was absurd. But Du Bois enacted a rhetorical tactic that defined black artistic and aesthetic practices as fundamentally informed by aesthetic experiences of black collective endurance of racist oppression. Du Bois argued that the practices emerging in the New Negro movement were ineluctably conditioned by African cultural habits; this connection allowed him to reimagine the figure of the "primitive" in ways that made the "savage" a co-equal in the remaking of the modern world. It was here where Du Bois took up Dewey's concerns over the Great Society, offering the African village as an ancient and contemporary architecture for the future. The artistic practices Du Bois enacted and recommended functioned as ways of instigating the endowment of New Negro voice and, perhaps, for bringing into being Dewey's Great Community as well.

During 1925, Du Bois seemed to be dedicating much of his considerable energies to harvest the crop that was planted at the Civic Club.[29] As I mentioned previously, Du Bois viewed the effort as a noble form of race labor, and he could be downright peevish toward folks he determined to be a threat to the well-being of the race. Lewis describes Du Bois's temperament thusly: "Seeing his people's predicament as that of an undermanned fire brigade facing an inferno, the editor came to regard uncoordinated and freelance undertakings within the race as nothing less than reprehensible."[30] In "The Social Origins of American Negro Art," Du Bois's topical sentence was a question meant to be a fulcrum for shifting the weight of the public conversation from discussing black writers to deliberating on the ethos of black art. "Is there any body of artistic expression which can be fairly called American Negro art?" he asked.[31] Let us note two implications here: first, Du Bois's answer posited collective aesthetic experiences as the ground for this body of artistic expression; second, Du Bois drew a troubling but effective distinction between "American artists of Negro descent" and black art. He was not always interested in making such a demarcation. In "The Contribution of the Negro to American Life and Culture," published in 1921, Du Bois took up "American literature by Negroes" as his subject.[32] In "Social Origins," Du Bois claimed that "Charles W. Chesnutt and William Stanley Braithwaite are both American Negroes who have done fine artistic work in the novel and poetry, but they could hardly be classed as contributing to any particular group expression." In 1921, Du Bois heaped high praise on Chesnutt and Braithwaite, but in "Social Origins" he pushed them aside. To be fair, Du Bois was remarkably consistent in his treatment of both men; the earlier essay presumed that "Negroes" produced "Negro art." The latter essay did not; it was more sensitive to the role of aesthetic experience in art and arose in the midst of conflict over the basic (and essential) "truth" of black art. Chesnutt and Braithwaite held fast to the belief that aesthetic experiences of blackness defiled art and crippled the artist. By 1925, it was time for Du Bois to cut them loose.

In contrast to the work of Chesnutt and Braithwaite, Du Bois proclaimed that, "there is without doubt a certain group expression of art which can be called American Negro. It consists of biographies written by former slaves and colored men of achievement, of poetry portraying Negro life and aspirations and activities, of essays on the 'Negro problem' and novels about the 'Color Line.' There are pictures and sculptures meant to portray Negro features and characteristics, plays to dramatize the tremendous situation of the Negro in America, and of course, above all, the group has expressed itself in music."[33] Du Bois gathered a wide assortment of cultural expression under the rubric of art and bonded them into a unified artistic practice through an appeal to history and emotion, realism and racism. These folks scattered across time and space in this passage responded to their individual life experiences in various ways; but there was also "a certain group compulsion . . . meaning that the wishes, thoughts and experiences of thousands of individuals influence consciously and unconsciously the message of the one who speaks for all." Two years earlier, in *Theatre Magazine,* Du Bois noted that the black dramatic instinct was not so much a biological trait as it was "a heritage, with common memories and experiences."[34] And, in an unpublished essay titled, "Contributions through Literature in Terms of Sociological Foundations," Du Bois, this time including Chesnutt in what is most likely an early work, specified common experiences of "work and human contact and organization" as the unifying principle for black culture.[35]

Why consider these common experiences aesthetic? In "Introduction to Folk Songs," a fragment apparently composed as a preface to another work, Du Bois explored the manner in which the black body mediated the transformation of pain and pleasure, therefore constituting aesthetic experience: "They [black folks] have known life with all its depths of sorrow and degradation and they have also experienced its finer and higher compensations in sunshine and love, sacrifice and toil." Du Bois's revision of pragmatism begins to become apparent. The transformation between states of being was a necessary phenomenon for aesthetic experience; but Dewey emphasized the pleasure of regaining harmony rather than the dread of impending disorder. Du Bois tested the body's durability by widening the expanse between pain and pleasure, between chaos and equilibrium, by characterizing the transformation as treacherous, as regaining one's footing means being pulled back from the brink of disaster. Du Bois, thus, made the black body in America the site of "intensely human" aesthetic experiences. Not only is the individual body subject to the torture of sadness and the elation of coming out on the other side, but the "group compulsion," so important to pragmatist aesthetics, becomes profound because it "was built on the sorrow and strain inherent in American slavery, on the difficulties that sprung from Emancipation, on the feelings of revenge, despair, aspiration and hatred which arose as the Negro struggled and fought his way upward."[36] Du Bois exposed a tension between a furtive aesthetic experience shared by "a great mass of millions of men" and the white supremacist system that sought to make permanent forms of black subjugation through slave codes, black codes, and Jim Crow.[37] On the one hand, the near-complete domination of black bodies throughout US history amplified Du Bois's assertion of collective, conscious and unconscious, aesthetic experiences. Each of the forms of black art outlined above called out the name of a specific degradation, and many hearers shuddered in response. Du Bois published numerous photos of mutilated bodies and descriptions of what he referred to as "deadly amusements," the spectacular ritual of cutting, stabbing, shooting, and burning black men and women to death in the South; these atrocities preserved Du Bois's outrage and relay to us the terror inspired by lynching. Through Richard Wright, Grace Elizabeth Hale is able to convey the unimaginable: "Hearing that 'the white folks' quietly shot his classmate's brother, Richard Wright recalled the impact all 'white death' had on young African American men: 'the white brutality that I had not seen was a more effective control of my behavior than that which I knew. The actual experience would have let me see the realistic outlines of what was really happening, but as long as it remained something terrible and yet remote, something whose horror and blood might descend upon me at any moment, I was compelled to give my entire imagination over to it.' "[38] We hear how one can be seized by the awful anticipation of an aesthetic experience and how the mind works to keep the experience afar and yet lively. Terror is an aperture to aesthetic experience and shapes artistic practices: "The Negro has given the world new music, new rhythm, new melody and poignant, even terrible expression of joy, sorrow and despair. The world dances and weeps at the beating of the black man's baton."[39]

Let us recall that there were complementary and competing aesthetic understandings implicated in Du Bois's rhetorical construction of black pragmatist aesthetics. Du Bois attempted to constitute the idea that black folk widely shared aesthetic experiences and these have and should condition the New Negro's artistic and aesthetic practices. These practices can make publics emerge if they move folks to acknowledge the ethical and emotional dimensions of speech, endowing the artists with voice. But lynching stimulated appetites in white onlookers and participants that were quite different from Wright's description of the terror experienced by black victims. For whites, the mutilation and consumption of black bodies ramified the aesthetic experience of white mastery, an experience bordering on the sublime as it "purified" and unified white subjectivities.[40] In the context of the more refined Civic Club affair, the primary duty of the New Negro was to satiate white modern aesthetic "hunger." New Negro artistry was commended by folks like Van Doren as a fountain of youthful naturalism to be consumed by those who can no longer drink directly from the spring. Dewey described the worldview in this way:

> There is much in the life of the savage that is sodden. But, when the savage is most alive, he is most observant of the world about him and most taut with energy. As he watches what stirs about him, he, too, is stirred. His observation is both action in preparation and foresight of the future. He is as active through his whole being when he looks and listens as when he stalks his quarry or stealthily retreats from a foe. His senses are sentinels of immediate thought and outposts of action, and not, *as they so often are with us,* mere pathways along which material is gathered to be stored away for a delayed and remote possibility.[41]

Dewey's "savage" exuded energy, vitality, and intensity; these were the forces Van Doren craved. Dewey described a life unmediated by system, society, mechanical regulation, and thus, "most alive." His "savage" was spared the social death endured by "us"; but there was nothing in his description that would safeguard savages' lifeblood if they were suddenly transplanted to the modern world; it was environment that mattered most. Taking advantage of both Van Doren's appetite and Dewey's conceptualization of the value of the "primitive" and his native habitat, Du Bois steeped the New Negro's pragmatist aesthetics into the eternal life force of African soil.

For Du Bois, the "origins" of New Negro artistry were nearly infinite. When describing the impact of slavery on Negro cultural expression, Du Bois paid tribute to the spirit of the slave: "Art expression in the day of slavery had to be very limited, a matter of wild strains of music with still wilder laughter and dancing."[42] This wildness soothed the soul and made New Negroes possible; but when we juxtapose the capaciousness of Africa with the "very limited" slave compound, we begin to understand the "still wilder" expression as an artistic practice energized by aesthetic experiences of slavery rather than, as was commonly held at the time, an essential characteristic of blackness. African culture inhabited the bodies of persons who were stolen and cramped aboard ships, whipped and raped and murdered; it should not be surprising that black expression gushed forth like a raging river in "wild strains of music." To understand the "origins" and to reinterpret them, Du Bois takes us back to Africa, for the first time, where we get our initial view of a village: "It was a thing of clay colored cream and purple, clean, quiet, small with perhaps a dozen or more homes. Authority was here and religion, industry and trade, education and art. It was not a complete thing from a modern point of view. It had little or no machinery, it lay almost defenseless against surrounding malaria. News service with the greater world, there was none." Originally titled, "The Essence of African Culture," this article romanced and reinterpreted African village life as the birthplace of the New Negro and as an alternative modernity. There was no hint of wildness in Du Bois's vision; there was order and peace, work, commerce, and faith. The village rolled into the surrounding world like water trickling into a stream. Since the village encountered and struggled with its natural environment, it was always changing. But its "beginning stretched back in time thousands and thousands of years and yet gathered to itself traditions and customs springing almost from the birth of the world." Timeless and changing, the village embodied the basic principles of pragmatist aesthetics. The village's sociality integrated art, religion, and education. Persons living here were socialized "completely" without destroying their humanity, without producing "esthetic hunger." Sounding like Dewey, Du Bois lamented that "when the nation attempts to socialize the modern man the result is often a soulless Leviathan."[43] Since it was a small, organically organized system, the village treated children individually, catering to their differing needs, cultivating their special talents. What emerged was a human being with self-respect and reverence for the village.

The figure of Dewey's "savage" materialized before us as well, transfigured into a worshiper of Africa's natural wonders: "The climate, the flora and fauna of Africa . . . [t]he sunshine of its central zones cloaks you like a golden blanket; it hangs heavy about your shoulders; it envelops you; it smothers you in soft but mighty embrace. The rain of Africa is a consuming flood, a river pouring out of heaven." The African must be keenly aware of these rapid and ferocious climate changes and behave accordingly: "In Africa the swift, the energetic are the Dead. In Africa the lazy survive and live . . . it is hiding from the fierce sunlight; it is shelter from the penetrating rain; it is defense from malaria." It was the body's violent confrontation with harshness and splendor, arriving at equilibrium through rest. It was African pragmatism. It was rational and contingent. The rhythm of the African's arbitration with her environment sired her aesthetic experiences and drew out a suitable practice that reconciled her body, mind, and community with the world that inhabited them: "It is this sort of thing that has given Africa beauty in exchange for slavery and disease; in exchange for that isolated provincialism which men call primitive culture. Deep in forest pictures and by the banks of low, vast rivers; in the deep tense quiet of the endless jungle, the human soul whispered its folk tale, carved its pictures, sang its rhythmic songs and danced and danced."[44]

There remained in Du Bois a partial investment in essentializing the heart of black aesthetics: "The sense of beauty which is the last and best gift of Africa to the world and the true essence of the black man's soul."[45] The last and best of Africa was also the "true" essence of its humanity. Such rhetoric may seem mystic, but Du Bois's aim was to constitute a black pragmatist aesthetics that supplied a "method" for a critical intervention in American social life. Shamoon Zamir argued that Du Bois sought to develop a "pragmatist sociology" that would force a "return of philosophical speculation to the realm of material existence."[46] Adolph Reed agrees with this assessment, noting that Du Bois's brand of pragmatism "can be construed as a 'humanized' positivism that invigorated the latter's notion of progress by emphasizing the importance of human action—an emphasis which, more likely than not, was rendered in practical terms to mean social engineering."[47] For both Du Bois and Dewey, a humanized positivism would insist on inspecting up close the concrete aesthetic and artistic practices inspired by aesthetic experiences and subjecting them to reasoned theoretical inquiry regarding their impact on social life. Shusterman sees Dewey as striving to conceptualize theory so that its value is as an intervention in practice: "as a critical, imaginative reflection on practice, emerging from practice and the second-order problems that practice always generates . . . what constitutes proper practice, and . . . how the practice should be continued or modified."[48]

The Public has been eclipsed by complicated mechanized processes that keep persons who were impacted by them from clearly perceiving the consequences of those processes. Common experience of the consequences of political action was not sufficient for the generation of forms of publicity; persons must have aesthetic experiences that were fulfilled through the expression and acknowledgment of the shared interests that were clarified by the experience. If we comprehend the machinery that Dewey described as constituting forms of aesthetic practices bringing forth near automatons, we can then treat Du Bois's rhetoric—what he would call his black art—as offering critical, imaginative reflections on those practices. By folding temporality, Du Bois invented a conduit through which primordial customs of Africa get announced at the gate of modern culture as methods for critical intervention in what Dewey and Du Bois each called "habits" of living. A habit was composed of the patterned accumulation of practices and experiences; habits were the result of training and make up the process of educating others. Quoting Du Bois's mentor, William James, Dewey suggested its most harmful effects: "'It dooms us all to fight out the battle of life upon the lines of our nurture or our early choice, and to make the best of a pursuit that disagrees, because there is no other for which we are fitted and it is too late to begin again. It keeps different social strata from mixing.'" Habits were "orderly and established ways of action";[49] they may be "intelligent,"[50] but they are stubborn: "habits of opinion are the toughest of all habits; when they have become second nature, and are supposedly thrown out of the door, they creep in again as stealthily and surely as does first nature."[51] Du Bois was in full agreement when he described race hate as "a vicious habit of mind."[52] So, what sort of intervention can alter such "brute training and drill"?[53]

In what amounts to a public confession of his own tremendous transformation while encountering the sorrow songs in rural Tennessee as a college student at Fisk University, Du Bois dramatized the kind of aesthetic experience necessary for the intercession of vicious habits:

> And there rolling down across the valley came music. It was as the Voice of Angels upon the Halls of God. It was the sorrow of riven souls suddenly articulate; it was the tears of slaves, the sobs of raped daughters, the quiver of murdered bodies, the defiance of deathless hope. I shivered and ran. I hurried along the stony creek, and up hard hills and through the grey and twinkling village. And ever as I ran the music, the terrible, beautiful music swept nearer. It became more human, louder, pulsating with life and vigor and yet more poignantly sweet. There was a building. . . . There within swayed and danced a people mad with song. It was the demoniac possession of infinite music. . . . O, it was bizarre. . . . I sat down cold with terror and hot with new ecstasy.[54]

Shocked and terrified, Du Bois was pulled along by the gravitational forces of something originating from an inner and outer compulsion. His daily routine—teaching black kids in a dilapidated schoolhouse—was forever altered for he cannot look upon their faces as he did before. Du Bois's transformation was recounted in many of his writings and marks the moment when he dedicated himself to social justice for black folk and wholly identified with blackness. The artistry of the New Negro had similar power because it fed off mother Africa's milk. Du Bois admitted in many writings that slavery dismantled African culture, amounting to "the entire break of millions of Negroes with their past: their language, their memories, their ideals and dreams, their habits of eating, bathing, playing, and even thinking," however, "this break was not complete."[55] The affective registers and force of

African art had "circled the world" and through the bodies of black Americans had been made "new." We have journeyed to Africa and back and are now prepared to hear—to acknowledge—the affective and ethical dimensions of black cultural performance, at once ushering into the world a public and endowing the New Negro with voice: "Have you heard the tom-tom in [Eugene] O'Neill's 'Emperor Jones'? Below this, this ecstasy of Fear, runs that rhythmic obbligato,—low, somber, fateful, tremendous, full of deep expression and infinite meaning; have you danced in your soul and have you heard a Negro orchestra playing Jazz? Your head may revolt, your ancient conventions scream in protest but your heart and body leaps to rhythm."[56]

Du Bois was taking advantage of the presumed "primitive" power of black art, the mysterious, magical force that Van Doren longed for and the thing that might satisfy Dewey's "esthetic hunger." But we should also recognize Du Bois's critical alteration in the temperament of the "savage." In "The Primitive Black Man," published in the *Nation,* Du Bois reiterated the reasonableness of "laziness" but insisted that African-inspired habits were not backward: "Primitive men are not following us afar, frantically waving and seeking our goals; primitive men are not behind us in some swift foot-race. Primitive men have arrived. They are abreast, and in places *ahead of us;* in others behind. But all their curving advance line is *contemporary, not prehistoric.*"[57] Du Bois reinvented the "primitive" as an alternative form of modernity, not by distinguishing it as an essentially different racial being but rather by emphasizing the "primitive's" capacity to generate differing aesthetic experiences and artistic practices. The Great Society was in such disrepair that Dewey fancied that, in order to instigate the Public, citizens may need to dream up "a new race of human beings to escape in the use made of political forms, from the influence of deeply ingrained habits . . . with their inwrought limitations of expectation, desire and demand." Dewey seemed to have a very limited imagination in terms of racial characteristics, but he was clear that a new "race" may bring new speech ways: "Communication can alone create a great community. Our Babel is not one of tongues but of the signs and symbols without which shared experience is impossible."[58]

Du Bois proposed a marriage of sorts between the "civilized" and the "primitive"; he emphasized that one of the chief benefits of the village system was its capacity to nurture richly efficient communicative practices: "Even the African city as it rose time and time again was a city of villages. Ancient Jenne, whence comes our modern word Guinea, 'had seven thousand villages so near to one another that the chief of Jenne had no need of messengers,' but cried his message from gate to gate and village to village until within a few moments it had gone a hundred miles to Lake Dibo."[59] If Dewey could put aside the hyperbole of Du Bois's sentiments, he might be inspired by the possibilities for New Negro pragmatist aesthetics to bring about the "perfecting of the means and ways of communication of meanings so that genuinely shared interest in the consequences . . . may inform desire and effort and thereby direct action."[60] New Negro aesthetic experiences and practices promised to provide a rupture in the Babel of the Great Society. For Du Bois, the aspiration was for black folk to constitute a black public composed of folks who "feed themselves upon a mass of literature which deals with themselves and their experiences in a particular way."[61] Shusterman understands this consumption as precipitating cultural transformation; one gets "new nourishment and alternative orientations."[62] The Great Community was conceived and begotten through "full publicity" of shared interests constitutive of "artful communication."[63] New Negro artistry offered fresh topoi for the invention of creative expressions that interrupt the hum of the machine; Dewey sensed this possibility while writing *The Public and Its Problems.* Dedicated to Albert C. Barnes, one of the white illuminati signing the covenant with Harlem's black intellectuals at the Civic Club in 1924, this work was informed by, even if largely unrecognized by Dewey, the vigorous affects bonding white patrons and critics to New Negroes. It would seem that at the heart of the solution to the Public's problems reside black pragmatist aesthetics. And it is precisely the "habit" of disregard that Dewey displays for African American pragmatic thought that I wish to repair.

The New Negro movement made great strides during 1925 and Du Bois was strutting too. He had imagined how black aesthetic practices could be enjoyed as aesthetic experiences, producing black voice and a black public. His rhetorical performances dramatized the manner in which folks should be inhabited by black aesthetics, be remade by them. In constituting a black public, the "truth" of black life was also altered from the "sordid facts" regarding sex and violence scattered across the pages of newspapers; this was so because when the materiality of living can be "beautifully expressed and transformed . . . into art, it becomes, from its very origin, new, unusual, splendid."[64] It was not the facts that become new; it was their meanings and values, their affective registers and alignments with our changed perspective. Black publicity led to black folk caring about the diverse needs of black folk: "The new Negro business man caters to colored trade. So far has this gone that today in every city of the United States with a considerable Negro population, the colored group is serving itself with religious ministration, medical care, legal advice, and education of children."[65] This self-interest arose through aesthetic experiences of blackness in New Negro art and life: "In drawing, painting, and sculpture the modern Negro artist is beginning rather late and half shamefacedly to paint himself and find himself not simply humanly beautiful but tremendously interesting in the dark and infinitely varied new types of this much mixed American Negro race."[66] For Du Bois, black pragmatist aesthetics yielded black self-love and care, being open to all the unknowable possibilities for black beauty. But we have all along been sensitive here to the complementary and competing aesthetic understanding of white audiences.

Writing in support of black social equality with whites, the essayist Sarah N. Cleghorn exposes us to a troubling phenomenon drawn from aesthetic experiences of artifacts of otherness: "Often when I take children to the Museum of Natural History, and note how they shriek and run away from the painted Indian masks exhibited there, I think of our characteristic American reaction to the question of social equality with Negroes. The children are at the same time fascinated and frightened; they are fascinated by their own fright. They are not intellectually, but emotionally deceived; their judgment is stampeded; they are mesmerized."[67] In the concluding chapter of *The Public and Its Problems,* Dewey explored the value of the pragmatic method as "experimental"; that is, as a way of testing and evaluating ways of social life and adjusting the fluid interests of groups with one another.[68] But in the American mind—including Dewey's—aesthetic experiences of blackness threatened to "stampede" judgment. Or, conversely, the habit of conceiving of aesthetic experiences as "positive" value drove one away from the "negative" space of race. Either way, the free play of experimentalism was itself eclipsed by the "characteristic American reaction to the question of social equality" with New (or old) Negroes. Du Bois conceived of these limitations to pragmatism much like Cleghorn—comprehensible in terms of the way children shrink from blackness. Here the children were encountering the cloistered effects of the museum, where otherness was preserved, made to stand still, to pose for white gazes. During the New Negro movement, the iconic space for such encounters was Harlem. But was this desire for the vitality projected into the soul of the other *necessary* for the constitution of the Public? Citizens must have a source of aesthetic nourishment that allowed for all other pursuits to be heightened; but if the New Negro was a conspirator in the constitution of the Public, if her or his aesthetic practices must stimulate the senses, can she or he also be a "normal" citizen? Or, does this "savage" always have to be peculiar and strange? The tension was (and remains) tremendous because the desire for the primal energies of the "savage" "scars" the subject of pragmatist aesthetics; her or his identity as American citizen was phantasmal—an imaginary concept that took shape in correspondence with New Negro "primitive" performances in service to the Public.[69] The terms of the New

Negro's integration were predetermined; her or his artistic and aesthetic practices must open wormholes to sacred times and utopist places.

We have now reached a silent space between Du Bois and Dewey. Du Bois insisted on a black public and invested nearly his entire oeuvre to bringing it into being. Without such black publicity, there can be no culturally distinct artistic and aesthetic practices to invigorate the Public. But Dewey was neglectful of black pragmatic thought; in his own terms, if black pragmatism goes unheeded by the Public, there can be no social knowledge of it. The Public was hampered by this omission and was in constant danger of stiffening itself against an aesthetic understanding of black life. Such rigidity hardened the outlines of "savagery," deepening its recession into lifeless myth—weakening whatever power it once held to generate aesthetic experiences. Without an artistic language for the production of shared interests and commonality, publics risked reifying their distinct interests. This dilemma still haunts us today as the American Public seeks to "solve" its immigration "problem" in a presumably humane and healthy manner; there are, of course, stark disagreements as to what "healthy" means and whose (public) health matters most. Pragmatism offers itself as a "method,"[70] not of resolution but of mediation; as a way to test and judge the ethical and affective character of practices meant to improve our lives. Dewey, thus, must acknowledge Du Bois (and other black pragmatists of the era like Alain Locke) if Dewey's notion of the Public can be enhanced by black voices. But as the velocity of the circulation of tropes of the New Negro increased, the tension among forces desiring their regulation or release burst some fragile alliances apart at the seams. It was on top of the violent shifts in New Negro terrain where Alain Locke's *The New Negro: An Interpretation* boldly sought to erect a defining discursive structure for New Negro aesthetic understandings.

4
"Negro Youth Speaks"
Alain Locke and *The New Negro*

Several years before her emergence as a prolific and eccentric writer, Zora Neale Hurston counted herself as one of the fortunate recipients of Alain Locke's counsel as an up-and-coming New Negro. Locke's advice and guidance began when he was briefly Hurston's professor at Howard University, where he encouraged her to submit short stories to the university's literature magazine.[1] Locke's influence on Hurston's aesthetic practices involved in the rooting up of Southern black folktales, songs, and rituals was intensely mediated by his complicated sense of propriety regarding when, where, and how specific qualities of "blackness" and self should be apparent in social life. Locke's biographers link this aesthetic sensibility to a deep self-consciousness: "The inwardness that attaches to a certain understanding of individualism was not necessarily that of a radical subjectivity—in which only the inward is true—but rather is seen by Locke as a term in a dialectic relation with how and under what conditions one should make oneself available or *visible to others.*"[2] In the late 1920s, Hurston was applying her training as an anthropologist and essayist to locate black folkways and narrate them in such a way as to display their basic dignity and elevate their value to American cultural life. Locke firmly believed that these folkways offered African Americans the keenest aperture through which they could sense the affective registers of African artistic practices, reinventing them as ways of making New Negro art. But these very aesthetic practices—and the racial values emerging through and around them—drew the intellectual and artistic interest of disparate cultural institutions and actors, generating the energy for friction among New Negroes and their benefactors. Such chafing was not only responsible for some difficult social relations among black and white folk striving to launch a black arts movement, it was constitutive of the very flows of power that specific agents like Locke sought to harness and regulate. Let us examine a brief case illustrating this point.

Writing to Hurston in Mulberry, Florida, in June 1928, Locke gratefully acknowledged the receipt of materials she shipped to him, some of which became Howard University museum pieces. Locke congratulated her "on your degree. That makes a period to that." This good feeling did not last long, however; when Locke turned to discuss Hurston's recent publication in the *World Tomorrow* titled "How It Feels to Be Colored Me,"[3] his enthusiasm was sharply curbed. Locke initially expressed "great pride and interest until I realized that maybe you had *opened up too soon.* I had that feeling because I had myself several times made the same mistake. The only hope is in the absolute blindness of the Caucasian mind. To the things that are really revolutionary in Negro thought and feeling they are blind."[4] Hurston's reply came from Magazine, Alabama, nearly two weeks later and suggested that the essay "came to be published [because] I had no money"[5] and faced severe financial hardships due to the funds she and others lost launching the one-shot literary magazine *Fire!!*[6] But what about this "mistake" of a premature opening up Locke noted? There are at least two senses of wrongdoing referenced here. Hurston benefited not only from Locke's tutelage but from Charlotte Osgood Mason's patronage—a wealthy New York City midtowner who felt a strong spiritual rejuvenation resonating in New Negro art and culture. Locke arranged the patronage and felt responsible for managerial duties involving Mason and a number of Harlem's budding stars. Hurston's research travels in the South during this time were, in part, funded by "Godmother"—as Mason was called by some of her "children";[7] these financial arrangements were often sutured to rigid imprimaturs regarding publication subjects and outlets. Mason dispatched to Hurston two hundred dollars per month to underwrite her work, treating the material she unearthed as her property.[8] Clearly, the appearance of "How It Feels to Be Colored Me" was a surprise to Locke and Mason. In this context, the "mistake" involved the apparent circumvention of Locke's and Mason's preapproval of the publication.[9]

Alternatively, Hurston's opinions about race could be enigmatic and unconventional, keeping Locke constantly on the look out for errant tones. "How It Feels to Be Colored Me" has come to be one of Hurston's most widely read and scrutinized essays. Locke was perhaps its first critic. In it, Hurston suggested that her feeling colored was radically contingent on fluid and changing relations and contexts. In Eatonville, Florida, the all-black small town where she was born, she noted that her feeling colored rarely registered. When she moved to Jacksonville at the age of thirteen, her feeling colored emerged out of a nearly all-white background. Yet even then, the feeling violated expectation: "But I am not tragically colored. There is no great sorrow dammed up in my soul, nor lurking behind my eyes. I do not mind at all. I do not belong to the sobbing school of Negrohood who hold that nature somehow has given them a lowdown dirty deal and whose feelings are all hurt about it." Taking perhaps an unwitting swipe at the presumed soul of the sorrow songs—the quintessential "colored" art form—Hurston painted a picture of how the affects of race are not mystical but profoundly social, based upon specific equivalences and differences. When in a jazz cabaret she got swept into the "jungle" by the wild rhythms of the band, and yet noticed how her white companion remained calm and detached, "my color comes. . . . He is so pale with his whiteness then and I am *so* colored."[10]

Locke's pragmatism and philosophy of value bolstered a rejection of racial essentialism, but he balked at Hurston's impulsive revelatory spirit: "At certain times I have no race," wrote Hurston in "How It Feels to Be Colored Me": "I am *me*. . . . The cosmic Zora emerges. I belong to no race nor time." Moreover, during these "certain times," the world disclosed to her that all of us—"white, red, and yellow"—were a relatively random compilation of stuff—"a jumble of small things priceless and worthless" and interchangeable:[11] "A bit of colored glass more or less would not matter."[12] Locke was again in general agreement but considered the vivid celebration of individualism as poorly timed—a "mistake"—because his rhetorical strategy as the impresario of the New Negro movement involved the transfiguration and reevaluation of New Negro art constitutive of a distinct *group experience*. Speaking of odd timing, one month prior to the appearance of "How It Feels to Be Colored Me," Locke published "Beauty Instead of Ashes" in the *Nation*. The essay posited that "American art has tapped a living well-spring of beauty" resonating through black folk "group momentum."[13] And in November of this same year in "The Negro's Contribution to American Art and Literature," Locke claimed that the importance of black culture to American literary achievement could not be divorced from a racially structured social order that functioned "to intensify emotionally and intellectually group feelings, group reactions, group traditions."[14] The affective dimensions of distinct black collective living were considered to be integral to attributions of New Negro beauty; these were contentious claims, however, even as they underwrote much primitivist thought. Indeed, it is clear from Locke's cautionary note to Hurston that he was relying on the primitivist enjoyment of her brief and furious dance in the jazz cabaret with "those heathen" to "blind" white folks from recognizing her "really revolutionary" appeal to a universal subjectivity.[15]

This mild tiff with Hurston opens up for us a number of key constraints on New Negro artistic sensibility and practice. Theoretically, Locke wanted to establish as "normal" just the sort of racial sentiment articulated in "How It Feels to Be Colored Me." The problem he perceived was specifically strategic, requiring the careful coordination of tactics designed to gradually yet robustly constitute alternate ways of making and unmaking "racial" relations. Locke recognized the serendipity of his historical moment where the intensified interest in Negro ways could be used to change conventional aesthetic judgments regarding race. He keenly felt that matters of "taste" concerning art and culture were held in place not by reason but by modes of valuing that were always already bonded to feelings. As an aesthetic value, taste was constitutive of emotions and could be altered by manipulating the way works of art were appreciated, by varying the means through which aesthetic values came into being. Locke emerged in the 1920s as W. E. B. Du Bois's "chief intellectual rival,"[16] not merely because he shared with the *Crisis* editor an academic pedigree, both holding Harvard doctorates—although Locke enjoys the distinction of being the first African American to be a Rhodes Scholar. Rather, Locke and Du Bois butted heads from time to time because they were ambitious and contentious strategists of racial uplift.[17] It is in conjunction with their rivalry that the Harlem Renaissance always needs to be assessed in part as a "movement," since movements commonly involve themselves with disputes over strategy. It is no exaggeration to note that Locke's promotion to the ranks of a key movement leader was triggered by the aesthetic production in 1925 of the "Bible" of the renaissance, *The New Negro: An Interpretation.*[18] The materialization of this work also intensified clashes over strategies and tactics mobilizing the trope of the New Negro.

This influential anthology labored to create and realign strategic interests in the New Negro by dramatizing and theorizing the presumed "evolution" of the "old" Negro into the "new." I argue that Locke staged this development by explicating the manner in which artistic and aesthetic practices showcased by the New Negro needed to be released from "old" aesthetic conventions, requiring the articulation of new modes of valuing black cultural expression. I contend that the affective registers associated with the "new" provided a sense of vitality felt as healthy and joyful to white folk. Meanwhile, the emotions bonded to the values of the "old" provided for a sense of folk tradition needed to underwrite the assertion by Locke that black collective life supplied racial norms as resources for American art. *The New Negro* animated and held in suspense emotions regarding change and stability, bringing together differential feelings and notions regarding American sociality so as to make known and apparent the processes of cultural pluralism—a dynamic open market for cultural exchange and reciprocity. Importantly, Locke posited the New Negro as not only a maker of "new" objects but as a subject productive of alternative modes of valuing, as a member of the avant-garde capable of rendering cutting-edge aesthetic judgments of the art of this "new" racial sociality. *The New Negro* thus staged an ambitious reimagining of relations between "old" and "new," universal and particular, subject and object, text and context. But before we can appreciate the working of Locke's rhetoric, we must better understand the dynamic and contingent milieu in which *The New Negro* materialized.

The New Negro's Coming-Out Party

There remains much difference of opinion as to when one can say that the New Negro movement actually began. But what is indisputable is that by 1924, Harlem was a hotbed of artistic activity. The *Crisis* and the Urban League's the *Opportunity,* edited by the University of Chicago-trained sociologist Charles S. Johnson, published as much New Negro work as they could muster and sponsored literary contests geared to drive up interest in black writing and attract black writers to the movement. Johnson and Locke became a potent team, working to recruit black artists and staging their arrival on the literary scene by manufacturing elaborate debuts (see chapter 3). The seed for *The New Negro* collection was planted and generously watered at one of the most famous New Negro spectacles held on March 21, 1924, at the Civic Club in lower Manhattan, one of the few dinner banquet venues that allowed interracial gatherings. The affair was billed as a celebration of the growth of black art and culture,[19] and it charmed folks like Albert C. Barnes, a Philadelphia-based art collector and benefactor to Lincoln University, and Paul Kellogg, editor of *Survey.* Barnes had become engrossed in recent years with the relations between African art and New Negro art, while Kellogg hoped to produce a special issue on Harlem life. Recognizing the mutual desire between Locke and Kellogg for a wider distribution and a heightened sensibility of black writing and intelligent discourse regarding its significance, Johnson engineered a meeting between the two men. This get-together became the impetus for Locke to put together "Harlem: Mecca of the New Negro," published a year later as a special issue of *Survey Graphic,* the magazine's visually accented periodical.[20]

By all accounts, the Civic Club affair was quite a party. It is also noteworthy as one of the moments where arts seemed to gain the decisive upper hand on radical politics as the vehicle for effecting changes in race relations; according to Arnold Rampersad, it was a "decision [that] . . . remains controversial."[21] Pragmatically speaking, the "decision" was a no-brainer in the sense that the trope of the New Negro transfixed some folks with the vision of a total social body awakening, a short-circuiting of the machinery of a numbing modern state. What I am suggesting is that there was *no* decision to be made in the "rational" sense of thinking it through and choosing the most "logical" course of action. The affair heated and expanded affects of race mobilized through the trope of the New Negro, and nearly everyone involved with the movement—present or not—felt a new kind of tingling sensation regarding new avenues of distribution and sensibility. Alliances were struck and enemies made. Walter White, an NAACP operative and a notorious " 'personal pusher,' " would later reflect on this occasion as the time and place Locke had "betrayed" him and where Albert Barnes backed the Howard University professor against White's own claims to expertise on African cultural artifacts. Locke may have agreed with Barnes about White being an intellectual " 'light-weight,' "[22] but since the publication of his novel *Fire in the Flint*, White was fast becoming a networking heavyweight among the folks who actually knew how to get published. White had aggressively cultivated an intimate circle of influential friends; among them were H. L. Mencken (who had helped get *Fire in the Flint* published), Carl Van Vechten, Carl Van Doran, Heywood Broun, and Sinclair Lewis. Positioning himself as the spokesperson of the movement, White probably felt terribly slighted by the manner in which Barnes had rebuffed him. After the *Survey Graphic* special issue became a sensation, he contacted Boni & Liveright to pitch the idea of him editing the work into an anthology. Apparently White was seized by a fit of conscience when he realized he was undercutting Locke because he withdrew the self-nomination; the idea, however, stuck and Boni commissioned Locke to convert the issue into an expanded collection. In December 1925, *The New Negro: An Interpretation* hit the bookshelves.

The episode of the materialization of this anthology was intense. Although Locke was elated about how the work came together and proud of his editorial largesse and skill mediating authorial personalities, he was in deep trouble at Howard University. Locke was consistently at odds with the university president J. Stanley Durkee over "salary and curriculum"; shortly after the Harlem special issue was on the newsstands, he and three other professors were fired.[23] At the same moment of his coronation as *the* New Negro, he was out of a job. Already contending with roller-coaster emotions regarding his private life and his professional aspirations, Locke was shunted between despair and delight.[24] The opening up and shutting off of vital opportunities gripped the black intelligentsia in general with a fierce affective radiation where "the surge of new feelings took many directions, and Locke's sense of value moved with it." But the New Negro was not the only racial force with which places like New York City had to contend: "The issue of immigration, and the restriction of it by Congressional action in 1924, caused the issue of racial purity to arise as an instrument of reactionary politics."[25] Since knees can jerk in several different directions and be flung by whites and blacks alike, the atmosphere enveloping Locke's aesthetic practices involving the *Survey Graphic* and the subsequent anthology was supercharged, causing some writers to feel suffocated by Locke's micromanagement. For example, when the *Crisis*'s literary editor, Jessie Fauset, submitted her contribution to the anthology, "The Gift of Laughter," it "almost provoked tears [from Locke]." Locke's review of it expressed dismay over her critique of black humor as aggressively steered by white desire for "buffoonery":[26] "You see a great many of us are joyous even if not socially happy, and even Dr. Du Bois regards this, rightly I think,—and I apologize for the 'even'—it is only his reputation that is bitter, not his personality—as our great instrument of survival . . . and perhaps one of our most valuable and conquering contributions." After providing Fauset with very specific edits, Locke addressed an even more sensitive facet of her essay, her censure of the graphic art of Winhold Reiss: "One more chaw at the bone. Surely you can't quite expect me to publish the paragraph on Reiss. It isn't because I violently disagree—for we are all entitled to our opinions, but for two other very pertinent reasons,—I wouldn't commit the discourtesy of rapping the Reiss drawings in a book to which they furnish the main illustrative material, and then the point is irrelevant to the subject under discussion."[27] Locke may not have *violently* disagreed, but he *did* disagree with the suggestion by Fauset that the representation of blackness ought to reside in the hands of black artists.[28] Moreover, Locke's aesthetic practices were shaped by his philosophy regarding the "pedagogic function" of aesthetic experience,[29] motivating him to push artists and writers to contribute to the New Negro in terms of a cultural "experiment" that would shake loose rigid racial sentiments. Fauset grudgingly complied with Locke's wishes in her essay but did not relinquish her assessment of Reiss's work. What we should accentuate is that the anthology was carefully crafted as an intervention into the production of aesthetic practices shaping New Negro art; it mediated quarrelsome beliefs and feelings about race and blackness; it was molded by an intellectual sensitive to what must *not be seen and what should not be heard*. Thus, the book worked and played with gaps, ruptures, and closures while depicting a coherent myth of the New Negro based around a distinct philosophy of value.

Values, Emotions, Aesthetics

The notion of affect occupies Locke's theory of value. During his formulation of *The New Negro,* he was buoyed by the intensity that held together new racial alliances and structured new social circuits. His intellectual pursuits at Harvard, Oxford, and Howard University came into vivid focus while residing in Harlem.[30] Locke possessed the mental capacities to imagine new cosmologies for American philosophy but reasoned that abstract journeys were forms of evasions from the vital lifework of the philosopher. For Locke, philosophies were "products of time, place and situation, and thus systems of timed history rather than timeless eternity." Locke was a pragmatist in spirit and in everyday practice but aggressively pursued theories of value. This quest invigorated him, but in the early twentieth century philosophies of value were molded by the ongoing and general intellectual turn away from metaphysics. Hence, many of his teachers and colleagues substituted either a "logico-experimental[ism]" for absolutes or embraced a "bloodless behaviorism." Either way, his attempt to think the matters of humanity and sociality needed to circumnavigate a "'philosophic Nihilism.'" This predicament was more significant than the imposition of an intellectual wasteland, more important than a good idea gone astray. Far worse than converting the question, "why do we do what we do?" into a description of what we do; this development actually threatened to aid the reification of value absolutes in social orders through a rationalized ignorance of how value absolutes are smuggled into communal, group, and institutional practices under the banner of "norms." For Locke, the philosophical dilemma here was not limited to the field of philosophy precisely because values are at the heart of human comity and conflict, human organization and the peril of world destruction. Locke's intellectual enterprise, then, was devoted to articulating a "middle ground" between a radical subjectivism, where values are (absolutely) relative, and a pure objectivism, where values are (absolutely) fixed.[31]

Pragmatically speaking, people's actions and attitudes are productive of norms that can be experienced as imperatives; we cannot grasp the significance of being by neglecting the urgency for action supplied by norms. The dismissal of absolutes must be disarticulated from an understanding of norms as opaque—as belonging solely to the individual or to the metaphysical realm. Norms are a key facet of the social. The "normative control" of speech and action, therefore, must be apprehended in the "immediate context of valuation."[32] When we search for answers to the basic character of social life, we must attend to the manner in which values emerge—we must focus on the places and modes involved in valuing. So, rather than inquire into the "content" of a value, seeking to establish value categories, we should ask what happens in the moment that value emerges. Taking a note from George Santayana,[33] Locke proposed that values come into life as a function of processes of experiencing "objects" or events; encounters with the world mobilize affective registers that we sense prior to our evaluation of the "object" or making a statement about the quality of the "object." The metabolism of the social maintains an ongoing organizing of these sensations into "feeling-modes,"[34] which we are habituated into recognizing as recurring in similar situations.

When I stroll into my favorite neighborhood bookstore, I not only have an expectation of what sorts of "objects" I will find there, I am also grasped by an anticipation of the sort of pleasure evoked by the event of being there. The "feeling-mode" of encountering the bookstore calls up the value that could potentially go by many different actual names. Of course, we tend to work out those names rhetorically so we may "agree" that this generic social time is a form of "freedom"—or not. Rather than contemplate the correctness or falsity of the name—the "content" of a value—we must shift our gaze toward the relationship among feelings, contexts, and values, between the affective dimensions of a specific encounter and the manner in which a quality of value materializes through competing claims regarding its "truth,"[35] as "the distinction between the evaluational experience and the evaluation of that experience constitutes the core of Locke's theory of values."[36] One of the reasons this line of thinking faced resistance from some members of Locke's intellectual community is that "this notion of a feeling-reference or form quality constituting the essential identity . . . of a value-mode is not easily demonstrable."[37]

Humans are more than creatures of habit; we are beings, as Georg-Hans Gadamer put it, with strong "prejudices." I prefer to write in the café of my favorite bookstore, while others prefer the privacy of an office. I prefer to have my thoughts "mingle" with the sounds of other folks thinking. Likewise, feelings are not experienced in isolation; they are associated with previous emotions and contexts. And when a feeling finds sympathetic alignments with other sentiments that emerged through other situated experiences, the affective resonance of the association provides accentuation—it presents the coalition of feeling-modes and value-modes as a "preference." Importantly, to say that something is "preferred" is not identical to saying that something is liked, wanted, yearned, or desired. It is to say simply that the experience of an event satisfies an expectation regarding a feeling-mode and that the "return" is triggered by a "quest for certainty."[38] We can profitably push this point a bit further and say that when a recognizable feeling-mode is felt, it aids in the determination of not only the value but of the kind of situation in which it emerged. If a writer prefers a "fortress of solitude" in which to write, my favorite writing place might evoke a coalition of feeling-modes implicated in the constitution of the evaluation that "this is a bad place to write." From here it is but a small leap to comprehending the operations of hegemony. If values are made up of preferred feeling-modes, then the social holds in dynamic tension interpenetrating preferred ways of living. Part of the labors of hegemony involves the rhetorical invention and deployment of universalizing discourses that mediate contentious values in favor of the most powerful preferences.[39] We have arrived at Locke's "gravest problem of contemporary philosophy . . . how to ground some normative principle or criterion of objective validity for values without resort to dogmatism and absolutism on the intellectual plane, and without falling into their corollaries, on the plane of social behavior and action, of intolerance and mass coercion."[40]

Locke's answer to the above quandary was to embrace the actuality of diverse modes of valuing and reinterpret the quality and significance of difference. By situating the social body as a force of intercession between fundamental individualism and a disembodied idealism, Locke sought to convey the conception that differences in values among individuals get amalgamated and altered by collective practices by groups. A single "reality" may indeed exist, but we should think of it "as a central fact and a white light broken up by the prism of human nature into a spectrum of values."[41] Human nature also supplies the essential poiesis required for the emergence of new values because feeling-modes cannot be "contained" by their "original" feeling-references. When one experiences a theorem regarding the possibilities for cold fusion as "divine," or a poem as fulfilling mathematical symmetry, one is situated at the nodal point for a "bleeding-over" of feelings "properly" belonging to a different value and context. Although Locke, as was common at the time, seemingly and unnecessarily delimited the field of aesthetics to the artistic, what he described was an aesthetic experience.[42] A moment seized by a quality of intensity that "short-circuits" the expected alignment of feeling-modes, creating an opening—a gap—an "absence" of value that we discursively "populate" by making an evaluation, by naming a "new" value. This view of values was accompanied by the refusal to treat the spectrum as a rigid graduation from "good" to "bad" or from "superior" to "inferior." Paradoxically, differences matter because they reflect a universal; different values *always and everywhere* emerge through the individual and collective striving of people in *particular places and times.* Rather than impose uniformity through value absolutes or commit ourselves to total relativism, Locke proposed we assume a perspective of value "equivalence" and multiplicity,[43] and "by proposing these basic value-modes as coordinate and complementary, value pluralism of this type proposes its two most important corollaries,—the principles of reciprocity and tolerance."[44]

There were few things more important to Locke than reciprocity and tolerance, especially regarding the implacable dilemma of the kinds of values evoked by experiences of race in a segregated world. Sitting at a dinner table at the Civic Club with the likes of Albert Barnes and Paul Kellogg in March

1924, Locke surely felt the suspension of "old" feeling-modes regarding race relations—an opening he sought to exploit through the rhetorical invention of the New Negro. The occasion was virtually perfect for the production of an aesthetic experience of race and blackness that would be constitutive of a break with convention and a reinterpretation of tradition. The *Survey Graphic* special issue was the initial phase of a spectacular distribution and amplification of black visibility and audibility. *The New Negro: An Interpretation* was the materialization of a kind of movement "manifesto," laying down the aesthetic and artistic practices for making up a vigorous New Negro dwelling place. Locke sought to animate and regulate the qualities of feelings productive of values of blackness sensed and understood as proper to the unfolding American century. To do this, he rearticulated the meanings and relations among black folk culture, African artistry, and modernity formalizing the New Negro.

Toward New Negro Affective Horizons

Due to the *Survey Graphic*'s emphasis on sociological trends, the special issue was parochial, featuring seven perspectives on the emergence of Harlem as a mecca. Following an introduction by Locke on the symbolic significance of Harlem as both a "race capital" and an integral facet of the diversity of New York City, the issue ruminated on the role of black labor, the continuing influence of Southern black folkways, the unique imprint posed by "Negroes" from the West Indies, and the materialization of black youth firing up the movement.[45] Readers would not encounter New Negro poetry, however, until one third of the way through it. The anthology, on the other hand, was markedly more cosmopolitan and concentrated more fully and immediately on aesthetic and artistic developments of interest to an expanding New Negro market. Notably, Albert C. Barnes's contribution, "Negro Art and America,"[46] was promoted by Locke from the middle of the pack in the special issue to a front-runner, becoming virtually the lead essay of the collection.[47] Locke was more than generous; he was offering the views of a prominent white aesthete as a key intellectual and emotive mode for how one should, in part, experience the volume.

Barnes's essay reflected the dreams of members of an elite white class for the noble savage to reawaken in them a lost zest for life. It first established the rational premises for the very existence of New Negro art: "A primitive race, transported into an Anglo-Saxon environment and held in subjection to that fundamentally alien influence, was bound to undergo the soul-stirring experiences which always find their expression in great art." For the remainder of the essay, Barnes was steeped in conveying the intensity and immanency of the soul-stirred: "He [the New Negro] has in superlative measure that fire and light which, coming from within, bathes his whole world, colors his images and impels him to expression. The Negro is a poet by birth." Barnes's desire for black art became rapturous when encountering the sorrow songs: "These wild chants are the natural, naïve, untutored, spontaneous utterance of the suffering, yearning, prayerful human soul." American sociality has provided the oppressive conditions for stoking the affects of black art and enjoyed the surplus resonance: "The cultured white race owes to the soul-expressions of its black brother too many moments of happiness not to acknowledge ungrudgingly the significant fact that what the Negro has achieved is of tremendous civilizing value. We see that in certain qualities of soul essential to happiness our own endowment is comparatively deficient." Electrifying and heart-stopping, blackness revealed its value to America as a "moving beauty," making evident the "essential oneness of all human beings."[48]

As the editor of *The New Negro,* Locke was attempting the feat of an escape artist. Barnes's prominent placement legitimized his sentiments as favorable and proper to New Negro art and culture. His essay functioned as a capacitor, capturing to itself tremendous affects and anxiety regarding the inhumanity of the machine age and inventing a release valve in the form of black expression. Locke sought to use this source as a generator for illuminating the entire anthology and the movement. Generally, it is this strategy that scholars criticize as helping "Harlem turn its back even more firmly on radical social movements."[49] Indeed, in this configuration, the heightened value of blackness to American culture was directly proportional to the felt sense that the affects of New Negro art are fortified in privation: "Only through bitter and long travail has Negro poetry attained its present high level as an art form." The tension was palpable. How can New Negro art uplift the race as ready for modern sociality and maintain its vivifying qualities? Setting up the anthology as the wellspring for white spiritual renewal, Locke had seemingly tied his hands behind his back, preserving the New Negro in the role of "mystic,"[50] a prophet or seer serving at the pleasure of the American social body.

The New Negro contains four sections that investigate and celebrate the intersection of black art and American literature, poetry and drama, music, and the symbiosis between Southern black folk culture and African folk art. Locke penned the foreword to the anthology and four key essays, three of which function as lead essays for the first three sections. His works, "The New Negro," "Negro Youth Speaks," "The Negro Spirituals," and "The Legacy of the Ancestral Arts," operated interdependently to use the affective registers radiating around the trope of the New Negro as free radicals, upsetting taken for granted racial and cultural aesthetic understandings; Locke's rhetorical performance demonstrated the kind of aesthetic practices appropriate to pluralism, reciprocity, and tolerance among complementary and competing community norms and values. Our acknowledgment of the affective and ethical dimensions of his speech endowing voice allows us to appreciate the problem of New Negro hegemony: the thrilling sight and sound of New Negroes were purchased through the imposition of forms of invisibility and voicelessness.

"The New Negro" began with Locke calling attention to the failure of conventional wisdom to understand black life; he blamed outmoded relations among the "Sociologist, the Philanthropist, the Race-leader" for poor social studies and race relations. Rather than pay tribute to the "watch and guard of statistics," traditional policy makers who are accustomed to quantifying a "Negro problem," Locke argued that these folks misapprehend the "new psychology," the "new spirit" among the "younger generation," perceiving it to be the result of a sudden "metamorphosis." This popular misunderstanding, Locke asserted, resulted from a persistent fiction; that is, "the Old Negro had long become more of a myth than a man. The Old Negro, we must remember, was a creature of moral debate and historical controversy. His had been a stock figure perpetuated as historical fiction partly in innocent sentimentalism, partly in deliberate reactionism." The aesthetic practices operating through the alliance of social science and social policy sought to reify a particular visible form of blackness—the Old Negro—partly because this form satisfied racial preferences among whites and partly because it was politically advantageous to whites. Held in place by these regimes, the Old Negro was "something to be argued about, condemned or defended, to be 'kept down,' or 'in his place,' or 'helped up,' to be worried with or worried over, harassed or patronized, a social bogey or a social burden."[51] What was remarkable about this opening passage was that Locke revealed and criticized a black folk performative tactic called masking.[52] Locke states that "the Negro himself has contributed his share to this [predicament] through a sort of social mimicry forced upon him by the adverse circumstances of dependence."[53] In the tradition of black folktales, the trickster is a hero who fools white sight and subverts white supremacist acts by donning a mask of ignorance, stupidity, and naiveté. Such performances were deemed by Locke to be motivated by the aesthetic practices of the regimes he was criticizing. As a tactic, tricksters had to await the right moment to act, to be mindful of the fluidity of hegemony and look out for openings. *The New Negro,* however, was meant to jar open its own spaces, to disarticulate the alliances among regimes mobilizing aesthetic practices formalizing Old Negro tactics. It was precisely the "dependence" upon those regimes of social order that needed to be made "old."

Even as Locke disclosed the Old Negro as a sight gag, a trick, he maintained that this tactic was once functional because it masked and, thus, enabled "the actual march of development" of the New Negro. Locke's functional analysis of value change conceived of the tension between old ways of life and the emerging differences in values as constitutive of "progressively corrective value norm[s]" where changes in modes of sociality might be sensed as sufficiently similar to tradition to be integrated into communal rites and rituals.[54] The formal features of Old Negro performances provided the "cover" for black folk "development" while that very functionality was continuously being tested by new communal goals and needs. Locke theorized that such stress eventually produced a "break" in the old that he dramatized in terms of the locomotion of the children of sharecroppers migrating from the rural South to the urban North. The march of black folk allowed them to "hurdle several generations of experience at a leap" and to behold "a new vision of opportunity . . . to seize . . . a chance for the improvement of conditions." Locke described the migration as more than relocation; rather, "with each successive wave of it, the movement of the Negro becomes more and more a mass movement . . . from medieval America to modern." In the trek from the premodern to the modern world, the New Negro cultivated "self-understanding," "self-respect," and was in the midst of "shaking off the psychology of imitation and implied inferiority."[55] For Locke, modernity presented a new aesthetic condition, where traditional formalisms underwent self-reflexive critique and the practice of critique was generative of the modes through which "subjects" and "objects" came into being. Self-reflexivity was a defining characteristic of modern subjectivity. Moreover, this self-reflexivity was constitutive of the aesthetic practices needed for the "proper" apprehension of modern art. There were two active forces Locke was tracking here: "The *widening* of the variety of styles and aesthetic has actually been accompanied by a *deepening* of aesthetic taste and a sharpening of critical discrimination."[56] Modernity let loose cultural pluralism and invigorated intense assessments of their particular values.

By casting aside the mask of the Old Negro, Locke's "changeling"[57] suddenly appeared "new" but was already potentially endowed with a modern voice. Locke's distinction between the old and the new continued in the essay "Negro Youth Speaks": "Youth speaks, and the voice of the New Negro . . . accents the maturing speech of full racial utterance." Introducing the section subdivided as "Fiction," "Poetry," and "Drama," Locke's essay conditioned the expectations of readers to sense and appreciate the coming artistic offerings as modern, fascinated by the affects breathed through the "break" with the old. In contrast to New Negro expression, the art of the Old Negro was "racially rhetorical rather than racially expressive." Constrained by the institutional regimes manufacturing Jim Crow paternalism and subjection, confronted by hideous caricatures of blackness in popular culture, black folk "felt art must fight social battles and compensate social wrongs." This impulse led to the normative practice of representing the race with "the better foot foremost." Locke contended that old artistic practices were forms of "posing" rather than exhibiting "poise."[58] They were once aligned sympathetically with a host of performances that sustained black community but gradually became unhinged from the feelings and values churned up by the actual march of development.

Conversely, New Negro artistic practices have "achieved an objective attitude toward life." They "take their material objectively with a detached artistic vision." The New Negro proudly articulated a "new aesthetic and a new philosophy of life" that was in "alignment with contemporary artistic thought, mood, and style." The New Negro writers were "thoroughly modern, some of them *ultra-modern* and Negro thoughts now wear the uniform of the age." The sizzle of the untutored and uncivilized was transferred to value-modes of modernity and transmitted through the trope of the New Negro. Locke, thus, reinvented black folk as modernists and warranted his claim by reinterpreting race as "an idiom of style" and a "contribution to the general resources of art."[59] Two senses of time operated in Locke's discourse. First, there was the sudden temporal displacement that accompanied a metamorphosis of the Old Negro. Second, there was the actual march of time. Locke's hermeneutics animated both senses; the magnetic polarities of old and new, of virtual and actual, building toward a dramatic release. Thus, the startling emergence of the New Negro "in his poetry, his art, his education, and his new outlook" provoked a radical reorientation of thought and social practice.[60] In an academic definition of the contemporary moment, Locke focused on affect: "The new Negro is not merely the younger generation, but the ever rising spread of the new psychology which in my judgment emanated not so much from the younger generation as from the *abrupt realization of the extreme change* of American sentiment and opinion on the Negro question. . . . It is, therefore, more a reaction to a reaction than is usually thought."[61] Two years after the appearance of *The New Negro,* Locke clarified the qualities of the extreme change: "The modern recoil from the machine has deepened the appreciation of hitherto despised qualities in the Negro temperament, its hedonism, its nonchalance, its spontaneity; the reaction against over-sophistication has opened our eyes to the values of the primitive and the importance of the man of emotions and untarnished instincts."[62] Again, let us note how affects of the "break" got transfused with feelings associated with the primal and vectored through the New Negro toward the horizon of an ultramodernity, a place where the New Negro "must know himself and be known for precisely what he is, and for that reason he welcomes the new scientific rather than the old sentimental interest."[63]

One can scarcely know what is meant by "primitive" here. It marked the "original" and the scientific, the modern black spontaneous subject painting with "vigorous realism."[64] It manifested a "changeling"; the disruption of value-modes and feelings compelled new race relations and aesthetic practices governing distributions of black visibility and tonality. The section being introduced by "Negro Youth Speaks" showcased the kinds of artworks Locke considered beautiful. "But there is an ethics of beauty itself,"[65] and we are faced with a choice regarding its presence. To heed it is to follow the emotional current associated with the transfiguration of the primitive deeply into American soil to encounter the disturbance of the very meaning of "race." When aligned with the Old Negro, race and blackness were (absolutely) immanent; but race was always an element in a trickster performance covering over the actual march of development. As a topic of the New Negro, "race" became a trope of modern art. Rather than a category used to fix persons by color, race was derived from cultural practices that can reasonably be grouped together.[66] In the "old" alignment of terms, feeling-modes, and value-modes, race was immobilized and segregated—a function of elaborate black codes. In the hands of the New Negro, race was a pragmatic and generative trope; the New Negro sought to "evolve from the racial substance something technically distinctive . . . [in] flavor of language, flow of phrase, accent of rhythm in prose, verse and music, color and tone of imagery, idiom and timbre of emotion and symbolism. . . . The newer motive, then, in being racial is to be so purely for the sake of art."[67] Art for art's sake was a very loaded phrase. It harkened back to a kind of metaphysics and formalism that Locke and many of his contemporaries, as I have said above, rejected. Locke's value theory, however, brought the matter down to earth and pushed against logics of formalism in favor of processes of valuing. Hence, "pure" art was possible only as a function of artists' relations with the ongoing experience of social life, an experience that historically involved the political deployment of race to produce groups, values, beliefs, and attitudes favorable to the maintenance of white supremacy. But since modes of valuing change due to shifting contexts and feelings bleed over toward "objects," there was no "authentic" content to which "pure" referred; rather, pure art indexed, paradoxically, a dynamic interpenetration of modes of creativity and valuation. Not only was the evocation of pure art itself challenged by the likes of Du Bois but so too was Locke's processes of analysis.

Locke's reformulation of modernism continued. Although he claimed that the so-called pure art motive was new, it was best exemplified in the universality of the Old Negro sorrow songs. This is why some key values of the Old Negro were not erased in Locke's strategic disjunction with the past. Because tactical performances like masking sustained black folk, Locke brought forward folk spirituality as affective resources for the New Negro. In the essay, "The Negro Spirituals," the sorrow songs were treated as emotional reservoirs with great pragmatic value. The sentiments and functions of these songs demonstrated the need for further study of folk tradition. As a "classic folk expression," the spirituals were a sign of black folk "genius" that can only "truly" be appreciated as "deeply representative of the soil that produced them."[68] Given his depiction of the New Negro as an ultramodernist who utilized race purely for the sake of art, Locke's argument hinged on his ability to characterize the spirituals as distinctive racial expressions and as giving rise to universal values.

In Locke's conception of cultural pluralism where "concrete human experience" grounded the distinctive, specific cultural labor bounded by common interests was a conduit to universalism.[69] The spirituals were "artistically precious things" that "stand the test of time" because they embodied black folks' appropriate responses to certain kinds of situations. As a means for the Old Negro to express the grief of the dispossessed and the faith of a people looking toward a horizon of possibilities, moreover, the spirituals redeemed the soul of the trickster because masking had great propriety in distinct and local practice. Similarly, they empowered singers to find ways to make something out of nothing. For example, Locke recounted the adventures of the Fisk Jubilee Singers, who were credited with not only bringing the spirituals to the world but also with raising enough money to save Fisk University.[70] Locke's narrative about the utility of the spirituals transformed them into "culture-goods,"[71] meaning that they circulated beyond their "original" cultural boundaries due to their emotive force and maintained the health of a black folk lifeworld from which they drew their intense resonance.

Locke explained that it was the character of the spirituals as life-affirming emotional utterances working effectively within specific lived experiences that allowed them to be "fundamentally and everlastingly human." "Indeed," he wrote, "they transcend emotionally even the very experience of sorrow out of which they were born; their mood is that of religious exaltation, a degree of ecstasy indeed that makes them in spite of the crude vehicle a classic expression of the religious emotion. They lack the grand style, but never the sublime effect." Locke brought into sharp relief the predicament that art faced due to the tension between the distinctive and the universal. Although the spirituals had been widely recognized due to their universal values, this appreciation was responsible for their transplantation from the black church into the theater. "And the concert stage has but taken them an inevitable step further from their original setting," away from the lived experiences that constituted them. As classical and universal expressions, impersonations were inevitable, but as the spirituals were distorted with "formal European idioms and mannerisms" on the concert stage, reactionaries double the damage by removing them also from their vital places and cramming them into the "narrow confines" of "arbitrary style or form" in the name of preserving tradition.[72] Locke was incredibly sensitive to this dilemma. In *Opportunity* in 1923, Locke praised the tenor Roland Hayes for having "cultivated his voice on its own pattern. It is *not an imitation of other models*, however great; but an intensive cultivation of a voice that had its natural limitations."[73] This sort of evaluation led to Hayes gracing the cover of the *Survey Graphic* special issue. But, by the time Locke and Mason shared an alliance driven by the aesthetic practices of New Negro promotion and regulation, things had changed. In a letter to Mason, Locke cut at Hayes, saying that he "sang like a white man."[74] This was not an appeal to racial essentialism; it was more a lamentation of the fact that the reciprocity of cultural pluralism was often productive of effects that might displease. But it also reflected Locke's sense that the energies of cultural transfiguration required careful and thoughtful administration.

Locke invoked the "vision and courage" of the New Negro to address the challenge of harnessing the powers generative of stability and change. The New Negro was both an ultramodern artist and a "sensitive race interpreter."[75] Embodying this rhetorician, Locke sketched the problem the New Negro solved. The spirituals were pushed and pulled in different directions because universalism was misperceived as uniformity, and cultural pluralism was misunderstood as rigid or radical relativism.[76] Within this polarized logic stained by the flight from metaphysics, universal values were treated as ahistorical and abstract, while cultural difference stood in opposition, privileging distinct group identity. This dialectic resulted in arbitrariness and relativism on both sides instead of "relative and functional rightness" because it extracted the spirituals from lived experience.[77] In exploring the spirituals, however, the New Negro would avoid either extreme through "the most careful study of the communal life as it still lingers in isolated spots." By highlighting the need to understand the situated performance of black art, Locke asserted social function as a criterion for aesthetic judgment. "We should always remember," he argued, "that [the spirituals] are essentially congregational, not theatrical, just as essentially they are a choral not a solo form." The spirituals were returned to the group life that generated them so that "modern interpretation [can] . . . relate these songs to the folk activities that they motivated, classifying them by their respective song types." Because these folk activities were responses to lived experience through time and in changing places, "there is and can be no set limitation."[78]

Importantly, the outline for a New Negro aesthetic practice emerged here. Locke's argument authorized the New Negro as a principal investigator. Such authority was readily tested by white critics who presumed to know better. Two months prior to the publication of *The New Negro,* Carl Van Vechten wrote to Locke to tell him that "we shall never agree on the subject of the Spirituals." The letter suggested that Locke and the novelist and cultural critic did not see eye to eye on the "interpretation and arrangement of the sorrow songs." Although Van Vechten seemed full of mirth, his opinion seriously mattered to the art world folks establishing the very terms through which the sorrow songs and their singers would enjoy visibility and voice.[79] Again, *The New Negro* competed with and appropriated old preferential aesthetic practices and judgments of taste. Locke's aesthetic practice posited that the proper treatment of the spirituals and other African American art forms was realized by experiencing their affective dimensions and by being open to changes in feeling-modes. Rather than perceive the joy and pain and dialect of the spirituals as corruptions of abstract concepts of piety or as exceptionally relative, Locke's discussion disclosed their sublimity and propriety. In the spirituals, eloquence was a form of reverence: "for all of their inadequacies, the words are the vital clues to the moods of these songs. If anything is to be changed it should be the popular attitude."[80] Moreover, Locke's system of value transfusion conceived of "song types" as emerging with feeling-modes and value-modes proper to the "folk activities." As folk culture migrated, "emotional judgments" of song types would inevitably produce a proliferation and diversification of qualities of values regarding the sorrow songs. One may reason that a specific value is "better" than another, but the functionality of the value in group life will induce feelings experienced as imperatives: "The role of feeling can never be understood nor controlled through minimizing it; to admit it is the beginning of practical wisdom in such matters."[81] In this manner, the primitive could be felt through tropes of the New Negro as actualizing black modern subjectivity, and the aesthetic realm can be understood to "objectively" involve ethical considerations—normative habits materializing through the production of taste and shaping social life.

Locke was accomplishing more than the reinterpretation of "logics" of meaning, he sought to explode the conventions of thought disciplining the relations between feelings and values that buttressed art world aesthetic and artistic practices. Beyond this blast radius, however, he wanted to set in motion a form of New Negro training: "We cannot accept the attitude that would merely preserve this music, but must cultivate that which would also develop it. Equally with treasuring and appreciating it as music of the past, we must nurture and welcome its contribution to the music of to-morrow."[82] Locke continued with this rhetoric of revaluing black art and the processes through which it materialized in the essay, "The Legacy of the Ancestral Arts," which rearticulated the character of African art and Africa's relation to black folk culture. Because "the American Negro brought over [from Africa] as an emotional inheritance a deep-seated aesthetic endowment," US sociality produced a black art that was "free, exuberant, emotional, sentimental and human." In contrast, African art was "rigid, controlled, disciplined, abstract, heavily conventionalized." This distinction had three related purposes. First, it transformed a long history of African creativity into a formal tradition. Indeed, Locke detailed the ways in which the well-defined discipline of African art had influenced the progression of European forms. Second, it offered African art as a classic model that can be the basis for New Negro *imitatio:* "Then possibly from a closer knowledge and proper appreciation of the African arts must come increased effort to develop our artistic talents in the discontinued and lagging channels of sculpture, painting and the decorative arts."[83]

Locke's point was that a New Negro ethos should inhabit a place of antiquity, making black artistry both old and new; thus, Locke's rhetoric infused the future with the past. What Africa offered was not romance nor "cultural inspiration or technical innovations, but the lesson of a classic background, the lesson of discipline, of style, of technical control pushed to the limits of technical mastery." African norms and practices were not called on in reaction to European hegemony; rather, they were to be New Negro topoi, "the guidance of a distinctive tradition."[84] Lastly, Locke ignited the affective vapors drifting upward from Africa's deep-seated aesthetic endowment to provide acceleration and forward momentum for New Negro artistic practices. In this sense, the New Negro had not merely arrived but was launched toward new horizons, lifted by African techne.[85] The trajectory for New Negro artistry was clear: "We ought and must have a school of Negro art, a local and racially representative tradition" that will fulfill "the promising beginning of an art movement instead of just the cropping out of isolated talent."[86] This fulfillment cannot be assessed in terms of brick and mortar; it must be judged and understood in terms of the progressive functionality of works of New

Negro art within powerfully contentious contexts circumscribed by stubborn values of race.

Voice and Voicelessness of The New Negro

As 1926 unfolded, Locke and the anthology received much high-profile attention. The New Negro stood out as a proud race nationalist, a figure to be admired, idolized, and listened to. The tremors caused by the vibratory force of its actualization thrilled some onlookers as if anticipating a new carnival ride or awaiting exultation brought about from a down-home revival; other spectators went queasy, noting a distinct air of elitism and disrespect for key aspects of folk culture like the blues.[87] Du Bois's criticism was by far the most disturbing to Locke and the most noteworthy for it signaled the intensification of the *Crisis* editor's sustained deconstructive efforts aimed at the aesthetic practices of "pure art." The praise for the work, however, was reminiscent of Locke's effusions two years earlier regarding what he considered to be an enormous breakthrough in the field of French "colonial literature."

In 1921, a hard-boiled account of the political and cultural conditions of black Africa shocked and won over French literati; Locke was entranced by Rene Maran's *Batouala* and published an essay in 1923 that announced the transformative character of aesthetic experiences of such works. In "The Colonial Literature of France," Locke trumpeted that Maran's novel ruptured a literary field that had been "narrower, [with] more stunted values . . . and . . . the worst provincialisms and prejudices of the Caucasian and European bias." To Locke, the novel indexed the materialization of a "pure literature" because Maran, a black Frenchmen, cultivated his artistic practices during twenty years of French colonial service spent among the persons and communities that inspired the book. His writing, Locke crowed, was constitutive of "a new attitude in the portrayal in fiction of widely divergent human cultures," amounting to a form of "aesthetic cosmopolitanism." *Batouala* was more than a singular accomplishment of "bold realism." It altered the strategic terrain on which aesthetic and artistic practices flourished: "For however rife this point of view may have been among artists and authors, without the creation of a *new taste* in the reading public it could never have come to public expression." In a sense, Maran appeared to Locke as a New Negro: "It was heroic work—and required to be done by the Negro himself—this revolutionary change from sentimentality to realism, from caricature to portraiture."[88]

Inspired by the first black person to win the French literary award, the Prix Goncourt, Locke, too, labored to create a new taste in the reading public. By making the New Negro old and new, primal, and an avatar of the avant-garde, folk and intellectual, regional and international, Locke fought against the calcification of values of race. Moreover, aesthetic judgments of New Negro works were carefully tended so as to evoke the sort of acknowledgment of the affective and ethical dimensions of speech that could endow voice. In Locke's philosophy, voice was not possible with the production of propaganda and, therefore, undermined the potential for communion among races. Propaganda not only sounded a false note to Locke's ears, it was the echo of white supremacist discourse; as with the mask of the trickster, an addressee or spectator was denied an "authentic" experiential encounter with the lived conditions of the person speaking. What one hears in such speech is not black voice but rather white terror provoked by a potential loss of a will to power. Speaking again about Maran's glorious arrival: "We predict the eventual triumph of the non-moralistic and purely aesthetic approach—art for its own sake combined with that stark cult of veracity—the truth, *whether it hurts or not,* for the sake of eventual peace of human understanding."[89] For Locke, New Negro art was generative of a "pure" kind of disclosure of universal humanism compelling acknowledgment. Voice is the sound of affect, and *The New Negro* made a mighty noise.

The New Negro: An Interpretation was aptly named. It pressurized a complicated and interlocking set of interpretations of race, blackness, art, and culture. It, therefore, was profoundly ironic. Its vigorous metabolism was in part constitutive of stresses among contributors, and Locke's aggressive mediation of them produced specific kinds of voicelessness. For instance, by the time the volume splashed down, Jean Toomer, the celebrated author of *Cane,* had begun to renounce his "blackness," he no longer wished to be represented as a Negro writer.[90] Locke's depiction of Toomer as an exceptional New Negro cut viciously against his emerging subjectivity as being beyond race. *The New Negro* arc of influence had near biblical proportions. Hence, Toomer's capacity to have a public acknowledgment of the affective and ethical dimensions of his speech was severely curtailed. Readers of the volume hear a kind of ventriloquism where the tropes and technologies of the New Negro altered Toomer's vocal register, keeping him sounding "dark." Similarly, Claude McKay was angry that Locke changed the title of one of his poems, "The White House," to "White Houses," morphing his political speech against the sovereignty of white power into a weak polemic regarding white hospitality. Both impositions of voicelessness were sustained when Locke edited *Four Negro Poets* in 1927.[91] The pamphlet put a spotlight on Langston Hughes, Countee Cullen, Claude McKay, and Jean Toomer. It represented an important development in the aesthetic practices of the distribution of the sensibility of the New Negro. Priced and marketed for popular consumption, *Four Negro Poets* reprinted "White Houses" against the strident objections of McKay and, once again, "blackened" Toomer against his will. There should be no surprise, therefore, that *The New Negro* raised the stakes for control over black artistic voices as they were made available through and disabled by dominating aesthetic practices. But even as it provoked voice and brusquely imposed voicelessness, and should be critiqued on those grounds, the anthology should also be judged for provoking some of the most enduring, wondrous, and acidic discourses about the very possibility of a New Negro. Disagreements over the very idea of New Negro art produced strong gravitational forces that eventually pulled young stars into grudge matches offered up by prominent literary forums.

5
"A Lampblacked Anglo-Saxon"
George Schuyler and Langston Hughes in the *Nation*

When Freda Kirchwey, the managing editor of the *Nation,* sorted through her mail on a crisp and clear October morning in 1925, she was both amused and annoyed by a submission from a rising journalistic star working for the *Pittsburgh Courier* and the *Messenger.* George Schuyler was probably an unknown black writer to Kirchwey when he submitted an article that was meant to peak her interest and test her tolerance. Kirchwey was on the fast track to running the entire magazine and dedicated to its liberal mission. In its pages she published stories about the need for female birth control, the state of modern morality, and the activities of the NAACP.[1] She was particularly excited about the New Negro renaissance bubbling up all around her, and she sutured its potential to change race relations to her desire to unseat late Victorianism's repressed sexuality. Kirchwey viewed her chair on the *Nation*'s editorial board as a sign of the coming freedom for women to be able to control and enjoy their bodies. This kind of release from the staid conventions regarding the "proper" movement, rhythm, and color of life seemed also to be at the heart of much New Negro art.

It was widely believed that "primitive" culture could animate deep "memories" of the supposed freedom that humanity enjoyed before the domination of the machine. Modern primitivism dreamed of a spiritual return to a time before humanity unwittingly chained itself to the assembly line and was forced to follow the rigid, unvarying rules of mass production; a time when people were more vigorous and more alive.[2] As a feminist who balked at Freudian analyses, Kirchwey did not long for the good old days; according to the biographer Sara Alpern, Kirchwey saw the "natural" condition of the primitive as promising relief from the artificial constraints regarding sexual pleasure and "exclusivity" imposed on the modern woman.[3] To her mind, the affects of blackness were "pure" energy waiting to revivify the entire Western world. One can imagine the consternation and, perhaps, anxiety that crept upon her as she began to realize the significance of Schuyler's essay, "The Negro-Art Hokum." This was a development that she might have brought to the attention of the *Nation*'s editorial board, especially the editor in chief Oswald Garrison Villard, grandson of the famous abolitionist William Lloyd Garrison and a member of the board of directors of the NAACP; Villard knew personally many of the black intellectual leaders who were proclaiming the "genius" of the New Negro.[4]

It would take nearly a year before Kirchwey was prepared to publish Schuyler's mockery of the New Negro and its putative art "movement." The delay was, in part, made possible by Schuyler's eight-month absence from New York while he reported on the living conditions in the "Negro South" for the *Courier.*[5] Kirchwey was also near emotional exhaustion because of her mother's failing health.[6] Whatever its principal cause, the delay turned out to be strategically advantageous; Kirchwey had no intention of undermining a "freedom movement" sharing a kinship with her liberalism, black intellectual activism, and the stimulation of lower Manhattan's metabolism. Arnold Rampersad comments on how attitudes like Kirchwey's impacted the development of New Negro regimes and aesthetic practices: "Very early, as the Jazz Age ripened in New York, Harlem was accepting the role forced on it—that of bookie, bootlegger, and bordello to white downtown." Sensing that the cultural climate had come to a rolling boil and not wanting to turn down the flames, Kirchwey settled on a course of action meant to produce "not so much a rebuttal of Schuyler" as an affirmation of New Negro art.[7] But who should authenticate the ethos of the New Negro? Perhaps due to a recommendation from Villard, she circulated Schuyler's essay among notable black leaders like James Weldon Johnson, Charles S. Johnson, and Walter White. By the spring of 1926, following James Weldon Johnson's advice, Kirchwey forwarded a copy of "The Negro-Art Hokum" to an award-winning poet and author of a recently published book of verse called *The Weary Blues.*

Enjoying new "celebrity" status and relishing his college days at Lincoln University, a small, all-male institution founded by Quakers in Pennsylvania, Langston Hughes was suddenly "distracted" from exams and perturbed by Schuyler's article.[8] "The Negro-Art Hokum" struck a nerve that wound along Hughes's spiritual travels; the very idea that there was no such thing as black aesthetics not only threatened Hughes's poetic style, it sought to do the unthinkable, to turn him away from "home." In works like *The Bluest Eye,* Toni Morrison describes the dread of being put "outside"; the deep-seated angst that arises when one has "no place."[9] Hughes had spent the first half of the decade escaping homelessness by living among the blues people: "To him, mind and body unite and flourish only with a plunge into the world—not for material rewards, but for the affirmation of ideals of joy, brotherhood, and justice, on which nature itself smiles."[10] Hughes's bond with ordinary black folk was profoundly emotional, as he explained in a letter to the noted white writer Carl Van Vechten about blues songs: "They always impressed me as being very sad," he wrote, "sadder even than the spirituals because their sadness is not softened by tears but hardened with laughter, the absurd, incongruous laughter of a sadness without even a god to appeal to."[11]

Kirchwey had chosen wisely, for Hughes was in a blues mood; within a week she received Hughes's "manifesto" for Negro art.[12] Now having a "response" to Schuyler, she published "The Negro-Art Hokum" on June 16, 1926;[13] it was followed a week later by Hughes's "The Negro Artist and the Racial Mountain."[14] I argue that taken together, "The Negro-Art Hokum" and the "The Negro Artist and the Racial Mountain" are constitutive of an epideictic ritual staged by the *Nation* in which Schuyler and Hughes made aesthetic judgments of acknowledgment and disparagement regarding the artistic practices of the New Negro. Schuyler and Hughes's discourses celebrated and denigrated specific and prominent values and beliefs associated with "race," "class," and "primitivism." Schuyler attacked dominant forms of racial reasoning through a deconstruction of "Negro," showing the term to be lacking any essential "racial" characteristic. Importantly, Schuyler performed a kind of "savagery" endemic to satire and owing some of its rhetorical force to primitivism. Hughes, too, appropriated primitivism; however, he applauded its "authenticity" and deplored the black middle class's imitation of American "civilization."

Both writers exhibited an artistic practice made up of their experiences of blackness; both writers received, to varying degrees, praise and blame for what they praised and blamed. But in the end, the epideictic ritual disparaged Schuyler's satirical speech, leaving him voiceless; the ritual, however, endowed Hughes's blues voice and, thus, functioned to bolster an assault on a civil rights orthodoxy that required black artists to serve racial uplift by painting only the New Negro's "best" face. I also consider whether this lingering aesthetic judgment of Schuyler made by the *Nation*'s audience and the regimes constituting its aesthetic practices is appropriate; by contemplating how Schuyler's "savage" satire was rendered voiceless, and by more fully acknowledging it, his ironic fate may be revealed to us. That is, his writing may contradict his claim of a "Negro-Art Hokum" by brilliantly satirizing his painful experiences of his blackness—by, perhaps, being "real Negro art."

Epideictic Rituals, Satire, and the Desire for the Primitive

It would be difficult to overstate the competing stresses being placed upon young black artists during this intriguing milieu, but, from the perspective of a publishing industry, works by and about the New Negro were, as Hughes put it, "in vogue."[15] The marketability of New Negro works became, more or less, directly proportional to the coherence of the "primitive" stance of the New Negro. Early in their friendship, Van Vechten often advised Hughes to "send as many jazz and cabaret things as you happen to have on hand" so that he may distribute them to outlets like *Vanity Fair.* Van Vechten saw no contradiction between what he considered to be the beautiful and the profitable.[16] Sponsoring the "debate" between Schuyler and Hughes represented, in part, an opportunity for the *Nation* to help firm up New Negro features—the characteristics that were increasingly desired, valued, and consumed by white audiences. Before we can attend to the appropriations and reinterpretations of race, class, and primitivism articulated through the epideictic ritual, we must turn to a consideration of how epideictic speech may provide this function and to why I deem the exchange to resemble an epideictic ritual.

Due to the recognized "fluidity of the genre as one unattached to any particular discursive setting," epideictic rhetoric has been subject over the years to different conceptions and assessments of its function and its value.[17] On the one hand, it has been considered an inferior form of public address where the mastery of the orator is showcased for the amusement of spectators. But epideictic speech has also been recognized for its capacity to teach moral lessons about civic culture and to cultivate in persons who attend to it an unfathomable sense of a community's values. It is this sometimes less appreciated notion of epideictic that helps us comprehend the significance of the exchange choreographed by the *Nation* at the apex of the New Negro movement. Rather than consider epideictic speech as oratory that chiefly honors or criticizes, I follow Lawrence Rosenfield's advice and seek to understand this event in terms of the "acknowledgment" and "disparagement" of key discursive features of the New Negro. Rosenfield conceives of epideictic speech as animating artistic and aesthetic practices that move hearers into the "proper" place in which to attend to the "radiance" of being and becoming—the "recognition of what *is* (goodness, grace, intrinsic excellence) or the refusal to so recognize in a moment of social inspiration." Rosenfield tells us what is at stake when listeners relinquish themselves to a "passionate openness to the world," a moment when we make a "resolute choice" to attend to (or ignore) "what's going on" right before our eyes.[18] We not only appreciate the inherent value of being, but we acquire the interpretive sensibility cultivated through our participation in the artistic and aesthetic practices of epideictic. The feeling Rosenfield describes as "exultation" due to the insight (*aletheia*) evoked by epideictic speech brings us to a consideration of the sensual knowledge—that is, the aesthetic understanding—that may arise from aesthetic practices.

Aesthetic practices give shape and authority to that which is sensed as the "right" and "wrong" topical materials located and drawn into forms of speech. When one decides to speak about a thing, one usually chooses certain features of the thing to be expressed; more than involving the picking out of what one wishes to say, rhetorical invention concerns the rearticulation of the "truth" of that which will be spoken. Since our self-understanding and our relations to others condition our discursive acts, the application of aesthetic understanding often takes the form of "taste." I have argued elsewhere that this process requires an aesthetic sensitivity that is brought forth and mediated by artistic and aesthetic practices through which one's subjectivity emerges.[19] This eventuality of becoming is not only imbricated in communication but resonates with affective qualities and intensities.

The "radiance" of what *is* shines forth as "a kind of love." This erotic connection between speakers and audiences is the hallmark of the poetic. From what I have said about aesthetic practices and aesthetic understanding, it is tempting to be an excessive lover of the poet. Rosenfield notes Aristotle's tendency to "link epideictic and poetry" because "both epideictic and poetry communicate experiences that are 'out of the ordinary' . . . though perfectly familiar." After all, the poet self-consciously works to instill in us a "childlike wonder" regarding life itself, a rapture that grasps us and that we behold.[20] Aesthetic theorists have long regarded this affective investment with the world in terms of aesthetic experiences that provoke thought and lead to aesthetic valuations, judgments, and the attribution of beauty.[21] The power of aesthetic understanding underscores Langston Hughes's search for a "home." Although there is some debate about the erotic motives and lasting effects of Hughes's homosexual encounters, nearly every scholar agrees that Hughes loved to commune with black people.[22] Or, perhaps more accurately, Hughes was captivated by how the "blues performance" was constitutive of intense affects associated with living "blackness."[23] Hughes was also attracted to the bold and vivid realism of the artistic practices of the blues.

When Hughes arrived in New York City in the fall of 1921, Harlem cried out to him and he answered: "he was immersed in the day-to-day culture of the people. He began to feel, as never before, the daily humiliations of black men and women; protected until now by his youth, or his white high school or university, or Mexico, Hughes was at that point in black lives where bitterness or cynicism begins to seem inevitable, even natural." Indeed, Hughes's wanderings through the nights of Harlem brought him in touch with more than the rhythm of "urban black speech," they acquainted him with the tempo of sacred time; the poet who often joked about the fact that he couldn't sing or dance could represent nearly perfectly in poetic song the blues spirit keeping his people alive. In a cabaret on what is now Malcolm X Boulevard in March of 1923, he reached into that sacred space and put down in words "The Weary Blues." Rampersad explains Hughes's epideictic motives: "Just as the classically trained black musician Scott Joplin had labored to notate ragtime in order to enshrine its beauty as art, so Hughes worked to link the lowly blues to formal poetry in order that its *brilliance might be recognized* by the world."[24]

There are three developments in our story here that we need to carefully notate. Hughes's journeys in search of aesthetic experiences of "blackness" took him all over the world, to Senegal and to Paris—and despite the fact that the Africans he encountered considered him an "American," he strongly "identified with the baffled hurt" they experienced as a result of European colonialism.[25] Secondly, Hughes's aesthetic experiences of blackness were imprinted upon his artistic practices making up his blues poetry like "The Weary Blues." Listen for awhile:

To the tune o' those Weary Blues.
With his ebony hands on each ivory key
He made that poor piano moan with melody.
  O Blues!
Swaying to and fro on his rickety stool
He played that sad raggy tune like a musical fool.
  Sweet Blues!
Coming from a black man's soul.[26]

Hughes's artistic practice matured between 1923 and 1925 even as his child-like wonder of the world intensified. During a junket to Washington, D.C., he was put off by the "black bourgeoisie" and embraced the black working class; it was during this period of his life when Hughes "theorized" a "black aesthetic"; while the black middle class seemed "Nordic and un-Negro," the working class appeared to him to be "the real thing." Hughes was so repulsed by the black middle class "that he wrote Jessie Fauset and Claude McKay . . . breathing fire against" it.[27] Hughes was so enchanted by the "authenticity" of the " 'low-down' folks"[28] that "he fashioned an aesthetic to suit, above all, their needs, not to amuse their masters." At a poetry reading at the Walt Whitman Foundation in New Jersey, Hughes described his writing as an "aesthetic of simplicity."[29] I shall return to this point in due time, but let us clarify the third development. Hughes's artistic practice was, in part, conditioned by the tenets of primitivism.

In the introduction to *The Congo and Other Poems,* Vachel Lindsay's notable collection first published in 1914, Harriet Monroe, editor of *Poetry, a Magazine of Verse,* heaped unconditional praise on Lindsay's enactment of a pioneering spirit that could move poetry back to its "proper place—the audience chamber, and take it out of the library, the closet." The relocation of poetry was accomplished by "appealing to the ear rather than the eye." Clearly, Monroe's hope was for a "return to primitive sympathies between artist and audience, which may make possible once more the assertion of primitive creative power . . . to fulfill its purpose and revitalize the world."[30] Like the editor of the *Nation,* Monroe seemed to be looking for something beyond verse; her desire for an earlier human condition—a longing for an opening to an original life force that seemed no longer present—was symptomatic of primitivism. There were many examples and "theories" that accompanied the disciplining of the "savage." Sigmund Freud conceived of primitivism in terms of latent sexual freedom; Franz Boas examined how primitive life honored nature by being in harmony with it. In both accounts, however, the primitive refers to the Western white subject's ongoing encounter with and evasion of the volatile and inspiring space through which forms of life burst into the world.

Primitivism designates the Other as inhabiting a "wild, unaxed" environment where life is hard, dangerous, luscious, and rich. Colonialists discovered these "strange" places and peoples and coerced labor for the acquisition of Western wealth; these sorts of aesthetic practices and social relations helped transform Western racial consciousness. The primitive is a peculiarly modern trope that marks a moment when white subjects recognized a difference in sociality among peoples that consisted of political economic alienation and domination of others; but near the turn of the twentieth century the Western imagination was fired by an intense interest in blackness. Robin Hackett, in *Sapphic Primitivism,* remarks that "Western Europeans repeatedly sought to define their own humanity in opposition to a monolithic usually dark-skinned being who was imagined to be supremely savage, barbaric, natural, *un*natural, exotic, or some contradictory combination of these."[31] Although opposed to the "civilized," the primitive can be a ferocious "cannibal" or a "noble savage," the source of death and disease or birth and regeneration.[32] The cannibal is perceived as "evil" and provokes fears of chaos; the noble savage, on the other hand, possesses a righteous soul that evokes the sublime; both forms of primitivism have received close scrutiny due to the raw sexuality ascribed to them. Anthropologists, like Bronislaw Malinowski,[33] "sought the universal truth about human nature and conceived primitive societies as the testing ground, the laboratory, the key to that universal truth."[34] If modernity has produced the civilized and is marked by an "art of the Machine Age," where the "precision" and "mechanics" of the assembly line dull the senses, then we should not wonder why Paris and England became enamored with African culture given the fact that the dark continent became the chief metonym for the primitive.[35]

It would be a mistake to treat primitivism as a dialectical counterpart to modernism, as if the former merely described a less developed form of social life. John Cooley rightly notes that the tropes of primitivism constitute aesthetic values: "'primitive' is also a value judgment. . . . The purpose of the contrast may be either to elevate or to denigrate the 'primitive,' depending entirely upon the concept of nature, of man, of race, and of civilization held by the observer."[36] Hence, explorations into the primitive are assessments of how the terror and titillation evoked by blackness (and otherness) have wrought modes of Western self-representation, modes that must be understood as arising from aesthetic experiences and belonging to artistic and aesthetic practices of the primitive. Marianna Torgovnick puts the point succinctly: "Short of reaching the true, essential Primitive (a goal even dedicated ethnographers have disavowed), the best we can do is uncover, from a political and cultural perspective, the kinds of work key terms like primitive have performed within modern and postmodern culture and the kinds of work they have evaded or shortchanged." We must, thus, go beyond understanding definitions of humanity deployed by primitivism and be sensitive to "a vaguer, emotional or 'intuitive' response to the primitive" as animated by a complex set of aesthetic practices in public culture. This perspective brings about a further recognition of the manner in which class and gender are implicated in the production of the primitive. Again Torgovnick puts her finger on the crux of the matter: "The masculine sexual metaphor of penetrating closed dark spaces no doubt helps account for the West's attachment to the trope of the center, heart, or core of Africa. African landscape is to be entered, conquered; its riches are to be reaped, enjoyed. The phallic semiology accompanies the imperialist topoi, a conjunction based on the assumption that if explorers (like Stanley and Tarzan) are 'manly,' then what they explore must be female."[37] Tracy McCabe and Amelia Defalco, in different works, have studied how Harlem and its residents performed the classed and sexed acts colonialists sought after in the heart of Africa.[38] It is important for us to keep in mind the work the primitive accomplishes in making claims of authenticity hinge on class distinctions and in fashioning Schuyler's satire.

Considered by many to be the "black H. L. Mencken,"[39] Schuyler thrived on saying "things that people did not want to hear," and his biographer Michael Peplow contends that "satire apparently came natural to Schuyler."[40] Well, perhaps, but we cannot ignore the fact that Schuyler's aesthetic experiences of his own blackness were singularly painful. In his autobiography, *Black and Conservative,* Schuyler relived for us his first racial encounter occurring at the Brighton School in Syracuse, New York: "On the opening day of the term I registered three firsts: I was called 'nigger,' which had never happened to me before; I had a fight with the offender, a pugnacious little Italian boy; and during the fisticuffs I had my nose bloodied. Being called 'nigger' hurt me worst of all." Born to a northeastern middle-class family proud of a heritage that did not involve slavery, Schuyler's nose would be bloodied repeatedly by racist reactions to his blackness and by the political economic infrastructure of racism. For Schuyler, being black meant being isolated and constrained. His early years in upstate New York were materially comfortable yet psychologically uncomfortable. He reported that the black middle class was small and cut itself off from the black working class, a group of folk deemed to be "riff-raff." Moreover, the "tiny" black middle class was riddled with divisions and petty jealousies. Like Hughes, Schuyler wandered in search of freedom—through the military, where he was a second lieutenant, through "Bowery flophouses" in New York City, where he came to the conclusion that "'common folk'" reflected the realities of social life, through the segregated South as a reporter for the *Courier,* where the only "pleasant experience" he could recall later transcended race.[41] Unlike Hughes, Schuyler was not filled with wonder as he roamed; he resented the superior attitude of ignorant white folk; he grew to loathe the palpable racism provoked by the mere presence of his black body. And he could not identify with the black working class. These tender aesthetic experiences of his blackness led him to retreat from the hurt by taking up the remote distance of journalistic observation and by donning the mask of the satirist.

In order to ascertain how Schuyler's artistic practice displayed a primitive motive, we should attend to satire's savage voice. American satire has a storied tradition—one that specializes in "demolition projects. The one thing we know about satire is that it promises to tell us what we do not want to know—what we may, in fact resist knowing."[42] Satire is the art of ridicule, scorn, and derision. Satirists curse the monuments of humanity hoping to not only bring them down but to lift up the rest of us. Dustin Griffin suggests that satire is epideictic, a "rhetorical art" because it seeks to "praise and blame, cast in a fictional war between good and evil."[43] Similarly, Edward and Lillian Bloom argue that satire functions chiefly as a call of conscience, "a plea for a return to our senses, moral, intellectual, and aesthetic."[44] John Clark implies that satirists possess a kind of oversoul enabling them to see the "truth" in the world and obligating their telling the "sad tale that culture is in discombobulation and decay." At the risk of pushing the point too far, Clark suggests that satirists are linguistic terrorists who will "never forgive the vocabulary of fools, the punctuation of profligates, the syntax of disorder or disgrace."[45] There is debate among theorists regarding the principles governing the genre; satire may work through opposition, exaggeration, or paradox. But for our purposes we may note three commonplaces among recent scholarship. First, satirists wear a "mask" to produce a particular kind of dramatic effect. The satirist's persona should not be elided with the "historical author" precisely because satire demands outrageous displays.[46] Second, satire is involved in letting loose "primitive" outbursts. In *Theorizing Satire,* Brian Connery and Kirk Combe remark that, "Most satirists . . . claim one purpose for satire, that of high-minded and usually socially oriented moral and intellectual reform; however, they [often] engage in something quite different, namely, mercilessly savage attack on some person or thing that, frequently for private reasons, displeases them. The veneer of civilized behavior serves to mask great primitive urges."[47] Lastly, satire often results in discursive incoherence so as to provoke thought about the ethical dilemma under scrutiny.

There is nothing incoherent, however, about the importance of the month of June in 1926 to the status and movement of the New Negro. The NAACP's journal, the *Crisis,* edited by W. E. B. Du Bois, was sponsoring an ongoing "symposium" regarding how the New Negro should be portrayed. Near the end of the month, at the NAACP's sixteenth annual convention in Chicago, Du Bois would deliver his own manifesto for Negro art. And, of course, the *Nation* would use Schuyler to provoke Hughes. Each of these events was constitutive of an epideictic ritual where the arts of praise and blame animated feelings of pride and shame. But it is toward the *Nation* to which we now turn to fully appreciate the voice and voicelessness occurring in that exchange.

Exaggeration, Contradiction, and Savagery: "Hokum" in the *Nation*

Schuyler honed his satirical bite and wit in the *Messenger* two years prior to inking "The Negro-Art Hokum." When his feature column, "Shafts and Darts: A Page of Calumny and Satire," debuted, he and the magazine's coeditor, Theophilus Lewis, were faithful to the satirist's convention of announcing up front the goals of satire: "[Our] intention is to slur, lampoon, damn and occasionally praise anybody or anything in the known universe."[48] Schuyler would be true to this calling for the remainder of his days and as the New Negro movement became a cause célèbre, he trained his sights not on the character of the artistry but on the aesthetic practices bringing art and artists into the world and shaping their relations to a consuming social body. "The Negro-Art Hokum" displayed exaggeration and contradiction; it hyperventilated against "racial difference," destabilizing the term "Negro" to disclose its precipitating agency—the desire of whiteness for blackness and its own superiority. Schuyler wielded a satiric club, hammering away at the institutions and logics of race; it was this savage satire that was largely responsible for the disparagement that left him voiceless; it is also the key to providing him with a more appreciative hearing and, perhaps, an acknowledgment.

"The Negro-Art Hokum" began with a shot across the bow of "the widely advertised profundity" of President Calvin Coolidge, the " 'seven years of progress' " of New York City Mayor John Hylan, and "the reported sophistication of New Yorkers," calling each as "non-existent" as Negro art " 'made in America.' "[48] A New Negro renaissance in this country, Schuyler scoffed as "self-evident foolishness." Although "Negro art there has been, is, and will be among the numerous black nations of Africa," in America "skeptics patiently" wait its rebirth. The juxtaposition of exaggeration and contradiction began in the first paragraph, a discursive relation that constituted semantic instability and provided the leverage for savage satire. Black Africans could produce "Negro art" because they apparently cultivated and shared an aesthetic sensibility that was *foreign* to American Negroes. But at the time of the writing of "The Negro-Art Hokum," Harlem was hosting publication parties and literary contests; the mecca for black life was embracing new black novels, Broadway shows, Charleston dance exhibitions, and high-profile poetry readings. And so, it seemed that the New Negro movement was not understood as "self-evident foolishness." Schuyler pointed to the "eager apostles from Greenwich Village . . . whose hobby is taking races, nations, peoples, and movements under their wing" and manufacturing cultural worlds to their liking.[49] Note here the dual tension between the satirist's insight regarding the self-evidentiary character of the "hokum" and the blindness of the masses, the eagerness of white consumers, and the patience of black skeptics.

Schuyler exploited and exaggerated a class distinction that portrayed middle-class blacks as "white-like," similar in kind and character to their white neighbors. Far from denying that the blues, jazz, and the spirituals were unique expressions of a group of people, Schuyler contended that "these are contributions of a caste in a certain section of the country. . . . They are no more expressive or characteristic of the Negro race than the music and dancing of the Appalachian highlanders . . . are expressive or characteristic of the Caucasian race." Indeed, Schuyler stressed that "any group under similar circumstances would have produced something similar." Pivoting sharply from folk cultural expression, however, "The Negro-Art Hokum" offered "literature, painting, and sculpture of Aframericans" as proof of Schuyler's claim, labeling them as "identical in kind with the literature, painting, and sculpture of white Americans: that is, it shows more or less evidence of European influence." And this was portrayed as perfectly reasonable because the Negro was "not living in a different world as some whites and a few Negroes would have us believe.... Negroes and whites from the same localities in this country talk, think, and act about the same."[50]

The creative tension cultivated and distributed through exaggeration and contradiction in the "The Negro-Art Hokum" began to build as Schuyler described the aesthetic experiences responsible for this sameness: "When the jangling of his Connecticut alarm clock gets him out of his Grand Rapids bed . . . when he toils at the same or similar work in mills, mines, factories, and commerce . . . when he wears similar clothing and speaks the same language . . . when he reads the same bible . . . when he gets the same or similar schooling . . . lives in the same kind of houses . . . when he responds to the same political, social, moral and economic stimuli in precisely the same manner as his white neighbor, it is sheer nonsense to talk about 'racial differences' as between the American black and the American white man."[51] This litany of sameness was, I believe, uniquely expressive of Schuyler's "soul." Recall that Schuyler's aesthetic experiences of his blackness left him feeling isolated and boxed in; thus, we can hear his *desire* for how black folk should have the same sorts of political, economic, and social opportunities as every other American, options largely denied in Schuyler's segregated America.[52] But there was much more here than the satirist's prescription for the ills brought on by the virus of racism. For if the satirist was read as he should be, that is ironically, we must question the rhetorical function of Schuyler's most famous claim: "that the Aframerican is merely a lampblacked Anglo-Saxon."[53] In the context of "The Negro-Art Hokum" and this epideictic ritual, it appeared as though this white-like condition of black folk was offered by Schuyler as a *good thing* precisely because he railed against the logic of racial difference; understood as satire, however, and removed from the interpretive structure of a "debate," the notion that "your American Negro is just plain American" opens up for us the manner in which satire destabilized the term "Negro" and challenged the supposed virtue of being an "American."

Ten months before the *Nation* received "The Negro-Art Hokum," the *Messenger* published "At the Darktown Charity Ball," a rollicking spoof of black high society.[54] In the short story, Schuyler let us eavesdrop on a conversation between two "gossips" who regularly attend charity balls sponsored by "the best people of Negro society," pitiful members of the "Hand-to-Mouth Club." Here were the "lampblacked Anglo-Saxons" to which he referred in "The Negro-Art Hokum." Having thoroughly internalized American values and beliefs, this "caste" exhibited snobbery, jealousy, and pretension. The Charity Ball was a forum for the display of all sorts of hokum. The gossips whisper about women wearing gowns that they cannot afford, "ladies of the upper ten [percent] sneaking out to domestic service to make ends meet." They also exposed "distinguished looking" men who were philanderers and adulterers—"gentlemen" who married absurdly "stupid" women because they appeared to be "almost white!" The "best" people of Negro high society were pathetic and hardly worthy of praise. The social world of the "lampblacked Anglo-Saxon" was replete with spectacular forms of vice and was the object to which Schuyler referred when he claimed that Negro art, "'made in America'" was "self-evident foolishness." Since Negro art existed among black African nations, this "foolishness" was the result of Americanization. Not only did the exaggeration of the white-likeness of the "lampblacked Anglo-Saxon" undermine American virtue, it provided some of the energy for the destabilization of the term "Negro."

The gossips at the Ball marveled over how whites "pass" into Negro culture so as to escape their dull and mundane existences in white society. As "pseudo-negroes," they were ranked among the "best" in Negro society and still enjoyed the privilege of "whiteness"—they "can go anywhere they please" because "the most rabid Kleagle would never recognize them for anything else but *exactly what they are.* Caucasians."[55] The satirist was clearly enjoying himself, for in racial terms these claims made virtually no sense. In "The Negro-Art Hokum," Negroes had a skin color that "ranges from very dark brown to pink"; and Negroes were identifiable as: American, Aframerican, Anglo-Saxon, and *Homo Africanus.* The Negro race included such notable persons as W. E. B. Du Bois, a New Englander; Claude McKay, a Jamaican; Aleksandr Pushkin, a Russian; and Alexandre Dumas, a Frenchman. One wonders what exactly was this Negro-ness that linked these men and could be appropriated by selfish whites—a Negro-ness that could be signified by nearly every skin tone? In a universe where "pseudo-negroes" with "pink" skins were readily recognized as being *really* Caucasians, how can "pink" Negroes even exist? Asked differently, in "The Negro-Art Hokum" to what did "Negro" refer? It could not signify skin color, nation, or African culture because in "The Negro-Art Hokum" the strongest influences constituting the "Negro" were Anglo European. To answer this question, we must consider how primitivism structured Schuyler's savage satire.

Satirists are often vicious because satire is rhetorical provocation.[56] Schuyler's toxicity cannot be adequately appreciated unless we come to terms with how the aesthetic experiences of his blackness conditioned his understanding of white power. In "Our White Folks," published by the famous satirist H. L. Mencken in the *American Mercury* a year after "The Negro-Art Hokum" appeared, Schuyler jeered at a host of assumptions about the proclaimed and celebrated primitive Negro. "We Ethiops," he wrote self-consciously, "are a childish, shiftless, immoral, primitive, incurably religious, genially incompetent, incredibly odiferous, inherently musical, chronically excitable, mentally inferior people with pronounced homicidal tendencies. We are incapable of self-government or self-restraint, and irresponsible except when led by white folks. We possess a penchant for assaulting white females and an inordinate appetite for chicken, gin and watermelon."[57] As the essay unfolded, Schuyler shifted his attention from the caricatures of blackness to the work they perform for whiteness.

As a socialist sympathizer, Schuyler was repeatedly irritated by how racial hatred kept the white working class from reaping the benefits of "labor solidarity" with black workers. Poor white folk would rather cling to "an empty color superiority" derived from "the famous one-drop theory, that distinctive American contribution to the science of anthropology which lists as Negroes all people having the remotest Negro ancestry, despite the fact that they may be, and often are, indistinguishable from the purest Nordic."[58] The ground pitched and rolled beneath Schuyler's feet as the term "Negro" was made to represent nearly everyone and no one; due to the "voodoo" of anthropology, this form of racial reasoning was nonsense, empty. As such, it was the near perfect object for the satirist's scorn. The mask the satirist wears is typically transparent so that we know the brutality is a contrived affectation, rendering it superficial, perhaps even trivial.[59] But Schuyler's savagery was not merely skin deep. In "Blessed Are the Sons of Ham," a farce regarding the day-to-day "honest-to-goodness thrill" black folk experience due to ongoing racial insults and inconveniences, Schuyler called himself an "unadulterated Negro"; we understand that the phrase signals his full ownership of the pain brought on by racist responses to his blackness. In fact, Schuyler, in an autobiographical moment when he lifted the mask, told us as much: "All these things used to infuriate me," he sighed, but "now I have a sense of humor." Even if we accept at face value his confession of having transmuted his fury into comedy, we should keep in mind that Schuyler also noted that the "thrill" of being called a "nigger" was "lasting. It's just as if it happened yesterday. . . . I can never forget it."[60] And so, despite his deconstruction of the term "Negro," Schuyler's savage satire was set off by an aesthetic practice motivated by what can only be called his racial memories—recollections of being an unadulterated Negro.

Scaling the "Racial Mountain" in the *Nation*

Although the *Nation* successfully spurred Hughes into producing his "manifesto," "The Negro-Art Hokum" did not inspire "The Negro Artist and the Racial Mountain." That honor goes to Harlem's other potential poet laureate, Countee Cullen. The son of a prominent minister, Cullen was Hughes's on-again-off-again friend, would-be lover, and chief rival for the spoils of the New Negro movement. In a review of *The Weary Blues* published in *Opportunity* in February of 1926, Cullen admired the fearless rupture the work created in literary tradition through "utter spontaneity" in form and sound. "This poet," announced Cullen, "represents a transcendently emancipated spirit among a class of young writers whose particular battle-cry is freedom."[61] But Cullen was conflicted about the impact such liberation was having on what he considered to be the divine poetic arts. In particular, Hughes's "jazz poems" were completely out of place, not belonging to Cullen's vision for the spirit of the New Negro. Like "The Negro-Art Hokum" would do in four months, Cullen threatened Hughes with homelessness by asserting that blues and jazz were made up of aesthetic practices that were a part of the low life that a poet should rise above:

> They [jazz poems] move along with the frenzy and electric heat of a Methodist or Baptist revival meeting, and affect me in much the same manner. The revival meeting excites me, cooling and flushing me with alternate chills and fevers of emotion; so do these poems. But when the storm is over, I wonder if the quiet way of communing is not more spiritual for the God-seeking heart; and in the light of reflection I wonder if jazz poems really belong to that dignified company, that select and austere circle of high literary expression which we call poetry.[62]

Although the midsection of Cullen's review granted that several of Hughes's more traditional poems were as "fine and polished as you like," his closing offered the central metaphor that would fire Hughes's imagination: "Taken as a group the selections in this book seem one-sided to me. They tend to hurl this poet into the *gaping pit* that lies before all Negro writers, in the confines of which they become *racial* artists instead of artists pure and simple."[63] Cullen had unwittingly supplied Hughes with the image he would seize upon for his "manifesto"; with Schuyler's "The Negro-Art Hokum" in hand and Cullen's "pit" before his mind's eye, Hughes transfigured the racial pit into the "Racial Mountain."

Hughes's "rebuttal" shared a potent commonplace with Schuyler's "The

Negro-Art Hokum" and yet was propelled by quite different motives. Like "The Negro-Art Hokum" it disparaged "lampblacked Anglo-Saxons"; it too saw "Nordic civilization" as draining the vitality out of humanity.[64] Hughes ridiculed the "aping of things white,"[65] as did Schuyler in the "Charity Ball" and elsewhere. Hughes, however, was not drawn to the satiric; he wandered in search of the erotic. His aesthetic experiences of black folk culture constituted in him a joyful love and respect for the ways in which song and dance seemed to "naturally" arise from the spiritual strivings of the masses. To Hughes, the primitive blues and jazz sounds were not barbaric; they were "noble," and the disregard they received from the black middle class was ignoble. To be sure, Hughes's understanding of race included essentialist concepts; but his primitivism did not strictly hinge on biology, it was more properly a reflection of his aesthetic experiences of blackness. And it was due to the fact that they were inspired by different aesthetic experiences of blackness that Schuyler and Hughes sharply parted company, leaving Schuyler isolated and voiceless. But let us first briefly examine their commonplace.

"The Negro Artist and the Racial Mountain" opened with Hughes relaying a conversation he had many times with Cullen about black art—an exchange that was undoubtedly partly responsible for Cullen's affections being unrequited: "One of the most promising of the young Negro poets said to me once, 'I want to be a poet—not a Negro poet,' meaning, I believe, 'I want to write like a white poet'; meaning subconsciously, 'I would like to be a white poet'; meaning behind that, 'I would like to be white.' And I was sorry the young man said that, for no great poet has ever been afraid of being himself." Beginning with a distinction held by both Cullen and Hughes between poetry and "Negro" poetry, Hughes moved through a series of logical demonstrations that revealed a basic agreement with Schuyler; that is, the strongest influence on the lifestyle of the black middle class were Anglo European values and beliefs. For Hughes, the "lampblacked Anglo-Saxon" felt a peculiar "desire to run away spiritually from his race . . . this urge within the race toward whiteness, the desire to pour racial individuality into the mold of American standardization, and to be as little Negro and as much American as possible." Like Schuyler, Hughes mocked the pretension of the black middle class, "the smug, contented, respectable folk" who were always uncomfortable in their own skins. A class that sought to minimize racial distinction so as not to be "like niggers." It was clear that Hughes disdained this New Negro home because the aesthetic experiences cultivated there lead to aesthetic judgments of disparagement of black beauty. Through the schools, churches, magazines, and books consumed in this home, "the word white comes to be unconsciously a symbol of all the virtues. It holds for the children beauty, morality, and money. . . . One sees immediately how difficult it would be for an artist born in such a home to interest himself in interpreting the beauty of his own people. He is never taught to see that beauty." The aesthetic experiences and practices regarding race in this New Negro home bring forth "a very high mountain indeed for the would-be racial artist to climb in order to discover himself and his people." This racial mountain not only impeded Cullen's "true" self-consciousness, it constricted Hughes's own voice. The masses for which he wrote do not really care that he writes. Cullen did have a point about the place of poetry in society, and Hughes acknowledged it through his grumblings over the "closed ears of the colored near-intellectuals": "Let Paul Robeson singing Water Boy, and Rudolph Fisher writing about the streets of Harlem, and Jean Toomer holding the heart of Georgia in his hands, and Aaron Douglas drawing strange black fantasies cause the smug Negro middle class to turn from their white, respectable, ordinary books and papers to catch a glimmer of their own beauty." Hughes's wondrous wanderings opened up his eyes to "the low-down folks" who do not seek approval from white folks. Hughes's primitivism was on full display as he celebrated in revival fashion the "so-called common element . . . may the Lord be praised! The people who have their nip of gin on Saturday nights. . . . Their joy runs bang! into ecstasy. Their religion soars to a shout. Work maybe a little today, rest a little tomorrow. Play awhile. Sing awhile. O, let's dance!"[66]

The "common element" were the source of Negro art, and they "furnish a wealth of colorful and distinctive material" for the artist who was free from the constraints imposed by the New Negro intellectual leadership. It was here where the commonplace shared by Hughes and Schuyler seemed to dissolve; although Schuyler wished to be rid of the folks Hughes referred to as the "Nordicized Negro intelligentsia," his savage satire also portrayed the "common element" in "The Negro-Art Hokum" as populated by imbeciles and "clowns."[67] Recall that Schuyler's Negro was delimited by white supremacy, referring to little more than the hegemonic operations of a racial reasoning shaped by the fears of and desires for blackness. Fully immersed in the erotic character of his aesthetic experiences of blackness, however, Hughes speculated that the "authentic" black artist could mine "the field of unused material . . . even among the better classes with their 'white' culture and conscious American manners" because for him there was a "Negro-ness" in surplus of white power. Hughes's explanation of the affects of blues and jazz poems revealed the cultural and spiritual sources of Negro art: "But jazz to me is one of the inherent expressions of Negro life in America: the eternal tom-tom beating in the Negro soul—the tom-tom of revolt against weariness in a white world, a world of subway trains, and work, work, work; the tom-tom of joy and laughter, and pain swallowed in a smile."[68] And so, Hughes wrote jazz and blues poems so that he could acknowledge the ethical and affective resonance of the expressions of "the Negro soul," endowing voice. The "revolt" against racism and modernism was accompanied by "joy and laughter, and pain"; these poems transfigured the inhumanity of "the white world" into the humanity of the Negro soul. The blues aesthetic was transformative and transhistorical; it was a source of black power and allowed for cultural memory. Hughes once described to Wallace Thurman how "the blues just naturally overtook me, like a blind beggar with an old guitar."[69] This was the power of the erotic, an affective force that moved through a joyful communion with others; being consubstantial with black folk felt "natural" to Hughes because it was not an imposition, it was a choice; thus, the blues aesthetic seemed "simple" to him because it fit the cadence of everyday life; the blues singer didn't rise above the topical materials of her or his speech, they were immersed in them.[70] Once enraptured, Hughes could also "sing" tales of how the Negro soul survives. We have arrived at the significance of Hughes's "manifesto": "to my mind, it is the duty of the younger Negro artist, if he accepts any duties at all from outsiders, to change through the force of his art that old whispering 'I want to be white,' hidden in the aspirations of his people, to 'Why should I want to be white? I am Negro—and beautiful!' "[71]

A Re-appreciation of Savage Satire as Negro Art

Hughes's "manifesto" did more than rally the younger artists' search for free expression of black beauty; as a contrived "rebuttal" to "The Negro-Art Hokum," it gave shape and force to the interpretive structure of an epideictic ritual ill equipped to appreciate Schuyler's savage satire. Schuyler was made to participate in an aesthetic practice that, in a sense, took the form of a New Negro revival; there was spiritual communion and bitter dissension over the basic character of New Negro art, but few attendants disputed its existence. Even Cullen who sought a quieter place of poetic worship asserted that the "pit" that lies at the feet of Negro artists was "real." The epideictic ritual generative of tremendous excitement by 1926 invited (or, in the case of Schuyler, commanded) diverse participants to elevate, denigrate, and meditate on the artistic and aesthetic practices of the New Negro movement. Although the black leadership and the black press generally disparaged Hughes's blues voice during this time, calling him a "poet low-rate," his eroticism spurred on the youth movement by promising black self-love. And as Alain Locke had predicted in the immensely influential anthology *The New Negro: An Interpretation,* it would be the younger generation that would round out the features of the New Negro.[72] Hughes's "The Negro Artist and the Racial Mountain" set him apart from nearly every other would-be black artist and inspired folks like Wallace Thurman, Gwendolyn Bennett, Aaron Douglas, Richard Bruce Nugent, Zora Neale Hurston, and others to venture out on their own in defiance of New Negro civil rights orthodoxy and establish new literary forums.[73]

As a satirist who swung a wrecking ball at nearly everything in his path, including black folk who got in the way, Schuyler found few commonplaces; the black masses ignored him and the black intelligentsia could not or would not understand him. In his autobiography, *The Big Sea,* Hughes, lamenting the castigation he received for his second book of poems, *Fine Clothes to the Jew,* noted that during the New Negro movement, black critics seemed incapable of appreciating the subtleties of irony and parody, unless it was "obvious like with George Schuyler's *Black No More.*"[74] As a coerced participant in the *Nation*'s epideictic ritual, Schuyler's satirical motive in "The Negro-Art Hokum" was not obvious; it must be perceived in relation to some of his other key writings about the New Negro at the height of the movement. For example, in a cartoonish short story appearing in the *Messenger* in June 1925, a few short months prior to his scripting "The Negro-Art Hokum," Schuyler shot darts at the racist and selfish consumptive desires backing the production of Negro art. "At the Coffee House" staged a conversation between a "shabbily dressed" white couple in a Greenwich Village café dreaming of literary fame and fortune. The woman advised the young man to write about "Indians, the South Seas or life in the jungle." The young man initially objected because he didn't "know anything about those subjects." But he was eventually persuaded by his scheming companion that the Negro renaissance was an era where you do not "have to know anything much about anything to be a literary success nowadays. . . . As long as you make it funny or very grotesque and creepy, it will make a hit. . . . If you write something funny," his friend elaborated, "do it in dialect and throw in plenty of references to chicken, watermelon, razors, gin, singing mammies, and all that sort of thing." The couple collaborated on such a novel and twenty-five editions later they enjoyed legendary literary status in Manhattan.[75] Read in conjunction with works like this, Schuyler's savagery was not simply meant to assault the logic of racial conservation and promotion; it was devoted to an onslaught on the basic character of the racist imaginary and on the manner in which New York City's art world was complicit in the manufacture of primitive delights.

I am inclined to agree with Michael Peplow, Schuyler's biographer, when he recalls how his friend's work was bonded to a counterstatement that did not exist when he authored it and was hijacked by the *Nation*'s epideictic ritual; Kirchwey's judgment of the right time to publish "The Negro-Art Hokum" resulted in Schuyler being "shabbily treated."[76] And to a great extent he still is. While Hughes is remembered as the Harlem Renaissance's brightest star, Schuyler is chronicled in one of the most notable African American literary anthologies as the writer who is "important primarily for having provoked Langston Hughes's famous rejoinder." Indeed, the anthology rightly notes that at the time of his death, "he was regarded by many blacks as a traitor to his race."[77] To be sure, this aesthetic judgment is also based on Schuyler's maniacal rants against the civil rights movement and Dr. Martin Luther King Jr. in the early 1960s. But let us be reminded that the satirist wears a mask and that savage satire is, in part, meant to be a call of conscience, "a plea for a return to our senses." We may differ with the possibility (or preference) for such a "return," but the affects of savagery should jolt us and suspend the commonplace indictment of Schuyler's traitorous legacy. Hence, for a brief moment, let us endure our anxiety regarding what might emerge and reconsider Schuyler's fate.

Despite some critics' claims to the contrary, Schuyler did not desire to be white; a fact to which much of his writing over the years and the title of his autobiography, *Black and Conservative,* testifies. He applauded W. E. B. Du Bois's *Gift of Black Folk* for helping black people to be proud of "the fact that they were Negroes."[78] This is more like the sentiment of the historical author; a black man supremely confident and secure in the belief that one's talents can take one anywhere. As a "black Yankee"[79] facing time and again the utter absurdity of racial hatred, the painful aesthetic experiences of his blackness, Schuyler did what came "natural" to him—he satirized his social world. In fact, he believed that satire was a perfectly appropriate response to racism: "The Negro is a sort of black Gulliver chained by white Lilliputians, a prisoner in a jail of color prejudice, a babe in a forest of bigotry, but withal a fellow philosophical and cynical enough to laugh at himself and his predicament. He has developed . . . the capacity to see things as they are rather than as he would have them. He is a close student of the contradictory pretensions and practices of the ofay gentry, and it is this that makes him really intelligent in a republic of morons."[80] Schuyler was describing his iconoclastic self; and this observation gets us closer to understanding the humanity of his savagery. Edward and Lillian Bloom remind us that the satirist's mask may also reveal affection and identification with the object of scorn: "In this large context, as we see many satirists, severity or harshness of tone need not imply rancor or an absence of social empathy. We think of those satirists who scold and berate, who sound caustic, bitter, and savage because they care enough about [humanity] to be angered by [its] errant betrayals of self and fellow creatures."[81]

Schuyler projected his savage satire into the nothingness that, in "The Negro-Art Hokum," was concealed by the incandescent trope the New Negro. What is at stake here is the propriety of satire as a response to being black in America. It seems evident that the most intense affects of race mobilized by the New Negro paralleled racial fantasies regarding the "proper" performance of blackness—that what one "sees" is what one gets. That blackness, although explosive, unsettling, and captivating, could be made to behave according to racial law; even as blackness is asked to run amok for the enjoyment of an audience, it cannot transgress the limits of authorized texts produced and distributed through dominant aesthetic practices of art world regimes. Wedged into the epideictic ritual perpetrated by the *Nation,* Schuyler's satire was judged to be decidedly out of place and out of bounds; thus it was met with disparagement. Such an aesthetic judgment failed to appreciate the fact that Schuyler's savagery was also self-reflexive. Clark explains that "the satirist archer becomes his own target. For it is certainly true (or at least we like to think it is so) that all too many a satirist is guilty of the very spite and malice that he lashes and impugns in others."[82] Considering the possibility that Schuyler's satire produced the sort of incoherence that landed him in his own crosshairs as a "lampblacked Anglo-Saxon," should we, here and now, still disparage Schuyler? I can imagine his savage satire flooding Cullen's racial "pit" with venom; I can picture it propelling black folk up and over Hughes's "Racial Mountain." Perhaps this is the satirist's gift; it was definitely Schuyler's motive—constitutive of the aesthetic understanding that "individuals and groups have been *seeking better places* since the beginning of time, and rarely if ever do they migrate consciously to a worse one."[83] In a very real sense, Hughes and Schuyler shared this migratory drive; for both sought better (dwelling) places. And who is to say that the blues aesthetic is more authentically black than savage satire? As an art under intense formative pressure by Schuyler's lived experience of his blackness, might we not call it black art? And if we do, let us listen for maybe the first time to Schuyler's satirical voice. But even as we hear Schuyler's hurt, the openness that haunts tropes of race were being subjected to powerful defining forces and sparking calamitous encounters among New Negroes, especially between the elders in search of stable communal life and the youngsters wishing to blast off New Negro orthodoxy.

6
"All Art Is Propaganda"
The Politics of New Negro Aesthetics

In his autobiography *The Big Sea,* Langston Hughes characterized the Harlem of the 1920s as a time and a place where "the Negro was in vogue."[1] This observation should be understood not simply as black life and culture being in fashion or in style; rather, we need to note that New Negro aesthetic and artistic practices were undergoing disparate and striking processes of habituation. When the University of Chicago sociologist Charles S. Johnson arrived in Harlem in 1922 and began editing the *Opportunity,* the Urban League's journal, the *Crisis* was the "prime mover" of the New Negro movement.[2] W. E. B. Du Bois assumed command of the burgeoning art movement by turning the journal into a venue christening young black writers; he held this unofficial post with his characteristic seriousness, so much so that he earned a reputation among NAACP board members as being, paradoxically, both obstreperous and sullen. Du Bois and Jessie Fauset, the journal's literary editor, systematically produced black authors through the circulatory system of the NAACP's muscular organ. But this pump also sought to make up rules for being distributed *as* a New Negro. Being in vogue, therefore, suggested the cultivation of particular forms of black subjectivity corresponding to prominent tropes of the New Negro. Heightened black sensibility was also bonded to consumptive acts of white folks formulated in conjunction with emerging aesthetic judgments of "taste"; the materialization of New Negro cultural "subjects" and "objects," then, necessitated alterations in the configurations of regimes operating in New York City's art world. Popularity of the New Negro entailed tremendous affects and provoked greedy and hungry acts of regulation and discipline in the name of bolstering more consumption of the trendy. Du Bois, however, was not interested in producing consumption for consumption's sake. The *Crisis*'s aesthetic practices associated with recruiting, editing, publishing, and awarding black artistry emerged in tune with Du Bois's sense of the duty he and other members of the Talented

Tenth felt toward bettering the life of black folk through the transfiguration of America's social body.

Du Bois's leadership faced many challenges originating from both within and without the NAACP. After the *Opportunity* began to mimic and perfect the aesthetic practices of the *Crisis,* molding New Negro artists and mobilizing their distribution, it would take barely a year for Johnson to wield such a "vast influence on the Harlem of the New Negro" that he was able to present Du Bois as "old school" at the Civic Club affair ostensibly organized to celebrate the publication of Fauset's *There is Confusion.*[3] In a review of *The New Negro: An Interpretation* in 1926, Du Bois described this event as generating aesthetic experiences for key New York City publishing agents inspiring the vision for the anthology and illuminating for Du Bois the actualization of new race relations that would redesign the strategic territory constituting black art's role in bringing about social justice. In Du Bois's tale, the editor of the *Survey,* Paul Kellogg, enjoyed fortuitous dinner conversation by being seated near A. Granville Dill, the *Crisis* business manager:

> The editor looked at the company with interest and Mr. Dill began to tell him who they were. It occurred to the editor of *The Survey* that here was material for a *Survey Graphic;* still he hesitated and feared the "social uplifters" of the United States with a mighty fear. But he took one step which saved the day: He got a colored man to edit that number of the *Graphic,* Alain Locke, a former Rhodes scholar and a professor at Howard University. Locke did a good job, so good a job that this Negro number of the *Survey Graphic* was one of the most successful numbers ever issued by *The Survey.*[4]

Du Bois's description of the genesis of the special issue, "Harlem: Mecca of the New Negro," and the subsequent publication of the anthology was laced, however, with residual resentment regarding once being muzzled by NAACP public image handlers. He recalled "vividly being asked by *The Survey* to furnish it for the New Year 1914 a statement of the aims of the N.A.A.C.P." He complied and included the goal of social equality, raising the terrifying specter of interracial marriage: "His [the Negro's] right to be treated as a gentleman when he acts like one, to marry any sane, grown person who wants to marry him, and to meet and eat with his friends without being accused of undue assumption or unworthy ambition." Apparently, the *Survey* "frantically" sought clarification from other directors of the NAACP, finding several who "did not agree" with Du Bois's framing of institutional goals, counting one person "who threatened to resign" if the statement made it into print. Thus, the statement was not published. Du Bois admitted that "much water has flowed under the bridge" since those unsettling turn of events involving *The Survey;* so why drudge them up fourteen years later in a review of *The New Negro*?[5]

The short answer can be discovered when we conceive of Du Bois's rhetoric as accentuating the flows of power always already imbricated in the invention and distribution of black speech. The politics of the aesthetic practices of the NAACP regarding the ideologies of social equality among the races—inevitably haunted by the mythology of black male sexual desire for white womanhood—triggered the disavowal of Du Bois's voice. Du Bois was often accused by NAACP directors of being too thin-skinned when gag rules were placed upon his speech as a board member. But his review revealed that his sensitivity to the politics of race was shared by the *Survey;* apprehensive of the "social uplifters," the recruitment of Locke as the special issue editor was framed as a tactic designed to drain energy away from critics who might feel as though the *Survey* should not speak *for* the New Negro. Du Bois's rhetorical inventiveness is evident here. Rather than uphold the widely held view that the special issue and Locke's *The New Negro* represented a radical uncoupling from conventional forms of performance conditions for black speech, Du Bois contextualized their emergence as accompanying a subtle shift in tactics regarding the maintenance of white power to discriminately endow some black voices and mute others.

In the review, Du Bois offered narrowly circumscribed praise for Locke's techne: "Mr. Locke has done a fine piece of editing. The proof reading, the bibliographies and the general arrangement are all beyond criticism." Du Bois hinted that Locke knew *how* to manufacture an anthology that exploited white dreams, but did not know *what* his aesthetic practices would eventually yield:

> With one point alone do I differ with the Editor. Mr. Locke has newly been seized with the idea that Beauty rather than Propaganda should be the object of Negro literature and art. His book proves the falseness of this thesis. This is a book filled and bursting with propaganda but it is propaganda for the most part beautifully and painstakingly done; and it is a grave question if ever in this world in any renaissance there can be a search for disembodied beauty which is not really a passionate effort to do something tangible, accompanied and illumined and made holy by the vision of eternal beauty. Of course this involves a controversy as old as the world and much too transcendental for practical purposes, and yet, if Mr. Locke's thesis is insisted on too much it is going to turn

> the Negro renaissance into decadence. It is the fight for Life and Liberty that is giving birth to Negro literature and art today and when, turning from this fight or ignoring it, the young Negro tries to do pretty things or things that catch the passing fancy of the really unimportant critics and publishers about him, he will find that he has killed the soul of Beauty in his Art.[6]

Given the severity of the "one point" on which Du Bois disagreed with Locke, it may seem odd to assert that these two African American scholars were generally of the same mind regarding New Negro artistry. Each man held fast to a kind of wish fulfillment for art to change American social order. Each man projected these dreams onto the faces of the youth of the Talented Tenth. Each man devoted time and intellectual energy toward the erection of black art institutes where the "fitting and proper" aesthetic practices would flourish, giving birth to the next generation of black artistry. And each man felt solely responsible for making it all happen. But, it was precisely the intensity of this singularity—this "one point"—that drove a wedge between them, taking on the hues of an expansive ideological schism. Although Du Bois and Locke were never friends, within the imaginary recalling the Harlem Renaissance they often appear as mortal enemies, holding rigid, diametrically opposed perspectives on the New Negro.[7] This conclusion is easily arrived at if one conceives of the ground of this dispute as paved exclusively—or primarily—with competing theories of literature and art. As Du Bois lamented in his review of *The New Negro,* historically there has been precious little commonplace for beauty and propaganda to peacefully coexist.

A much more robust understanding of the significance of Du Bois's refutation is made available through an orientation that accentuates the manner in which Du Bois worried over the politics of New Negro aesthetics. We should pay attention to how emerging aesthetic practices occupying regimes of artistic publication and distribution conceived of the relations among blackness, art, and the possibilities of social equality in America. Indeed, Du Bois could not have agreed with the sentiment in "Enter The New Negro," published in the *Survey Graphic* special issue wherein Locke asserted that "the Negro mind reaches out as yet to nothing but American wants, American ideas."[8] The cleave to which I am alluding was emergent in Du Bois's contribution to *The New Negro* called "The Negro Mind Reaches Out," where he seemed to have specifically appropriated Locke's phrase from the special issue as his title in the anthology to redirect and re-qualify the extension of black consciousness and intellect. Du Bois's essay began by reassessing his famous prophecy published in *The Souls of Black Folk* that the "problem of the twentieth century is the problem of the Color Line."[9] Du Bois states that "most men would agree that our present problem of problems was not the color problem, but what we call Labor, the problem of allocating work and income in the tremendous and increasingly intricate world-embracing industrial machine that our civilization has built." The color line, however, was not obliterated in this rearticulation of global social order; it was refracted through the increased intricacy of imperialism because the aesthetic practices of industrialism made available populations of color as exploited labor and colonial subjects that were swept into the "shadows" of England, Portugal, Belgium, and France: "Modern imperialism and modern industrialism are one and the same system; root and branch of the same tree. The race problem is the other side of the labor problem." This is so because labor solidarity has historically been scuttled by the amplification of race hatred. Du Bois highlighted how global imperialism has been fueled and shaped by the sort of racism worn into the grooves of US sociality. "American ideas" about race were for Du Bois, key obstacles standing in the way of "industrial democracy." Although a quarter of a century had slipped by since his famous claim regarding the stubbornness of racial exclusion and after apparently displacing it in the beginning of the essay, Du Bois completed its remarkable return: "And thus again in 1924 as in 1899 I seem to see the problem of the twentieth century as the Problem of the Color Line."[10] Du Bois surely would have understood Locke's strategy calling for New Negroes pledging allegiance to American values—Du Bois had expressed similar sentiments many times before. But when Locke stitched this suggestion regarding the rightness of American values to the fabric of New Negro art and beauty in the special issue, Du Bois broke ranks.

This chapter is concerned with Du Bois's rhetorical sensitivity regarding the fluid dynamics of hegemony in terms of how tropes of pure aestheticism functioned to produce and legitimate aesthetic judgments of racial "authenticity" based on New Negro artistic practices. To Du Bois, the putative autonomy of art concealed the urgency of its practical and social labors regarding how specific features of black life and culture became selectively amplified while other aspects were dampened. The production of the "Bible" of the Harlem Renaissance,[11] *The New Negro,* raised these stakes to stratospheric heights precisely because it signaled widespread interest among white power brokers in New Negro aesthetic and artistic practices. The picture of "pure" artistry shone in *The New Negro*—despite Locke's revisionist efforts regarding so-called pure art mobilized through his philosophy of values—provoked in Du Bois an excruciating dilemma.[12] On the one hand, New Negro artistic practices "purely for the sake of art" insinuated the production of a "universal" and distinctively black art. Du Bois favored displays of New Negro sophistication and education as infallible signs of a readiness for social equality with white folks, but tropes of the middle class were routinely sensed and judged by white folks as basically too familiar and lacking intense resonance; thus, such performances were understood as not distinctively (or "authentically") black. Meanwhile, as works like Fauset's *There Is Confusion* were criticized for having "the usual faults of the propaganda story,"[13] because they focused on struggles of educated blacks, the stories of the "low-down" folks were increasingly judged as expressive of the "true" Negro racial essence, rendering both its universality and its distinct blackness. The sediment of such aesthetic judgments settling in forms of taste authorized the amplification and hyper-visibility of intense "low-down" adventures of sex, drugs, and violence. Framed as the result of a "free" and "pure" artistic motive, explosions of the passions emerged as "universal truths" regarding blackness; and the black elite who denied these "truths" were criticized for being gripped by the ideologies of a false consciousness promoted by propaganda. To Du Bois, the hegemony of pure art undermined an acknowledgment of the ethical and affective dimensions of his speech as a black intellectual, fomenting voicelessness. This plight was not merely personal; it was a problem for the social. In this chapter I explore the contours of this predicament by first describing a public debate regarding the relations among art, aesthetics, and obligations to social justice. I then critique an address, "Criteria of Negro Art," delivered by Du Bois as an intervention in the establishment of what he considered to be white poor taste.

How Shall We Feel toward the Negro?

The popularity of the *Survey Graphic*'s special issue on Harlem stoked many fires, some of them chokingly personal. In the summer of 1925, the *Crisis* published a scathing review of a work by a British art historian loosely based on his experiences in military service to the Crown in the Caribbean. Haldane MacFall's novel *The Wooings of Jezebel Pettyfer* was not only trashed by the reviewer, Emmett J. Scott, as a despicable novel, the author was personally attacked as a person who obviously hated Negroes.[14] Carl Van Vechten dispatched a letter of protest to Du Bois claiming that although he knew nothing of the island of Barbados, the setting for the novel, he found the work to be "credible" as "a work of art." Van Vechten's defense of MacFall was far from altruistic; by the fall of 1925, the Knopf author and essayist had immersed himself in Harlem life, claiming to be an honorary New Negro and planning to pen his own "Negro" novel.[15] MacFall's work may have been set among unfamiliar scenery, but it animated familiar affects regarding blackness—the sort that, for Van Vechten, "awaken . . . interest and arouse . . . imagination."[16] Van Vechten sought to establish his taste as "credible," as an aesthetic judgment derived from aesthetic experiences of the affective registers of New Negro artistic performances. Du Bois and Van Vechten briefly shared a commonplace; each critic desired a public conversation about the propriety of the aesthetic and artistic practices emerging in the movement. Jessie Fauset coordinated the communion by soliciting questions from Van Vechten concerning ideological flashpoints that had become so hot so as to cause some New Negro social gatherings to meltdown. The questions were distributed to several prominent artists, publishers, and critics, and the responses were published in a recurring series called "The Negro in Art: How Shall He Be Portrayed? A Symposium."

Although the symposium's title provided a guiding query—how shall Negroes be portrayed—the exchange, lasting eight issues, dramatized a dance of discourses choreographed by an *unasked* question—an inquisition into the affects of blackness. In the opening passage of *The Souls of Black Folk,* Du Bois asserted that improvements in US race relations were stymied by a suffocating silence due to an American evasion of the chief question gnawing at the heart of white folks: "How does it feel to be a problem?"[17] Similarly, the symposium's racial tropes orbited the tremendous affects radiating from the void. Van Vechten submitted seven questions to Fauset, but they essentially amounted to two problematics: First, what sort of ethical concerns were provoked by New Negro aesthetic and artistic practices? Second, what implications arose from these practices that impacted American racial sociality? The series was kicked off in February 1926 with the publication of the seven questions under the title "A Questionnaire." The introduction revisited claims of artistic freedom traditionally authorized by the notion that any artistic practice was "permissible so long as the work was pleasing and the artist sincere." The prologue interjected a caveat. "But the Negro has objected" on the grounds that "while the individual may be true and artistic, the net result to American literature to date is to picture twelve million Americans as prostitutes, thieves and fools and that such 'freedom' in art is miserably unfair." It was clear that Du Bois's interest focused upon the aesthetic practices of cultural regimes promoting and distributing artworks that satisfied fantasies, constituted subjectivities appropriate to those fantasies, and rendered aesthetic judgments in the form of "miserably unfair" tastes. The introduction ended with a reminder that the *Crisis* was itself a regime set on disrupting these iniquitous practices: "Meantime let our readers remember our contest for $600 in prizes and send in their manuscripts no matter what attitude they take in regard to this controversy."[18]

It was entirely fitting to lead off the symposium in March with Van Vechten's response. Ignoring the structure of the questions he submitted, Van Vechten agreed with two premises structuring the open forum—that some portrayals of the "lower strata" of black life provided "reason enough to feel sensitive," and that these stories have been overemphasized by publishers. Van Vechten, however, found "a very excellent reason" for the prominence of such practices: "The squalor of Negro life, the vice of Negro life, offer a wealth of novel, exotic, picturesque material to the artist. On the other hand, there is very little difference if any between the life of a wealthy or cultured Negro and that of a white man of the same class."[19] We are presented with a neo-Kantian paradoxical aesthetic judgment. If there were "little difference if any" between a "cultured Negro" and a "white man of the same class," rendering them formalistically as poverty-stricken artistic "objects," race emerged as both class structured and abstract. Tropes of blackness enjoyed great "wealth" in social privation while tropes of whiteness distributed material capital in a state of affective indigence. These affective registers were animated by New Negro tropes producing an intense desire for narratives of squalor and vice, constituting the lives of folks in the "lower strata" as essentially black.

This configuration of racial tropes bonded to the New Negro had profound implications for aesthetic and artistic practices. NAACP board member Mary White Ovington took up the question of the tastes of publishers, saying, "What publishers, at least the best, want today is art, not propaganda. They don't want to know what the writer *thinks* on the Negro question, they want to know about Negroes."[20] The satirist H. L. Mencken sharpened this point razor thin. After affirming the "freedom" of artists to be realistic, he claimed that publishers do not refuse to handle stories of educated blacks, "The objection is to Negro characters who are *really only white men,* i.e., Negro characters who are false."[21] Recalling Van Vechten, educated black folk behaved as the "false" characters that Menken considered "really only" white folks. So, under what conditions might a publisher accept a narrative about educated black folks? The white playwright Du Bose Heyward offered a potential solution to this riddle when he revealed that "there is a growing public everywhere in America for literature dealing sincerely with any aspect of Negro life," so long as the work was accomplished with "skill and insight. . . . The point is that it must be treated *artistically.* It destroys itself as soon as it is made a vehicle for propaganda." Referencing his own work on poor black folks in *Porgy,* Heyward revealed the manner in which the artistic practices to which he alluded and subsequent attributions of beauty nevertheless aligned with affects of blackness; the characters in *Porgy* emerged through "*my* feeling *toward* my subject."[22] In order to be felt as authentically black, it would seem that stories of cultured Negroes would need to become uncouth, performing blackness through squalor and vice thus, the "cultured Negro" as a valued literary object is a paradox, a no one living no where. Van Vechten's friend and publisher, Alfred Knopf, seemed to feel this fuzzy logic; he dismissed the contention that publishers were repelled by stories of middle-class Negroes as "senseless."[23]

This alignment of tropes revealed a secondary paradox. On the one hand, Mencken and Ovington objected to unrealistic portrayals, calling them propaganda; but more than one white respondent noted that the racist stories of Octavius Roy Cohen were "caricatures," "exaggerations,"[24] and "untrue,"[25] but not propaganda because they tickled white sensibilities; Mencken observed "they have amused me immensely" and thus are judged as "reasonably accurate."[26] We can clearly see here that it was the coordination and translation of affects of blackness into narrative that accounted for aesthetic judgments of art and propaganda. Since affects of blackness were felt as dampened as the black body traveled up the social strata, the aesthetic practices shaping New Negroes deployed artistic practices moving in the opposite direction, in a line appropriate to this alignment of terms. For example, the North Carolina novelist Julia Peterkin asserted that "it would be better for Negro authors to demonstrate that their race has things the white race has not in equal degree and that cannot be duplicated." Peterkin closed her response with a strangely romantic contradiction: "I write about Negroes because they represent human nature obscured by so little veneer; human nature groping among its instinctive impulses and in an environment which is tragically primitive and often unutterably pathetic. But I am no propagandist for or against any race."[27] Rather than understand her advocacy for her artistic practices as self-interested, a campaign made rational in accordance with its relation to a structure of emotions, Peterkin's point of view was imbricated into a wider universalized discourse regarding racial "truths."

There is one further sentiment that occupied major figures in the symposium worth mentioning here. Walter White and Countee Cullen testified that publishers ought to be criticized for not attending to works figuring educated blacks. Cullen's reply in particular was sophisticated, pointing out the myth of monolithic blackness and querying readers about why several respondents did not perceive any racial value regarding the squalor and vice of poor whites. Each of these writers sniffed out the long-term danger inscribed in the logic of the aesthetic value of the "squalor of Negro life." Cullen worried about the "popular trend of seeing no cleanliness in their squalor, no nobleness in their meanness, and no common sense in their ignorance."[28] Langston Hughes suggested a similar problem in his very brief response, saying, "It's the way people look at things, not what they look at, that needs to be changed."[29] There was no a priori connection between the value of blackness and deprivation and filth. But since each writer, to differing degrees, leveraged the authority of pure aesthetics, the problem of the politics of aesthetics lingered. The author whose work may have most directly triggered the symposium, Haldane MacFall, saw his reply to Van Vechten's questions in print in June. Writing in defense of himself, MacFall provided an autobiographical account of his military service in Jamaica meant to undermine claims regarding hostility between him and persons of color. His story involved Jamaican soldiers coming to his aid when his life was threatened by a man under his command. The harrowing event led the author of *The Wooings of Jezebel Pettyfer* to this conclusion: "Anyway, if I hate Negroes, the Negroes did not hate *me,* since they were prepared to risk their lives to save me from harm." Along with the fact that MacFall disarticulated his paternalism from white supremacy, he also confused the actions of his subordinates as governed by affection instead of colonial power.

By the time MacFall's self-indulgent encomium appeared in his journal, Du Bois was convinced that the dictates of "pure" art were having too much sway over the aesthetic practices of the New Negro. In the forward to *The New Negro,* Locke characterized young Harlem artists in terms suggesting that critics such as him have the taste to judge aesthetic value of blackness: "So far as he is *culturally articulate,* we shall let the Negro speak for himself."[30] To Du Bois, Locke's strategy for revising the basic character of pure art was dangerous because it kept intact the presumption that higher orders of the imagination regulated aesthetic judgments rather than one's situated senses. At a time when Harlem's streets teemed with newly arrived and impressionable young writers hoping to make a name for themselves, Du Bois feared that any accreditation of pure art conferred authority on the already established agents and regimes of the art world. Du Bois was concerned that this sort of rhetorical performance reinforced traditional forms of aesthetic values and taste by not explicitly calling them into question. Importantly, the reification of what Joel Spingarn, NAACP board member, called a "childish formula like that of 'art versus propaganda'" allowed white supremacists to "objectively" compare culture as an "unbiased" measure of civilization.[31] The concealment of a racist politics within aesthetics put Du Bois in a tizzy: "When the matter of race became a question of comparative culture, I was in revolt. I began to see that the cultural equipment attributed to any people depended largely on *who estimated it*."[32] This recognition of the politics of aesthetics grew sharper during the months of the symposium. Du Bois also became aware that his call for propaganda in the face of continued certifications of pure art solidified the schism of art and propaganda, pitting black intellectuals in a dispute over "theory."[33]

After having stayed on the sidelines during the exchange in the *Crisis* about the ethos of black art, Du Bois delivered the "Criteria of Negro Art" on the Spingarn Medal Award night at the annual meeting of the NAACP in Chicago on June 29. I explore this address as an attempt to constitute race as a disruptive force collapsing the distinction between so-called pure art and propaganda. First, Du Bois constituted distinct African American artistic and aesthetic practices, affiliating them with the ethical capacity to manufacture the objects and agencies of social justice. Second, Du Bois argued that black culture made available to American sociality alternative aesthetic understandings of everyday life. He also linked them to the capacity for an American polity to deliberate on social justice. Lastly, Du Bois critiqued specific political functions of aesthetic practices of the art world, exposing them as impediments to the public deliberation necessary for the ongoing reconstitution of social justice. In sum, Du Bois reinvented tropes of race that at once authorized black art as a form of public discourse and posited it as an expression of "universal" ideals of democracy. This analysis helps to endow Du Bois's voice by acknowledging the ethical and affective dimensions of his speech. Voice is useful to rhetorical and cultural studies of race because it encourages an assessment of the aural character of discourse; it reminds us of the hating and loving relations often conditioning racial identifications, and that these relations coordinate fearful and lustful communities. It reminds us that the power and prestige of race must be appreciated in terms of its capacity to stimulate and translate these affects into ways of knowing and living.

Beauty, Blackness, and the Social Body: Why "Turn Aside to Talk About Art"?

During the *Crisis* symposium, the arguments about the proper role and character of black art were framed so as to make the whole affair seem like a fairly innocent dispute over literary license and decorum. Despite some irreconcilable differences, the question of race art remained principally a question of artistic judgment. As a question of aesthetics, new Negro artistry worked to avoid topics and forms that might attract the label of propaganda. And those black and white elite who relished a spirited debate over aesthetic theory soured when Du Bois raised questions about the politics of aesthetics. This troubling dichotomy was offered up by the presumed idealism of pure art and the apparent sophistry of propaganda, and was immediately collapsed by Du Bois as he took the podium:

> I do not doubt but there are some in this audience who are a little disturbed at the subject of this meeting, and particularly at the subject I have chosen. Such people are thinking something like this: "How is it that an organization like this, a group of radicals trying to bring new things into the world, a fighting organization which has come up and out of the blood and dust of battle, struggling for the right of black men to be ordinary human beings—how is it that an organization of this kind can turn aside to talk about Art? After all, what have we who are slaves and black to do with Art?" Or perhaps there are others who feel a certain relief and are saying, "After all it is rather satisfactory after all this talk about rights and fighting to sit and dream of something which leaves a nice taste in the mouth." Let me tell you that neither of these groups is right.[34]

In this opening passage, Du Bois rehearsed his themes of racial exclusion, racial exploitation, and social justice. In a satirical tone, he mimicked the voices from both sides of a mutually supportive dialectic. On the one hand, "some in this audience" supposedly were anxious about his speech, thinking that the "blood and dust of battle" hurt "art" and, therefore, should be left to those persons better suited to its pursuit—those who are readily capable of bracketing their social activism away from artistic practice. These members of the audience thought "art" should be shielded from the debilitating effects of polemics. They also suffered from a racist psychosis asserting that "we who are slaves and black" cannot judge "art," Du Bois implied, because they saw little (purely) beautiful about the black imagination. On the other hand, there were others who felt "a certain relief," happy to put the topic of civil rights aside and "sit and dream" of the pleasures of consuming exotic and racy blackness. Pure art and propaganda (race rhetoric) were alluded to here as serving the motives of people who promoted nonpolitical (pure) art and who believed that black protest corrupted art. Some folks thought that the NAACP denigrated art, while other folks believed that questions of aesthetic judgment marked a complete departure from the civil rights agenda. But for Du Bois "neither of these groups is right."

Having bluntly declared that these presumptions were false, Du Bois enfolded black art into "the great fight we are carrying on." Moreover, he invested both the art and the civil rights struggle with a progressive spirit captured in a visual arc. Du Bois argued: "You and I have been breasting hills; we have been climbing upward; there has been progress and we can see it day by day looking back along blood-filled paths." Du Bois sought here to make initial rhetorical use of the trajectory of historical idealism—the taken for granted notion of the perfectibility of society so ingrained in progressivism.[35] But as soon as this momentum was established, it lost its principal thrust. As Du Bois noted, "But when gradually the vista widens and you begin to see the world at your feet and the far horizon, then it is time to know more precisely whither you are going and what you really want. What do we want?"[36]

This question created a void in the text, robbing progressivism of its idealistic energies and opening up presumptions of American virtue to critical reflection. This contemplative pause compelled Du Bois's audience to suspend its belief in the "truth" of American Manifest Destiny protected by "pure art" and to consider another's perspective. "What is the thing we are after?" he asked. "Do we want simply to be Americans?"[37] For Du Bois the answer was no. To be simply an American would represent a retreat from the sort of critical reflection he sought to enact. To Du Bois, the typical American suffered from a sort of pathology brought on by an infatuation with the "tawdry and flamboyant," an utterly materialistic craving that "maddens humanity."[38] But if Americans were spiritually corrupted, black folk, "pushed aside as we have been in America,"[39] had the capacity to make available a kind of cure to American society. At this point, at least two questions logically arose. First, what did social illness have to do with beauty? Second, what properties did black art possess that qualified it as remedial?

In this speech, Du Bois's answer to the first question was oblique. Years earlier he had critiqued the civilized world for manufacturing the "ugly."[40] But what did he mean by ugliness? In numerous essays and books, Du Bois disclosed the ideology of "civilization" and critiqued its requirements for oppression.[41] In each of these cases, Du Bois specified either American or European forms of social order, and his critiques were influenced by his strong socialist ideals. The affiliation of oppression with ugliness, however, probably dates back, as Arnold Rampersad speculates, to Du Bois's Calvinist upbringing. As a social theology, Calvinism pits the hideousness of sin against the beauty of the civic good.[42] In this context, the presence of injustice signifies the negation of beauty. In the speech, Du Bois argued that persons living in this "civilized" world, due to widespread oppression, had "their lives distorted and made ugly."[43] Ugliness and beauty were thus antithetical aesthetic judgments of the quality of the social. Du Bois's perspective here is consistent with Terry Eagleton's concerns regarding the ideology of the aesthetic and the actualization of forms of subjectivity fit to live and thrive in such a social order, making the aesthetic practices themselves appear natural.[44]

Questions still remained, however, about the capacity for black art to make the world beautiful. "Who shall restore to men the glory of sunsets and the peace of quiet sleep?" Du Bois asked. In the speech, Du Bois invoked the spirit of the New Negro to answer the question. He asserted: "We black folk may help for we have within us as a race new stirrings . . . of the beginning of a new appreciation of joy, of a new desire to create, of a new will to be."[45] Du Bois tapped into ideas well established in the minds of his elite black and white audiences and siphoned off the optimism affiliated with the New Negro movement. Black folk could help to make the world beautiful because the New Negro was progressive and sought in art "universal truth." But the "truth" of civic beauty was not disclosed through transcendence; rather, it was disclosed in aesthetic practices and artifacts. In many essays of this period Du Bois referenced as beautiful and virtuous some distinct African American cultural norms. For example, in "The Essence of African Culture," Du Bois complimented the African village system for offering the world a sociological balm for the irritation associated with the mechanization of modern cities. He also argued that African children were nurtured as self-conscious citizens with a healthy "reverence for authority."[46] A primitivist desire for black culture was predicated on white psychological trauma.[47] In "Criteria of Negro Art," however, this trauma was transfigured into an ethical predicament. Thus, the presumed racial difference of black folk culture did more than soothe the angst of white folk over self-alienation in an industrializing world; its distinctiveness also offered a "new [social] determination for all mankind."[48]

To this point, Du Bois had portrayed American society as ugly due not only to racial prejudice but also to the inhumane aesthetic practices of "civilization." The forms of social order to which Du Bois alluded satisfied the needs of a privileged few; however, the "mass of human beings" were being "choked away" from beauty. Du Bois asked: "Who shall right this well-nigh universal failing?"[49] The answer to this question was fairly clear by now. If beauty was negated by injustice, then racial oppression negated the beauty of blackness in particular. But it wasn't just black folk who suffered. The select negation of some black voices by making them "white-like" or by essentializing race within the "lower strata" of black life signaled a "universal failing." It was at once a failure of a universal construct and a failure felt by all Americans. The capacity for America to imagine social justice was "distorted and made ugly." Thus, the coherence and the performance of distinct

African American aesthetic and artistic practices in public became essential requirements for the reinvention of the (beautiful) social.

Yet Du Bois forestalled an idealistic closure that presumed all speakers had an equal opportunity to name the beautiful. The theoretical constitution of distinct cultural norms for black public voice did not come with a proviso that such a voice would be endowed. What chance did a black speaker really have to speak of social justice? In the address, Du Bois put the query this way: "After all, *who* shall describe Beauty?"[50] If he didn't know it beforehand, Du Bois learned in this decade that it was futile to affirm the social good in principle if one lacked the authority to enact it in practice. For black intellectuals, the problem of public speaking was compounded by the history of Western aesthetics privileging the cult of observation—the truth-values associated with "proper" sight, perspective, or judgment.

"We Who Are Dark Can See"

Du Bois suspended the trajectory of American perfection with the question, "What do we want? Do we want simply to be Americans? Once in a while through all of us there flashes some clairvoyance, some clear idea, of what America really is. We who are *dark can see* America in a way that white Americans cannot. And seeing our country thus, are we satisfied with its present goals and ideals?"[51] In this part of the speech, Du Bois appropriated the authority of the artistic imagination and used it to sanction an African American perspective on the social good. Traditionally, the value of distant surveillance has rested upon the presumption of a unilateral epistemological link between knower and known; the knower sees the known and speaks its "truths." This relation also implicates the truth-value of literature.[52] In a letter to Du Bois in 1925, the black writer Charles Chesnutt referred to this norm in his attack on the "propaganda" that Du Bois supported, saying that "if the story does not ring true and does not convince the reader, it is not a good story."[53] Chesnutt's comment preserved dominant aesthetic value because it treated as objective and universal the character of aesthetic perception. This statement presumed that everyone should see the same things in the same way.

In his speech, Du Bois performed a narrative about history and culture that troubled the presumption that dominant aesthetic judgments of race and blackness were universally correct. He created a transformative space where the judgments about the worth of blackness could be revised. Du Bois's rhetorical strategy was constitutive of a public dialogue that had intensified during the New Negro movement regarding the significance and value of a black perspective on social life and had two complementary facets—dark and light. The virtual absence of African American voices in American public address strengthened the notion that there was no black thought of public value. Metaphorically, light connotes sight and spoken truth, while darkness signifies their absences.[54] It is this taken for granted relation that Du Bois reconstituted so that "dark can see" and light (whiteness) must listen. Indeed, this rhetorical strategy contained both antiracist and antielitist dimensions. Inverting the truth-values associated with light and dark, Du Bois recognized how Platonic idealism affected thinking about race. The Enlightenment, embodied by the guardians of the cave in Plato's famous allegory, was depicted as a form of aesthetic understanding maintained by domination.[55]

Du Bois also argued that art is constitutive of life's ethical dilemmas. I have already discussed how Du Bois conceived of beauty as a value associated with the quality of social life. The myth of "pure" art, however, was also maintained by a refusal to recognize the relationship between literature and the ethical and political contexts that gave rise to it. Thus, Du Bois had to address the character of the service beauty performed for social justice and knowledge:

> What has Beauty to do with the world? What has Beauty to do with Truth and Goodness—with the *facts of the world and the right actions of men*? "Nothing," the artists rush to answer. They may be right. I am but a humble disciple of art and cannot presume to say. I am one who tells the truth and exposes evil and seeks with Beauty and for Beauty to set the world right. That somehow, somewhere eternal and perfect Beauty sits above Truth and Right I can conceive, but here and now and in the world in which I work they are for me unseparated and inseparable.[56]

This passage is strongly reminiscent of Plato's resistance to any notion of artistic autonomy. Du Bois appropriated this philosophical legacy in his argument against pure art. Both Plato and Du Bois subjected art to ethical critique but for slightly different reasons. Plato was concerned with how the poetic corrupted reason through a powerful evocation of aesthetic pleasure. Although Plato equivocated about his feelings regarding poetry, he generally held that all of the mimetic crafts (especially rhetoric) were twice removed from the transcendent forms constituting the beautiful. Artistic vision, then, was both dangerous and inferior to philosophical insight and needed to be controlled by intellectual or political elites.[57] Du Bois's own perspective on art was no less ambivalent. He shared Plato's desire to bring the poetic into the ethical and social world. But Plato prized above all the status of the transcendent even as he recognized his sinful love of art. Du Bois, on the other hand, worked to invent race in sociological and cultural terms and understood that the poetic could effectively do this work for precisely the reasons that Plato disparaged. As we shall see, Du Bois was skeptical of Platonic idealism and exerted great energy explicating the political economics of aesthetic judgment.

At this point in his speech, however, the intimacy between art and life allowed Du Bois to introduce black history into art. The reason that beauty has everything to do with the "facts of the world" was clarified when Du Bois associated literary material with history. Black folk, said Du Bois, had been compelled by aesthetic judgments of white supremacy to forget Africa and black history: "We thought nothing could come out of that past which we wanted to remember; which we wanted to hand down to our children. Suddenly, this same past is taking on form. . . . We are remembering that the romance of the world did not die and lie forgotten in the Middle Age; that if you want romance to deal with you must have it *here and now and in your own hands.*"[58]

Du Bois proposed that the aesthetic experiences of one's life condition the aesthetic and artistic practices of literature. But, the experiences of black folks' lives were dimly perceived because of the racist presumptions of white folk. The confidence that white folks had in the powers of their own observations blinded them to the "truths" of black life. It was this void in American public discourse and aesthetic understanding that Du Bois hoped to fill in the speech. By recounting specific episodes of racial injustice and racial heroism, Du Bois destabilized the confidence of the white observer and dramatized the rational infusion of art and life. Consider Du Bois's sad tale of the consequences of racial passing: "I once knew a man and woman. They had two children, a daughter who was white and a daughter who was brown; the daughter who was white married a white man; and when her wedding was preparing the daughter who was brown prepared to go and celebrate. But the mother said 'No!' and the brown daughter went into her room and turned on the gas and died. Do you want Greek tragedy swifter than that?"[59]

Here Du Bois posited for public deliberation the material tragedy of black experience, misperceived and misunderstood by white observers. Du Bois also informed his audience of previously negated historical dramas, like that of the forty thousand black men who "fought and won and lost German East Africa" in the First World War.[60] Du Bois retrieved the particularity of black living from within the transcendent action of "pure art." He articulated its negation as an ethical concern within a deliberative forum to arouse a genuine rhetorical audience. To Du Bois, the problem with the "souls of white folk" was constitutive of the very same social relation that cultivated black folk "clairvoyance." The irresistibility of white authority moves us "more and more, day by day, to making the statement 'I am white,' the one fundamental tenet of our practical morality," Du Bois asserted.[61] Lamenting how society had been shuttled further away from the basis of genuine public dialogue, Du Bois suggested how a rhetorical audience must listen sincerely to diverse public voices. The tendency for white intellectuals to presume to know, and thus claim to speak the "truth," about black folk aggravated Du Bois for many years, prompting him to demand a more sensitive ear. In *Dusk of Dawn,* Du Bois articulated the surest path to the resuscitation of genuine public dialogue: "It will not be easy to accomplish all this, but the quickest way to bring the reason of the world face to face with this major problem of human progress is to listen to the complaint of those human beings today who are suffering most."[62]

Thus, "Criteria of Negro Art" embodied Du Bois's continuing efforts to get white folk to heed, acknowledge, and thus endow a black public voice. Du Bois sought to establish as presumptive the need for "authentic" and diverse cultural expression in American public address. Du Bois's authority to say so was itself derived from his rhetorical performance. "*Who* shall describe Beauty?" he asked, and Du Bois's answer was African Americans like himself:

> I remember tonight four beautiful things: The Cathedral at Cologne, a forest in stone, set in light and changing shadow, echoing with sunlight and solemn song; a village of the Veys in West Africa, a little thing of mauve and purple, quiet, lying content and shining in the sun; a black and velvet room where on a throne rests, in old and yellowing marble, the broken curves of the Venus of Milo; a single phrase of music in the Southern South—utter melody, haunting and appealing, suddenly arising out of night and eternity, beneath the moon.[63]

The montage of sights and sounds making up Du Bois's "four beautiful things" captured Plato's sense of the panoply of universal values that compose the transcendent realm. Scholars have made much of Du Bois's own expressive transcendence of the material world.[64] And so, perhaps Du Bois's vision was an appellation of universal beauty. If so, it also deformed modern notions of universal beauty by invoking African and black folk culture as requisite elements. This reading also returns us to classical teachings, since Plato held that ideal forms necessarily took on varying shapes in the material world.[65] But what is most important in this speech is not Du Bois's gesture toward the heavens. Rather it is his examination of the kinds of political, cultural, and psychological work that is performed in the name of pure art in the historical world—in "normal life."[66]

Du Bois "remembers tonight" not objects or places in the past; instead, he recalled a perspective on how to conceive of an aesthetic judgment of the civic good that did not yet exist. Du Bois's "four beautiful things," then, referred to a range of creative possibilities that could come true, but only if black and white folks were critical of the aesthetic and artistic practices of race communities engaged in during the activity of *sensus communus*. The cathedral, the village, and the Venus of Milo were ancient and timeless reservoirs of beauty—each contributing equally to Du Bois's mosaic. Historically, however, European foundations of "civilization" conflicted with African communalism.[67] This discord could be measured in terms of European colonialism in Africa, but it also could be *heard* in the American sorrow songs of the Deep South.[68] Indeed, the Southern melody owed its spirituality to the unhappy acquaintance of Africa and Europe. But this "utter melody, haunting and appealing," also drew some of its emotional depth from black folk suffering in Jim Crow America. The "universal" quality of the sorrow songs could only be truly appreciated as a function of its localized practice in "normal life." By attending to the historicity of its utterance, we could hear its melody "suddenly arising out of night and eternity." Far from a transcendent synthesis of forms, Du Bois's collage exhibited the enduring character of history; it orchestrated the sights, sounds, and affects of cultural dissonance and harmony—giving rise to new voices and new visions of the civic good. "Such is Beauty," Du Bois announced, referring to the creative tension seized in this imagery. "Its variety is infinite, its possibility is endless."[69]

With his authoritative public interpretation of diverse beauty, Du Bois constituted himself, and others like him, as legitimate public black intellectuals. His authority was generated by the invention and orchestration of racial aesthetic experiences, practices, and values that were indivisible from the structure of American social relations. But this dynamism also set in motion the modern quest for stability.[70] And so, as the manifold features of an eternal and perfect beauty (momentarily) appeared before the audience, Du Bois voiced skepticism about any finalized notion of beauty, including the progressive idealism suggested by his own portrait of diversity. He did this by revealing the pernicious dominating tendencies of pure art.

Disclosing the Politics of Aesthetics: "All Art Is Propaganda"

Du Bois articulated the promises of a beautiful society as potentially redeemable if black aesthetics reconditioned what counted as beauty. However, the spirituality of black folk and the raw materiality of white power conditioned his skepticism about the perfection of "pure" artistry. The "unhappy consciousness" of Southern sorrow songs and the brute force of white supremacy alerted him to the unscrupulous operations of politics of aesthetics.[71] To fully understand Du Bois's argument, we must quote him at length:

> With the growing recognition of Negro artists in spite of the severe handicaps, one comforting thing is occurring to both white and black. They are whispering, "Here is a way out. Here is the real solution of the color problem. The recognition according Cullen, Hughes, Fauset, White and others shows there is no real color line. Keep quiet! Don't complain! Work! All will be well!" I will not say that already this chorus amounts to a conspiracy. Perhaps I am naturally too suspicious. But I will say that there are today a surprising number of white people who are getting great satisfaction out of these younger Negro writers because they think it is going to stop agitation of the Negro question. They say, "What is the use of your fighting and complaining; do the great thing and the reward is there?" And many colored people are all too eager to follow this advice; especially those who are weary of the eternal struggle along the color line, who are afraid to fight and to whom the money of philanthropists and the alluring publicity are subtle and deadly bribes. They say, "What is the use of fighting? Why not show simply what we deserve and let the reward come to us?"[72]

At this juncture in the address, Du Bois explicated the levers producing the hegemonic torque of pure art. The public recognition of some black artists warranted the claim that race prejudice was being eroded. Publicly defined as pure artists, not propagandists, their success served as legitimate evidence of a decreased need for Du Bois's brand of "agitation." The more that this transaction was encouraged by white patronage, the more artists themselves might assent to its logic. But, for Du Bois, therein lay the "deadly" rub. If white aesthetic tastes dictated the development of black artistic expression, the "authentic" historicity of black life could be reinvented and recalled as "evidence" of the rightness of those tastes. Du Bois demonstrated that the movement toward satisfying white aesthetic desires was not an emancipated impulse of pure art but rather was steered by the psycho-economic imperatives of the culture regimes.

Du Bois asserted that the positive public awareness of selected black artists overshadowed the normative practice of racial exclusion. As Du Bois explained: "There is in New York tonight a black woman molding clay by herself . . . because there is not a single school of sculpture in New York where she is welcome." And her predicament was typical: "There was Richard

Brown. If he had been white he would have been alive today instead of dead of neglect. . . . There is a colored woman in Chicago who is a great musician. She thought she would like to study at Fountainebleau. . . . But the application blank of this school says: 'I am a white American.'" Young black writers routinely faced the argument that their literature about the subjects they "knew best about" had to be mangled, made into hideous caricatures of the original to be published because "white publishers catering to white folk" wanted "Uncle Toms, Topsies, good 'darkies' and clowns."[73]

In terms of the values articulated in Du Bois's rhetoric, this cultural milieu was anything but beautiful. Du Bois understood that "a few recognized and successful Negro artists" would be able to rise out of obscurity, but the normative racist practices he outlined denied the cultivation of true beauty. It is tempting to suggest that Du Bois believed that there was no way to transcend racial oppression. After all, he expressed the political and historical impediments to this kind of sublimation throughout his address. But this pessimism would be wrong. Du Bois was laboring not to kill the beautiful but to clarify the conditions under which it could provide hope for life. This is why, in the face of the severe odds he aligned against himself, he could turn to make a provocative moral charge: "Thus it is the bounden duty of black America to begin this great work of the creation of Beauty, of the preservation of Beauty, of the realization of Beauty." This task was essential to "Truth" and "Goodness," and could not in good conscience be ignored. As Du Bois noted: "The apostle of Beauty thus becomes the apostle of Truth and Right not by choice but by inner and outer compulsion. Free he is but his freedom is ever bounded by Truth and Justice; and slavery only dogs him when he is denied the right to tell the Truth or recognize an ideal of Justice."[74]

Du Bois once again appropriated Platonic idealism and constituted a pious trinity made up of the life struggles of black folk (Truth), artistic expression (Beauty), and social justice (Goodness). Contrary to the subordinate role Plato assigned art, aesthetic practices functioned in Du Bois's alignment as actualizing and distributing modes of ethical discourse because they could make sensible the social good—"an ideal of Justice." But since all forms of discourse were subject to censure in the service of domination, and the artist, "not by choice," took up a localized perspective on the world "ever bounded by Truth and Justice," art was always already radically contingent. The artist as an "apostle" served this piety by recognizing that their "freedom" was constitutive of social obligations; black artists, in particular, were compelled by the "specter of slavery." Penitence was achieved through a devotion to the pursuit of "Truth" and "Goodness"—the political and ethical ideals of social justice. This is precisely what Du Bois meant when he boldly announced that "all Art is propaganda and ever must be, despite the wailing of the purists. I stand in utter shamelessness and say that whatever art I have for writing has been used always for propaganda for gaining the right of black folk to love and enjoy."[75] By transfusing art and propaganda, Du Bois showed that aesthetic practices, removed from public interrogation by claims of philosophical perfection, reinvigorated forms of domination. It was the public deliberation of such operations of power that redeemed the possibility of eternal beauty.

Du Bois's moral romanticism was sweeping, but his skepticism was equally resolute. He argued that the younger artists needed to be released from the implacable paradox of pure art, and black audiences needed to make aesthetic judgments of a work not with the criteria of white publishers but "by our own free and unfettered judgment." But then he repeated his warning about the way that dominant discourses appropriated potentially disrupting influences: "Just as soon as true Art emerges; just as soon as the black artist appears, someone touches the race on the shoulder and says, 'He did that because he was an *American,* not because he was a Negro. . . . *He is just human;* it is the kind of thing you ought to expect.' "[76] In an important way, Du Bois has brought us full circle. We have returned to the troubles of a black public voice and the place of race in public deliberations of social justice. The bright and shining semblance of "American" again cast its long, ugly shadow over the accomplishments of African Americans. Du Bois was not giving up the fight in this return, nor was he being truculent. The metabolism of the text preserved the energies of Platonic idealism, holding in creative tension the potential for a better world and the doggedness of social injustice. In the end, the muting capacities that metaphysics generated for the material world were mediated by the disputatious activity of the materiality of race. Du Bois enacted a deliberative process in which the aesthetic experiences and practices conditioning human beliefs and actions were exposed and subjected, time and again, to critique by interested others in order to sustain the possibility of beauty. Du Bois would almost immediately recognize that such sustenance was evaporating.

The "Criteria of Negro Art" was published in the *Crisis* in October 1926. Although the speech was delivered concurrent with the high-profile presumed disagreement over the character of the New Negro movement in June between Langston Hughes and George Schuyler in the *Nation,* its publicity lagged far behind.[77] The timing seemed ill fated since the central question by the fall was which New Negro star would emerge next. Van Vechten's *Nigger Heaven* was advertised in the very issue in which "Criteria of Negro Art" was published, marketed as a "book you cannot afford to miss."[78] The irony was intense, and it stipulated the pressures that aesthetic regimes like the *Crisis* faced. Since the novel's publisher, Alfred Knopf, owned a vital publication outlet, the journal could not pass up its revenue without causing a massive stir among NAACP directors, some of whom were allied with Knopf and other publishers. *Nigger Heaven* appeared to great fanfare shortly after "Criteria of Negro Art" was published; it lit up Harlem's skies with fireworks.[79] And it advertised the titillation of Van Vechten's playground for tourists from downtown.

"Criteria of Negro Art" warned against such inflamed excursions. The traffic up Seventh Avenue thickened and must have turned Du Bois's stomach. His review of *Nigger Heaven* in December expressed unbridled contempt because its popularity signified the kind of "deadly bribes" he feared would multiply. Du Bois is generally regarded as prophetic due to his vision of the ills of segregation in many of his writings, but his sense of how "decadence" might encroach upon and rearticulate the aesthetic and artistic practices of the movement was just as farsighted as his claims about the legacy of the "color line." But Du Bois's distaste must also be appreciated in terms of his discomfort with the homosexual (and hyper-sexual) tendencies of folks like Van Vechten and his "rival" Locke.[80] Although "Criteria of Negro Art" was theoretically and ethically forceful, it could not stem the flow of racial tourism in part because it amplified the affects of blackness. To an authoritarian like Du Bois, the surge of white interest served as an imperative to stiffen and assert the criteria as virtual laws regarding how the Negro *must* be portrayed. He was not alone; many members of the black press expressed consternation about white tastes shaping black art. But there would be no way to undo the work of elite white aesthetic judgments about the value of black art objects. Indeed, in the coming years, Du Bois would appear to many Harlem newcomers as an objet d'art—a late Victorian relic. As the radiance of the New Negro expanded, his influence shrank, seemingly releasing into the open New Negroes unconcerned with being strictly in the service of the race. Du Bois would, of course, continue to write valiantly against these politics of aesthetics, but another kind of writing was already on the wall; that the more intense the affective registers of race a writer could generate, the more gravitational pull they asserted. The danger here was, as Du Bois suspected, as deadly as collapsing stars.

7
"Paul's Committed Suicide"
A Utopist Tragedy in Wallace Thurman's *Infants of the Spring*

In a letter dated October 8, 1928, Alain LeRoy Locke advised Scholley Pace Alexander, business manager of the soon-to-be-published literary magazine, *Harlem: A Forum of Negro Life,* about the new venture's proper place in the New Negro movement and warned Alexander about the influence of his partners and friends, Wallace Thurman and Richard Bruce Nugent: "About the magazine, I can only say try to keep it balanced—all of you are temperamental—do not exploit that to the verge of eccentricity—for after all the eccentric is not beautiful."[1] Locke expressed admiration toward their collaboration on *Harlem,* alluding to the doctrine of African Americans "putting one's best foot forward"[2] to promote social equality during the Harlem Renaissance, but the letter is both cautious and ironic. Locke portrayed W. E. B. Du Bois as closed-minded and dogmatic in his attempts as editor of the *Crisis* to regulate the ways in which black art served the ends of civil rights. "Have controversies," Locke explained, but, unlike Du Bois who cultivated a "creed of me and my dog . . . give both sides."[3] Deterring Alexander and friends in this letter from being "eccentric" and from giving in to the polemical, Locke seemed to be trying to mitigate the impact that extreme ideologies have on black literature. Such counsel was consistent with the figure of the African American intellectual Locke sculpted two years earlier in his influential anthology, *The New Negro: An Interpretation,*[4] which presented the black savant as an arbiter of competing positions and a mediator of conflicting voices, ensuring that both sides get heard.

But from the perspective of the "friends," Wallace Thurman and Richard Bruce Nugent, getting a hearing was thickly imbricated with competing interests regarding the New Negro. Writing to Locke shortly after *Harlem* appeared, Nugent was morosely poetic about human desires, aspirations, and the endowment of voice. Admitting to being seized by "a terrible crisis psychologically," the openly gay writer and graphic artist flitted from dismissing the new journal as "God-awfull" to expressing hope that he may still receive the Guggenheim for which he applied with Locke's help.[5] Locke's admonishment of the "eccentric" concerned something else, something unspoken, and something off-center, unconventional, deviant—queer. The "temperamental" natures of Thurman and Nugent needed to be carefully attenuated, for their lifestyles were perceived by black middle-class agents of social change as indulgent and unhealthy, decadent and strange. But Locke was also very much aware that such unconventionality fed the appetite for emerging New Negro works. And so, in his recommendation to the Guggenheim folks, he signaled that Nugent's "quite unusual sense of color" warranted "your serious consideration."[6] To Locke, however, their "eccentricity" could become a distraction from the aims of beauty and a corruption of the objects of beauty. Thurman and Nugent's queerness was in part constitutive of the "culture of homosexuality"[7] that was cultivated among a coterie of young bohemian-styled black intellectuals migrating to upper Manhattan. Their desire to express their eccentric ways in black artistic practices, therefore, was unsettling to those who hoped that the New Negro movement would produce a mainstream black American nationality, a modern subject deemed worthy of social equality.

Furthermore, what is apparent in several correspondences involving Locke is that queer Harlem was a sort of open secret, constitutive of a discourse of indirection, innuendo, and subject to sudden, thunderous silences rather than candidly acknowledged.[8] We should note that queer speech was subject to complicated forms of New Negro administration. On the one hand, civil rights orthodoxy persevered in redirecting the resonance of such works toward the sometimes inchoate aims of social equality. On the other hand, the enthusiasts supporting New Negro artistic autonomy sought to ignite an unbridled bonfire releasing into the air the excited spores of New Negro harvest. This tension was productive of tremendous affects of (queer) blackness experienced emotionally as titillation, terror, triumph, and trauma. Although Nugent's on-again, off-again depression was always in part due to artistic frustration, he confessed to Locke of suffering otherwise: "You can see by this erratic note that I am in a *state.* No *one* is at the bottom. Just an incoherent, vague unrestful and slightly depressing 'state.'"[9] In two months' time, Nugent would report on a deepening emotional crisis, one requiring him to mask its unpleasant sewage from others: "Am passing thru [sic] one of those awful spills of depression during which I am irritable (and hide it), have an insane desire to weep (and hide it) and feel as tho [sic] there is no one on earth that gives a damn. A perfectly stupid way to feel and so easily explained psychologically as to appear childish, either from the angle of a homo- or duosexual's juxtaposition to life or an artist's."[10] Nugent's self-diagnosis is very helpful to us. His depression was linked to his feelings of both artistic and sexual blockage and alienation, and to the felt imperative to conceal his feelings. In this sense, questions about the impact of queer desire on the aesthetic and artistic practices constitutive of New Negro voice should not be limited to literary theory and criticism; such queries must be understood as addenda to the public moral argument sponsored in 1926 by the *Crisis* literary editor Jessie Fauset, titled "The Negro in Art: How Shall He Be Portrayed? A Symposium."[11] This nearly year-long debate involved a consideration of the "proper" topics for the invention of an African American home and of obligations that black artists have toward the cultivation of a positive racial identity. Literary notables like Langston Hughes, Countee Cullen, Carl Van Vechten, and Sherwood Anderson, although taking up sometimes significantly different positions, expressed negative opinions about what some observers would perceive as the *Crisis* editor's underlying resolution, that black artists *ought* to be propagandists; that black cultural expression *should* be shaped by the explicit concerns of civil rights and racial uplift. And so, much of Locke's correspondence during this era was ironic because he was not purely interested in a fair hearing of both sides as much as he was concerned with cultivating rhetorical capacities and placing limits on the inventive possibilities of queer speech. Locke believed some boundaries mercilessly bludgeoned queer subjectivity, thus, folks needed to be instructed on how to use and be mindful of their powers; he also felt they were necessary for the maintenance of a straight, middle-class, respectable ethos—the New Negro's "dwelling place."[12]

Although Locke's biography provides ample evidence for his felt need to be self-protective and inward, the bright lights of the New Negro stage might have provoked an increased sensitivity toward public faces. His friendship with Countee Cullen in the first years of the second decade of the twentieth century was in part chronicled in their regular correspondence—letters that describe their liaison and transmit its intensity; this time period figures for us a mode of experiencing the complex and complicated pressures exerted on their bodies, and of understanding a key relationship conditioning Locke's "haughty caution"[13] of and devotion toward the New Negro. The pressures to live up to and exceed the expectations and aspirations of true believers in New Negro doctrine colluded with the desires to be happy in one's skin and released of shame, fear, and condemnation; the New Negro seemed to promise both futures as virtually available, but the everydayness of queer Harlem offered up routine denials of their communion and their unplanned and passionate rendezvous.

Countee Cullen was a Harlem-born, adopted son of a prominent minister of a church. He first met Locke during the holiday season of 1922; he and

Langston Hughes had already become friends through the auspices of the 135th Street Library in Harlem. Cullen's world twirled and widened with Hughes providing "a charming childishness"[14] that helped Cullen maintain his wide-eyed wonderment at what God had delivered unto humanity, and Locke wavering between establishing discipline and administration on the one hand, and being a confidant and friend with benefits on the other hand. These discordant tones did not produce dissonance in Locke's case. Each role resonated with the high-frequency buzz of the New Negro. The former administrative post defined expected New Negro attitudes and behaviors by expressing them as "laws" of racial loyalty; "legal" evidence of group advancement resonated in tune with New Negro elders' intensely felt satisfaction at moving the Race forward. The youths' yearned-for intimacy mingled with the excitement over having won a chance to set the world on fire. The New Negro social body, therefore, received contentious feedback impulses that got ordered in terms of their productive relations to incipient values. New Negro "preferences" were fractured and litigious precisely because they were constitutive of parallel and potentially polarizing drives, coordinated pushes by the older generation and the youth. The case of Locke and Cullen (and Hughes) was underwritten by a "nuanced and flirtatious"[15] social contract. Cullen identified his expectations in a letter after their initial meeting: "I hope [our visit] was enjoyable as it was in itself merely a prelude to a greater intimacy between you and me."[16] Cullen was one of the few very young black artists who felt a moral obligation to shine as a first-rate New Negro. He shared this affective register with Locke, and much of their private conversations were involved in tactically outlining performances in self-defense of the disciplining efforts of the heteronormative sociality of the New Negro. Before Locke basked in the spotlight of having achieved *The New Negro: An Interpretation,* he established relationships with the actual young men and women who would soon earn the right to be described as heralding in a renaissance. Locke's sense of taste was cultivated within a context calling for racial excellence, yet yearning for what Cullen understood to be popularly thought of as the chimerical, the grotesque. Locke's queer speech played in the shadows and his aesthetic judgments shaped part of the hermeneutical situation encountered by many of the folks engaged in queer Harlem lives.

This chapter explores the emergence of queer voices during the height of the New Negro movement. I argue that although Harlem was revered as an African American homeland that nurtured black artistic possibilities and was celebrated as an after-hours playground for Greenwich Village "decadents" seeking safe haven for experiments with the exotic, New Negro aesthetic and artistic practices were inhospitable toward the cultivation of a black gay "home" and queer voices. This chapter examines the struggle over Harlem dwelling places and over the conditions for inventing and performing queer rhetorical voices. I first situate these rhetorical efforts within the complex and intriguing milieu of mid-1920s Harlem and gay New York. Then, I perform a textual analysis of Wallace Thurman's roman à clef novel *Infants of the Spring.* In this fictionalized account of Thurman's Harlem experiences, the younger generation of black artists tries to mediate an imposing racial consciousness with the "freedom" promised by bohemian living. Thurman dramatized the failure of the New Negro movement as, in part, resulting from the inability to negotiate a shared dwelling place for both queer and racial voices. Coolly received and harshly reviewed, the book, ironically, represents this failure.[17] *Infants,* however, does make a queer sound; it interrupted the orthodoxy of New Negro discourses by confessing to the movement's secret. It ushered out of the closet the manner in which queer "deviance" was constitutive of a preoccupation with a "respectable" African American ethos. By reflecting on queer homelessness and voicelessness, queer Harlem's "decadence" is posited as a function of the New Negro's obsession with race, forcing queer desire to be overindulgent to be acknowledged—portraying it literally and figuratively in excess of the racial bodies meant to contain it. *Infants* revealed such experiences through a utopian vision where black queer life may be free of racial boundaries and can imagine new ways in which folks can belong together, but queer life was also put out in the middle of "no where," "no place," subject to a tragic, silent death.

"That Fear . . . Always at My Heels."

Tracking Locke's footsteps, Cullen looked forward to being a Rhodes Scholar. Indeed, Locke's example hardened his resolve to provide such racial representation: "The goal of the Rhodes' appointment is before me night and day, it figures in my prayers and in my day dreams. . . . I steel myself in the belief that I *will* receive it—but should I not reach the end for which I shall employ all honorable means, let me hope that our strengthened friendship, yours and mine, will dull the edge of that keen disappointment."[18] Cullen clearly wore the colors of the New Negro and sought to raise its banner. But these aspirations were difficult to live up to and they were bonded to performance conditions regarding New Negro propriety that pushed Cullen's emotions in strongly divergent ways. He regularly reported being "a rather depressed young man"[19] overtaken by the frayed edges of his desire: "I am feeling as miserable at this writing as I can imagine a person feeling."[20] And there were two interrelated reasons for such misery. First, Cullen immersed himself in Edward Carpenter's *Iolaus: An Anthology of Friendship,* a work recommended by Locke that struck a nerve: "I read it through in one sitting, and steeped myself in its charming and comprehending atmosphere. It opened up for me soul windows which had been closed; it threw a noble and evident light on what I had begun to believe, because of what the world believes, ignoble and unnatural. I loved myself in it."[21] The anthology takes its name from the legend of Hercules; Iolaus was his charioteer and "his faithful companion."[22] The work surveys the character of friendship in Greek and Roman societies and figures eroticism among men as heroic and beautiful. Cullen wanted to share this revitalized self-adoration with a friend, Ralph Loeb, due to visit, but by Saturday night Cullen felt stood up. In a letter to Locke dated March 3, 1923, he wrote, "I know you will understand how I feel. But I suppose some of us erotic lads . . . were placed here just to eat our hearts out with longing for unattainable things, especially for that friendship beyond understanding." Locke was most certainly guiding Cullen through the young poet's sense of rightness and goodness, allowing Cullen to participate in the production of aesthetic experiences that helped convert his feelings about himself into caring sentiments. But the materialization of a "normal" desire was not accompanied in this case by an object, and Cullen, in the end, sensed that he had perhaps said too much: "P.S.—Sentiments expressed here would be misconstrued by others, so this letter, once read, is best destroyed."[23] Cullen's longing for intimacy was exacerbated by his failure in the classroom: he flunked Geology and his hopes for the Rhodes scholarship evaporated. He confessed to Locke the grave sense of letting the race down: "And there I was a sort of colored hope to you and others, wasn't I. . . . But I will make up the disappointment to you in poetry if my muse is good to me."[24] Cullen's mindset was made worse by the voicelessness that beset him: "I experience the gamut of human emotions but I cannot register them for the world."

Despite forays into literature sympathetic to male homosexuality, Cullen felt there was no place for queer speech in his poetry. As was the case with some racial material, Cullen saw very little aesthetic value in his queer longing. In the fall of 1923, Cullen was getting around a circle of notables very nicely. He reported on a visit with Jessie Fauset—whose first novel was due in the spring—and he had received a note from Jean Toomer, whose enigmatic work, *Cane,* appeared in September 1923. Although Cullen appreciated "parts of it immensely," saying that the work flowed from the imagination of a "genuine poet," Cullen nevertheless channeled stock criticism of middle-class blacks hoping art would showcase New Negro respectability:

"but I do wish he would look, if only for a few seconds, beyond the muck and mire of things."[25] The range of feelings Cullen endured included perhaps a smidgeon of jealousy when Locke successfully reunited with a German-born lover, Rudolph Dressler: "You must be enjoying yourselves, you and Rudolph, reveling in the ecstasies of a perfect friendship which is enough to inebriate your senses."[26]

Cullen's emotional state must be calibrated with Langston Hughes in mind. To Cullen, Hughes was a "virile, brown god."[27] Hughes was a restless deity who sailed to Africa in mid-1923 and then was off to Paris in the winter of the following year. He gifted Cullen with poems from distant ports of call; commenting on a recent batch of verse from Hughes, Cullen seemed lovesick: "No poems by Langston have ever smitten me with as much fire and veracity as those last over—perfect cameos of light and color. I have heard from him but once since he left, and that by way of a card. . . . The letter he promised me keeps me in painful anticipation."[28] By the holiday season—a year after meeting Locke—Cullen reported having gone through a "terrible ordeal" crippling his "creative work, which is what really *is* the only thing that counts, I seem to be absolutely lost, dazed as it were." The damming of the creative juices reserved for New Negro publicity was linked to being "harassed as I am . . . both mentally and physically." Even private correspondence was often deliberately obtuse when it came to sexuality; Cullen was rarely explicit, but he confessed to contemplating "compunctions that may not be overridden by any ailments." In this way, Locke filled a cathartic role with which Cullen felt "freer than with any of my friends, because whereas most of my friends are sympathetically on notice, you are the only one for whom I am not compelled to wear a placard on my back."[29] Without the imperative for formal identifications or sympathy imposed on one from well-intentioned friends, Cullen experienced momentary relief.

During this year, Cullen had also been serving as Locke's go-between with Hughes. Although Locke and Hughes exchanged letters and cards, by the time Hughes sailed for Paris in 1924, Locke was distressed over not yet meeting the sojourning poet. The note sent to Hughes in February was quite revealing of Locke's anguish and loss of composure:

> At increasing cost,—for pride is my master-sin, I have opened my arms three times to you, closed my eyes in confidence, and waited. And three times, I have embraced thin air and blinked and then stared at disillusionment. Shades of my ancestors,—what whoredom is this! I know you are the same person, I feel that you are the right person, I realize that you were nearer this time than ever before, and that perhaps for the first

> time and last time you really wanted to,—but I will be too cheapened to accept if I say "Come" again. I do not recognize myself in the broken figure that says "come,—come when you can, come soon."
> The spring quarter begins March 13th.
> I cannot describe what I have been going through—it has felt like death—but out of this death and burial of pride and self there has suddenly come a resurrection of hope and love.[30]

Locke and Cullen were kindred souls in terms of how each was flung between heights and depths of emotions associated with potential queer excursions and meetings. Given his own violently shifting emotions about love lost and found, Locke may have bristled at Cullen's youthful parochialism when he asked the elder professor, "Were you like this—hot and cold by turns—when you were young?"[31] In any event, Cullen counseled Locke to be patient with Hughes because "Very few people can reach you. Do bend down a bit. Langston is really worth while, but there are various factors which have contributed toward this irresponsible streak in him. You two have never met, and still your ideas and spiritual personas are continually in contention." Clearly Cullen identified the affective currents responsible for Locke's pining. He and Hughes had already embarked upon an energetic encounter that, from Locke's point of view, needed to be fleshed out to make his vision of "whoredom" come into focus. This volatile sense of emptiness and restlessness was captured and intensified by the limits imposed by each man's sense of New Negro propriety and the danger each was prepared to face. For instance, in a letter where Cullen celebrated Locke's rendezvous with Dressler in Germany, the young poet demonstrated he'd gleaned enough of Locke's caution to offer this advice to his mentor: "I have been seriously thinking your situation over. And I urge you to act prudently. This admonition is necessary because you have enough of the artist in you to be scornful of consequences. There are some people in Washington who would give their hope of heaven for a chance to hurt you. So I advise you to surfeit yourself this summer and to abandon any projects that might prove chimerical and disastrous in a cold place like Washington—this for your good and Rudolph's."[32]

There are no official statements regarding Locke's sexuality playing a part in his firing at Howard University in 1925, but word of his sexual orientation could not have endeared him to the university's president and its trustees. Similarly, in the fall of 1924, Cullen's "need deepens." So much so that on a car trip to Boston with Harold Jackman, Eric Walrond, and Louise Thompson, Cullen disclosed a "revelation so far as Eric is concerned. He was most surprisingly sympathetic and aggressive, but I am afraid he offers no lasting solution; he is too exacting (I almost said abandoned) and there are some concessions I shall never make. What a price to exact for a meagre mess of talent!"[33] We are left to speculate about the concessions Cullen was not willing to make, but what we can surmise is that the toll road Walrond was exacting a price to travel upon was populated with some places Cullen refused to visit. The opportunity offered him "no lasting solution."

Cullen's head was spinning as his eyes fixed upon a potential spouse with whom he could at least satisfy one important New Negro expectation—a marriage that advanced New Negro respectability. And perhaps he also found the cover he longed for. In a letter dated September 20, 1924, he wrote: "Recently I met Yolande Du Bois—and I believe I am nearer the solution of my problem. But I shall proceed warily."[34] Cullen was almost certainly identifying for Locke something that they had discussed before: the possibility of fashioning a domestic arrangement—a dwelling place—wherein one could be safe and set loose. In this work, I have been involved in an exploration of the predicament of voice by contemplating and appreciating the affective dimensions and ethical obligations attendant to speech. Cullen's rising star was, in part, shooting for a specific kind of horizon, a roof under which he could create and enjoy some happiness. A month after meeting Yolande, Cullen was much less optimistic about a serviceable abode: "all that has come to naught—as yet. And then there are complications—her age and experience above my own, and then that fear which is always at my heels."[35] But what was the object of this fear—toward what thing did it extend? There was no object (once again). The fear radiated to the precise frequency of the anxious vibrations emanating through what Nugent above called a "state." We have been listening to how Locke and Cullen made sense of the affective currents whisking them about and coursing through them. Honorable service to New Negro aesthetic practices operating as technologies of discipline seemed to have ordered their emotions so as to have them readied as what Heidegger called a "standing reserve."[36] The everyday practices of avoiding suspicion inhabited every step. Under such conditions, the emergence of sex as a subjective impulse was shaped as a partially gratified, mostly frustrated capacity for making social spaces inhabitable. This observation is important as we think about how the Harlem tourist trade became a spectacular industry; how it promoted dancing, music, and nonstop revelry as a commodity. If we turn toward this sheen, we see bright flashy smiles and we hear deep-throaty laughter. This sort of carousing was, of course, trendy and faddish and subject to staging. Hughes saw this too: "Harlem Nights became show nights for the Nordics. All of us know that the gay and sparkling life of the so-called

Negro Renaissance of the '20's was not so gay and sparkling beneath the surface as it looked."[37]

The dwelling places of the New Negro can be understood, then, as some of Harlem's more prominent and contested fabrications. But, Harlem manufactured all sorts of productions for white consumption. And if we look "beneath the surface," our vision is swept downtown toward Greenwich Village. George Chauncey describes the transformation of the Village during Prohibition from a backwater working-class neighborhood into a thriving bohemian community of artists and intellectuals.[38] Villagers liberated themselves from the rigid norms and social practices of late-Victorian mores, flaunting nontraditional lifestyles that were considered "unmanly" due to the celebration of single "free-lovers and anti-materialists. . . . [Villagers] had forsaken many of the other social roles and characteristics prescribed for their class and gender in ways stereotypically associated with homosexuals." This Bohemia, then, protected homosexuality as one of its queer tastes, but was often mistakenly identified with it. Hence, the Village attracted scores of homosexual and heterosexual folks who sought escape from middle-class sexual and social repression. This was, in part, because it "constituted a *liminal space* where visitors were encouraged to disregard some of the social injunctions that normally constrained their behavior, where they could observe and vicariously experience behavior that in other settings—particularly their own neighborhoods—they might consider objectionable enough to suppress."[39]

Hedonists flocked to the Village to gawk at the "queers" and to play among them. Indeed, some residents "complained that their less scrupulous compatriots had begun to cater to the tourist trade, decking themselves out in the costumes visitors expected of bohemians, selling their verse and etchings to the unsophisticated, and offering tours of a fabricated 'Bohemia' to the gullible."[40] As queer performances by "'pseudo-Bohemians' interested . . . in a mindless escape from the conventions of bourgeois society" became increasingly commodified, vice squads stepped up the moral policing of most of New York. But due to racist neglect and disinterest, the moral authorities, like the Committee of Fourteen, allowed the underground liquor, gambling, and sex trade to go largely unchecked in Harlem. Gay and lesbian Villagers, seeking refuge from what was becoming a queer stage show, ventured into Harlem where "gay life was livelier and more open" than downtown.[41] It is precisely this queer "migration" that helped sponsor queer Harlem and hardened its resistance to the orthodoxy of the New Negro. And so, what is of interest here is not just the raced and sexualized performances for the benefit of tourism and social activism, but how attempts to fabricate queer dwelling places and cultivate voices should be placed in relation to these practices. Although the New Negro movement is usually indexed to the early 1920s, its ideological tenets can be traced back to the nineteenth century and can be observed in letters like the one that Charles W. Chesnutt penned to James Weldon Johnson in 1913, congratulating him on his "Emancipation Anniversary poem, 'Fifty Years.'" In the letter Chesnutt beams, "I can only add, after endorsing all [that the other critics] say, that it is the finest thing I have ever read on the subject, which is saying a good deal, and the finest thing I have seen from the pen of a colored writer for a long time—which is not saying quite so much. If you can find themes which will equally inspire you, why may you not become the poet for which the race is waiting?"[42]

Here we see how literary accomplishment was identified with African American social advancement. But Chesnutt's congratulatory remarks also referenced the interpretive task of locating the proper topics—the themes that will inspire—for rhetorical invention. In a sense, it was not just the poet for whom the race was waiting, but there was also the anticipation of kairos, the right time and place enabling writers to find the right words to touch the hearts of readers. The year 1913 was not the time. Responding to a request in 1924 for a copy of *Autobiography of an Ex-Colored Man,* Johnson explained that when he published it anonymously "fourteen years ago there was little or no interest in the Negro. In fact, we had reached the deepest depths of apathy regarding him so far as the general public is concerned."[43] Convinced that black social advancement was always overdue, W. E. B. Du Bois dedicated, as early as 1916, significant editorial space in the *Crisis* to the publication of black writing;[44] and by June of the same year, he joyfully reported a substantial increase in the literary works received by his office.[45]

By the time that Wallace Thurman moved to Manhattan from California in September of 1925, Harlem was enjoying a reputation as a black mecca,[46] but it was on the brink of a significant controversy regarding the architecture of this New Negro home. For the purposes of this chapter, we need only understand that with the publication of "the Bible of the emerging Harlem Renaissance,"[47] *The New Negro,* artists were impelled to integrate African cultural forms with American modernist aesthetics. Locke posited that pagan topics and feelings allowed black folk to take advantage of the wealth of emotions that connected black Americans to their ancestral roots. To Locke, Africa's legacy offered a strictly defined topical structure for the sort of interpretive acts that make up writing. Locke's appeal to African artistic classics to inspire and guide the younger artists was largely hailed as a monumental breakthrough in the philosophy of black aesthetics. It seized the advantage over Du Bois's mantra of "propaganda" by seemingly paying homage to the "higher" ideals of art; Locke's return to Africa resonated in keeping with the spirit of primitivism at the bottom of much ravenous attention that white folks paid Harlem. And thus it posited racial experiences as legitimate resources for art. *The New Negro,* therefore, ushered in a full-fledged advertisement for Harlem and for the very idea of a modern black America. Locke was nearly prophetic when he proclaimed that the younger generation evidenced a "new psychology" regarding race consciousness,[48] but in the case of Wallace Thurman, this new mentality fostered very little interest in the racial uplift mission at the heart of New Negro dogma.

Underlying Wallace Thurman's rejection of New Negro racial philosophy was a complicated matrix of desire. Thurman wished to be free of racial constraints, free of middle-class values, free from the perceived ignorance of the masses, and free from dictates of authoritarian regimes in general.[49] He also yearned to be a writer, a *great writer,* and, soon after he arrived in Harlem, he secured a job as utility man at a brand-new little magazine called the *Looking Glass,* edited by his new friend, Theophilus Lewis. The magazine quickly collapsed, but Thurman's friendship with Lewis was to last a lifetime. Lewis, a part-time drama critic, returned to work at the *Messenger* and took Thurman with him. It was in the employment of the quasi-socialist, quasi-progressive magazine that Thurman was influenced by George Schuyler's conservatism and impressed by his creative resemblance to H. L. Mencken, whom Thurman studied at the University of Southern California. Schuyler's acid-dipped criticism of the New Negro advanced the *Messenger*'s generally antagonistic posture toward black leadership's rear guard.[50]

Taking up this iconoclastic temper, Thurman attempted to live out his "bohemian lifestyle and his self-defined outsider-critic status." Encouraged by disapproval from members of the Talented Tenth generation, and increasingly surrounded by young intellectuals who also "advocated emancipation from the demands of racial propaganda," Thurman embraced through his writing the notion "of an intellectual aristocracy . . . the Artist-Iconoclast [that] set the elite in opposition to the mob, the individual to the mass, the artist to society, rebellion to conformity, excellence to mediocrity, and scepticism to mindless assent." Hence, Thurman's critique of the constraints of group identity took shape as attacks on New Negro proponents, producing among a cadre of young black bohemians an antipathy toward "the black middle class as subject matter for the artistic interpretation of the African American experience."[51]

The problem with smashing idols becomes evident when one grasps for new images and symbols, when one searches through the rubble (rupture) for a coherent picture of who one wants to be. Snubbing a range of topics made available by New Negro convention, artists like Langston Hughes, Richard Bruce Nugent, Aaron Douglas, Zora Neale Hurston, Eric Walrond, and Dorothy West were encouraged by Thurman to try out in the *Messenger* new themes of free-spirited urban living. Such experimentation was met with suspicion from Locke, but it was excited by the arrival of one of the most marketable and combustible works of this era, Carl Van Vechten's *Nigger Heaven*. With such an incendiary title, Langston Hughes recalled later that most black folk didn't even have to read it to hate it.[52] Du Bois in particular thought it to be a betrayal of the generosity afforded Van Vechten by black folk.[53]

But Thurman felt the book represented an odd sort of truth: that the New Negro was a disturbingly shallow sensation made up of the trivial and the inane; he insinuated in his review that it captured the spectacle of Harlem revelry as experienced by a white ("Negro") spectator reporting his findings to whites. Thurman's review concluded with the speculation that the novel "should have a wide appeal and gain much favorable notice."[54] Not surprisingly, then, most of its favorable reviews came from white readers who, incidentally, after 1926, constituted the majority of readers of Harlem Renaissance works.[55] *Nigger Heaven* set Harlem on its edge and Van Vechten seemed to be loving every minute of it; in a letter to James Weldon Johnson he called the attention "wonderful so far," while noting that Harlem was "seething in controversy."[56] Eric Garber argues that from the perspective of downtown this storm lit up the northern skies and had to be witnessed up close; thus, the novel intensified the sexualized consumption of black bodies.[57]

Van Vechten had touched a raw nerve in Harlem's social body. How *shall* the Negro be portrayed? Should it be a prim and proper embodiment of the "dead conventional Negro-white ideas of the past," as Hughes put it;[58] or, shall black subjects be shaped by the imagined excesses of their bodies, as drunken, lewd, and violent creatures of Harlem's wild nights? Although this dichotomy is a false one, Thurman and his fellow travelers, Nugent in particular, seemed caught up in its dialectical energies. When in 1926, Thurman, Nugent, Hughes, Hurston, Gwendolyn Bennett, John Davis, and visual artist Aaron Douglas collaborated on the one and only issue of *Fire!!,* Locke was invited to subscribe, not editorialize. Thus, Thurman can be seen to embrace explorations into flawed and pathetic black individuals, even of the *Nigger Heaven* variety, precisely because his sharp pivot away from the obligations of racial uplift occurred in rhythm with the tempo of the "decadent" Jazz Age. Freed from the obligations constitutive of New Negro civil rights discourse, the editors of *Fire!!* set out to free other young artists by shocking the New Negro social body with a vital aesthetic experience.

Voice and Voicelessness of *Infants of the Spring*

In exploring the conditions under which voice (or voicelessness) occurs in public discourse, I have posited that voice is the sound of affect and is a phenomenon endowed by the public acknowldgement of the ethical and affective dimensions of speech.[59] Voice is a dialogic event in which persons are reoriented toward one another by the shared acknowledgment of the obligations and anxieties incumbent in building dwelling places. There are two dimensions of public speech that require acknowledgment in order for voice to be realized. First, the emotions associated with being on the line, with publicly addressing an issue or event, need to be acknowledged so as to stimulate the affects of voice. Second, the ethical import of taking a position and representing it rhetorically demands acknowledgment in order to fulfill voice. Voice is essentially a phenomenon of public hearing in which speakers must often interrupt ongoing conversations that do not make room for them in order to be acknowledged. Another way to understand the makeup of an ongoing conversation is to hear its cacophony, its drone of noises. This is its cauldron of voices. Imagine that it has a highway of circuits, a signification array, interlocking sets of master narratives carrying those noises. The underpasses contain shadows in which one finds the homeless. From the underpass, we may create many tactics of disruption: hide, hack, evade. And in 1920s Harlem, New Negro buzz ushered in its tonal wake hospitality centers where the sounds of queer desire and demise still echo. We can pick them up and track forward toward the distinct sounds of their speech, their emotional *contents.* It is here where we will face the imperative of voice, its call for an act. But before you imagine how you might answer or ignore such a call, let us remember that we have contents available; and so let us complete the metaphor and offer contexts—the streets, stores, and homes of Harlem and treat them as temporal spaces in which new possibilities for *addressivity* and *answerability* are brought into being.[60]

It is to such a moment that we now turn. *Infants of the Spring* was published in 1932, a few years after the crest of the rising tide of black artistry in Harlem. As such, its reception was tepid and the book seemed to be quickly forgotten. Although flawed due to its laborious dialogue and narrative incoherence, *Infants* is the only novel about the Negro renaissance written by a black author during the movement. It is also noteworthy because the novel recreated a home for homoeroticism. Thurman, however, placed such strain on his characters that in the end nearly everyone in the book imploded from the pressure. We experience through the workings of Thurman's caustic imagination how a black queer utopian dream ended in a tragic half-life; and how black queers who dare to dream otherwise passed away, out of blackness, out of Harlem, out of sight, and out of mind. But *Infants* is here to remind us of this passing by telling the story of queer housing, conviction, and eviction; our passage into *the* queer Harlem home should begin by keeping such passing in mind.

"Raymond opened the door with a flourish,"[61] and with this grand gesture, the reader is escorted into the hub of black bohemian living. Raymond Taylor, Thurman's alter ego in *Infants,* is our tour guide and commentator throughout the novel, serving as both object and subject of Thurman's critical gaze. Through Raymond, Thurman invited us into his home, his infamous studio at 267 West 136th street, a house for indigent black artists nicknamed by Thurman and Hurston as the "Niggeratti Manor."[62] The Manor seemed to represent a kind of crucible where unconventional black thought was applied to the exigencies of trying to live up to one's hopes of being a significant writer and a New Negro. Raymond immediately shows it to be a place where the vibrant and the vulgar radiate in red and black and where intellectual conversations about race and art are liberally lubricated by gin. Raymond's studio is also homoerotic, adorned with Paul Arbian's drawings of "highly colored phalli."[63]

Hence, the first glimpse the reader gets of the Manor is framed by a composite of the signs of decadence and homoerotic "deviance." Thurman not only displayed his home to us, but by introducing us to the characters Samuel Carter and Stephen Jorgenson, he instructed us on how white tourists often behaved while visiting. Sam, perhaps modeled after Leland Petit, a homosexual and a frequent visitor to the Manor, embodied gay, white, paternal sentimentalism:[64] the "social service workers, reformed socialistic ministers, foreign missionaries . . . all so saccharine and benevolent."[65] Stephen symbolized both Thurman's desire for his Canadian-born friend and lover, Harald Jan Stefansson, and Carl Van Vechten's rapacious appetite for black culture. As we get to know Raymond, Sam, and Stephen, we begin to appreciate how a queer ethos and voice were cultivated in *Infants* as well as how they were subject to destruction and dissipation.

Queer voice in *Infants* is instigated by the articulation of a bold rhetorical interruption. The Manor is not simply red and black; we are told that the colors are "loud."[66] Red and black allude to the aesthetic and ethical challenge made by Thurman and friends with the magazine *Fire!!*. Aaron Douglas's red and black cover art stood in sharp contrast to the subdued graphic designs of the *Opportunity* and the *Crisis.* Michael Cobb describes *Fire!!* as a "self-consciously asserted . . . aesthetic rupture" of New Negro discourse.[67] *Fire!!* was designed to be completely different and, since Thurman and Nugent decided to write stories about prostitution and homosexual love for the first issue, it was explicitly meant to shock. *Infants* reproduced this disruption of New Negro respectability and decency by beginning with a loud, flamboyant, striking sound.[68] Samuel is predictably annoyed by the vulgarity of this queer resonance, but Stephen is drawn to it. He closely inspects the "colored phalli," appreciating the artist's handling of color; this explicit interest establishes the foundation for the queer desire that will soon blossom between Raymond and Stephen.

Wallace Thurman and Richard Bruce Nugent moved into the Manor in November 1926 and lived there until 1928, "forming the core of Harlem's black bohemia."[69] The Manor must have been particularly alive during the first month since *Fire!!* was due out on the 15th. In the novel, Raymond shares this space with Paul Arbian, Pelham Gaylord, and Eustace Savoy; each character performing an uncomfortable routine assigned to the black body. Eustace is a struggling singer who believes that the spirituals are too "primitive" to be worth his time. Raymond "had no sympathy whatsoever with Negroes like Eustace, who contended that should their art be Negroid, they, the artist, must be considered inferior."[70] Pelham, on the other hand, has no talent to be corrupted by anxieties associated with blackness; but he yearned, nevertheless, to write like the others, to acquire "queer tastes," a desire that *is* corruptible. He wants to be *of* the "Niggeratti," someone who could sound like an eccentric. But according to Raymond, Pelham was born to be just a servant. Paul Arbian is the fictional counterpart to Richard Bruce Nugent; the name "Arbian" sounds out Nugent's initials, "R," "B," "N."[71] Because Thurman felt that Nugent epitomized bohemian living and since Nugent was openly gay while living at the Manor, Paul Arbian is iconic; he stands for a range of possibilities and he typifies a set of problems for a queer home.

In order for queer voice to be actualized, the loud sound of the rhetorical rupture that echoes through the first few pages of *Infants* must be accompanied by the acknowledgment of the ethical and affective dimensions of queer speech. In *Infants,* the ethical dimensions of speech are disclosed by the challenges to New Negro racial philosophy offered by the inhabitants of the Manor. In particular, *Infants* dramatized boundary crossings, the violation of social rules and conventions associated with interracial and homosexual communion. Similarly, a queer abode materialized as a black bohemian utopia, a dwelling place for those on the fringe of the New Negro movement.[72] Thurman used characters' bodies and narrative action to destabilize the very idea of rule-bound behavior. When Paul enters the novel, his movement and body instigate queer voice and its attendant affects.

"Ain't he a beauty, Eustace?" Paul announces, referring to Stephen. "Have you ever been seduced?" he asks the startled but amused newcomer. "Don't blush. You just looked so pure and undefiled that I had to ask that," says Paul.

Enamored of Stephen's white, virginal presence, Paul sits at his feet to gaze at the man "fashioned like a Viking" and offers him a tip on style: "take that part out of your hair and have it windblown. The hair, not the part. Plastering it down like that destroys the golden glint."[73] Paul's performance is disruptive (he literally interrupts the ongoing conversation in the room) and, despite the attention paid to Stephen, it is narcissistic; it brings notice to himself. Thurman reinforces the idea that Paul's gaze is self-reflexive by concentrating on Paul's body: "Paul was very tall. His face was the color of a bleached saffron leaf. His hair was wiry and untrained. It was his habit not to wear a necktie because he knew that his neck was too well modeled to be hidden from public gaze. He wore no sox either, nor underwear, and those few clothes he did deign to affect were musty and dishevelled."[74] As an effeminate man, Paul, in contemporary terms, can be said to be "flaming"; that is, he is on fire.[75] As such his manner matches the shade of fire-engine red on the cover of *Fire!!* and splashed across Ray's studio walls. Sutured within this alignment of signifiers, Paul is at home.

Paul's fictional style was inspired by Nugent's distaste for what was considered the "proper" attitude and place for Harlem's black literati.[76] Hence, Paul displays the bohemian's penchant for crossing over the lines. Indeed, Nugent "cared not for any societal structure which dictated his behavior."[77] Liberated from social norms, the inhabitants of the Manor no longer needed to negotiate so intensely when and how they entered Harlem circles. The Manor was open all day and night and, in the book, such unencumbered access to others rapidly engenders a friendship between Raymond and Stephen that is described in the language of pastoral romance: "They [Raymond and Stephen] had become as intimate in that short period as if they had known each other since childhood. In fact, there was something delightfully naïve and childlike about their frankly acknowledged affection for one another."[78] This fondness has been discussed by other critics as homoerotic, even though Thurman referred most directly to racial taboos associated with their friendship.[79] Despite the "potential for exploitation" when white folks invaded Harlem, Garber notes that "with its sexually tolerant population and its quasi-legal nightlife, Harlem offered an oasis to white homosexuals. . . . This identification and feeling of kinship . . . may have been the beginnings of homosexual 'minority consciousness.' "[80] I'll take up the character of this felicity in a moment when I explore the affects of queer speech. What is important at this juncture is that Raymond and Stephen's "kinship" serves as the impetus for Stephen to move into the Manor.

While trying to convince Stephen that Harlem's charm is due to the fact that it is just "New York . . . black New York," Raymond challenges the logic of racial tourism: "[Negroes] have the same social, physical and intellectual divisions. You're only being intrigued, as I have said before, by the newness of the thing. You should live here a while."[81] The author's voice can be heard in Ray's words here. In the *World Tomorrow,* Thurman wrote that "in Harlem we find a community as American as Gopher Prairie or Zenith. . . . It permits of everything possessed by that stupendous ensemble—New York City—of which it is a part."[82] There are two concepts being posited here. First, Raymond's explanation of Stephen's consumptive habits ties them to the maintenance of Harlem's novelty, masking its "true" character. Since the moment of his arrival in New York, Thurman was a critic of the artificial character of the New Negro movement and believed that it was the mission of intellectuals like himself to debunk it.[83] *Infants,* therefore, explores the perils of posing. For example, Stephen tries to understand Paul's need to be the center of attention by focusing on how racial consciousness produces his hyperbolic performances: "Paul has never recovered from the shock of realizing that no matter how bizarre a personality he may develop," Stephen tells Raymond, "he will still be a Negro, subject to snubs from certain ignorant people . . . being a Negro, he feels that his chances for excessive notoriety à la [Oscar] Wilde are slim. Thus the exaggerated poses and extreme mannerisms. Since he can't be white, he will be a most unusual Negro."[84] Paul's queer excesses are in part precipitated by the containment field produced by his black body responding to both New Negro doctrine and white consumption. In order to be recognized as more than black, he is excessive.

Paul's posture is a counterpart to the New Negro pose. In perhaps the most widely studied chapter in the novel, Dr. A. L. Parkes, Alain Locke's character, asks Raymond to convene a distinguished salon so as to "establish the younger Negro talent once and for all as a vital artistic force." Artists in attendance included Langston Hughes as Tony Crews, Countee Cullen as Dewitt Clinton, and Zora Neale Hurston as Sweetie May Carr.[85] The meeting begins with Dr. Parkes praising the group's potential, but like in the letter with which I opened this chapter, Dr. Parkes warns of decadence damaging the movement and suggests a return to African cultural forms as topics for invention. Commentators have taken the ensuing melee as a metonym for the New Negro's debacle. I wish to note how Thurman dramatized this scene so that it can serve as a refutation of the claim made by Locke in the anthology *The New Negro,* that this new confidence was no longer a "pose" for the benefit of racial protest, but rather that New Negro artists have attained "poise."[86] Thurman observed that Sweetie May Carr was popular to white folk because "she lived up to their conception of what a typical Negro should be."[87]

> "It's like this," she told Raymond. "I have to eat. I also wish to finish my education. Being a Negro writer these days is a racket and I'm go-

> ing to make the most of it while it lasts. . . . My ultimate ambition, as you know, is to become a gynecologist. And the only way I can live easily until I have the requisite training is to pose as a writer of potential ability. *Voila!* I get my tuition paid at Columbia. . . . I find queer places for whites to go in Harlem. . . . They fall for it. . . . Thank God for this Negro literary renaissance!"[88]

In a sense, Sweetie May tells us she is wearing a mask, hiding from view the fact that the New Negro embodies strategies for individual and group advancement. Furthermore, *Infants* shows us that it was the pressure to conform to this racial mission and yet remain unusual that stifled queer speech.

Raymond and Stephen's relationship also testifies to the notion that to better understand Harlem's real self, one must live in Harlem. The Niggeratti Manor, as the place where such living is made possible, materializes queer living as an alternative aesthetic practice with great aesthetic value. That is, it allows for queer forms and practices to emerge and breathe. The capacity for ways of life to provoke and sustain mutual understanding and affection among people perceived as different must be comprehended as *Infants*' chief ethical challenge to sexual and racial orthodoxy. The prime example of this confrontation in the novel is the donation party. Modeled after Harlem's infamous rent parties, the cost of admission to the Manor's donation party is food rather than rent money. The party starts slowly, but by midnight is in full, hedonistic swing. Taking stock of the festivities, Raymond is encouraged by the interracial crowd's collective boundary crossing; the Manor seems to sway back and forth, coaxing lovers into embraces, singers into song, and writers into verse: "The party had reached new heights. . . . Color lines had been completely eradicated. Whites and blacks clung passionately together as if trying to effect a permanent merger. Liquor, jazz music, and close physical contact had achieved what decades of propaganda had advocated with little success." The party in the Manor made emergent both the time and the place for the birth of a new form of social life. Raymond contemplates the idea that here there is "social equality." He notices how comfortable Paul seems, hand in hand with "Bud," his "bootblack" friend with "the most beautiful body I've ever seen."[89] Scholars have noted how rent parties "were the best place for Harlem lesbians and gays to socialize, providing safety and privacy."[90] But in *Infants,* the liminal space of this challenge to strict rulebound racial and sexual decorum is fragile and conflicted because queer aesthetic practices here are constitutive of excesses and overindulgences, tendencies linked to the pressure of New Negro conformity and appetites for exotic "others." As such, dis-ease is also present and grows stronger as the party wears on. The crowd confuses a group of school teachers who wander in, "as it did most of the Harlem intellectuals who strayed in and who all felt decidedly out of place."[91]

In order for *Infants'* queer voice to be actualized, the affective dimensions of its speech are in need of acknowledgment. To this end, Raymond describes a kind of euphoria (which is also the name of the woman who owns the Manor) that morphs into vertigo and then sickness.[92] "Tomorrow," Raymond mumbles to himself as he surveys the crowd, "all of them will have an emotional hangover. They will fear for their sanity, for at last they have had a chance to do *openly what they only dared to do clandestinely* before."[93] Thurman's work suffered here from narrative incoherence, but managed nevertheless to convey Raymond's nagging suspicion and anxiety that right before his eyes the Manor was being transformed into a "sex circus," a place where spectators come for a scandalous show.[94] As Raymond's mood turns blue, we recognize that the Manor may no longer be a safe place for homosexual communion; rather than be free of social constraints about how one can be with racial and sexual others, the Manor is a kind of theater where Raymond and friends are prescribed to act outlandishly. And so, we see Raymond's pleasure vacated. At the precise moment when he is most giddy regarding his recognition of the gifts of black queer living, Raymond notices that Stephen has left him. He dashes throughout the house searching for his roommate and constant companion, intruding upon "the fanciful aggregation of Greenwich Village uranians Paul had gathered in Raymond's studio to admire his bootblack's touted body, and irritated and annoyed two snarling women who had closeted themselves in the bathroom." He interrupts others' sexual delights while his own disappears. Raymond becomes nauseated, as "the music, the noise, the indiscriminate love-making, the drunken revelry began to sicken him. . . . It is going to be necessary, he thought, to have another emancipation to deliver the emancipated Negro from a new kind of slavery."[95]

Thurman is not clear here, but his disorientation and disgust are triggered by the recognition that Harlem's queer aesthetics are sponsored by an oppressive body politics. Dr. Parkes demands that one wear a New Negro mask, while the bohemian utopia of the Manor offers an orgy of flesh and drink. On the one hand, one's blackness makes one an instrument of the Race. During a visit to the Manor, Dr. Parkes lectures Raymond about the donation party fallout: " 'This is a new day in the history of our race. Talented Negroes are being watched by countless people, white and black, to produce something new, something tremendous. . . . Scandal stories in the newspapers certainly won't influence the public favorably.' "[96] On the other hand, one's blackness is a consumable commodity in the tourist trade. Either way, one's body is not one's own. Rejecting the demands of the racial body, therefore, seems paradoxical. Stephen later confesses to Raymond in a letter that he had to leave the Manor on the night of the party because he too was feeling ill; rather than consuming the other on visitations to the Manor like the party-goers, Stephen is especially queasy because he has overeaten. "I am fed up on Harlem and on Negroes," Stephen writes. "I can stomach them no longer." On the other hand, we may also appreciate Stephen's malady in terms of a Burkean transformation of key terms: exotic and alien. In addition to being full, Stephen is also empty. His always-there sense of alienation—necessary to the enjoyment of the erotic—has finally *consumed him*. Either homesick or nauseated, he is sick of blackness and no longer feels at home in the Manor.

The promise of Raymond and Stephen's homoerotic love is scuttled in *Infants* by explosive body politics. The naïve and innocent character of their friendship is despoiled by the harsh reality of "race business." Stephen explains in his letter that, "I have no prejudices, you know; yet recently my being has been permeated with a vague disquiet. I feel lost among Negroes. . . . the major thing is not my disquiet, but my growing dislike and antipathy. . . . I have lived recently in a suddenly precipitated fear that I had become unclean. . . . So complex and far reaching has this fear become that I rushed in a panic to a doctor."[97] Stephen's emotions sprint a wide scope of registers, but are animated by a chief affect of blackness—a growing sense of being taken over. Stephen got in the blocks when these affects produced aesthetic pleasures associated with the exotic; he was in full stride at the turn through an ambivalent illness due to a suddenly overpowering alienation; we see him here in a paranoid fever, haunted by the thought that his white body might have been infected by even a drop of the stuff that has just made him sick. Although Thurman (and I) may seem heavy-handed here, it is important to note that *Infants*' queer voice barely has an opportunity to express love and joy before racial and sexual anxieties turn it into a bitter, fearful timbre. This tone can also be heard in Thurman's acrid commentary while with the *Messenger,* regarding how black bohemia ultimately undermined the necessary discipline to cultivate truly gifted young writers. The affective registers of *Infants*' voice are haunting precisely because we hear it faintly coming out of nowhere. In the book, Raymond and Paul create a queer utopia, a no place;[98] this bohemian invention, this queer "home" is groundless, disorienting and, in the end, the Niggeratti are dis-eased in it and displaced, that is, evicted from it.[99] As an object of spectacular consumption, the Manor is no longer a closet that protects and harbors; it is a stage on which black queer life is open to enjoyment and exploitation.

Euphoria Blake closes the Manor due to gossip that she is running a "miscegenated bawdy house"; she fears that the scandal that worries Dr. Parkes is hurting her reputation. "I must make money," she explains to Raymond. "That's all a Negro can do. Money means freedom. There's nothing to this art stuff. . . . I only want to make money."[100] No longer feeling that the Manor would be a "monument to the New Negro,"[101] a symbol of "an intellectual aristocracy . . . engaged in the search for Truth (as opposed to money) as a means of social progress,"[102] Euphoria becomes depressed. And, she gets angry. Paul's surprise at his unexpected homelessness leads to insults directed at her materialism and her fear of social reprisal. She kicks him out of the Manor in a fit of rage.[103] The affects that vivify queer voice in *Infants* rapidly descend from the heights of dreams and fantasies to the depths of despair. Raymond is alone and distraught about having to leave the Manor; he suffers a mental breakdown and is bedridden. Thurman seems to struggle with his own morass in the novel and seems unsure how to make sense for the reader of the destruction of a utopian vision. The raced and queered persons in *Infants* cannot seem to avoid the body politics consistently rising up to devour them, but the reader cannot be entirely sure if Thurman's anxieties about his own very dark skin provoked the cannibalism or if this orgy of racial bodies in *Infants* conveyed the pressure of New Negro doctrine. I will return to this ambivalence in a moment, but we must first examine Paul's fate in relation to the acknowledgment of voice.

In the novel's final chapter, Raymond is awakened in the middle of the night by a frightened voice on the phone that tells him, "Paul's committed suicide." Paul had left Harlem for Greenwich Village. Raymond catches the train there immediately; he is oddly detached from the death as a life-ending moment for a friend. The novel dampens Raymond's emotions in favor of contemplating the acknowledgment of queer voice. Raymond voices this contemplation: "Had Paul the debonair, Paul the poseur, Paul the irresponsible romanticist, finally faced reality and seen himself and the world as they actually were? . . . He had employed every other conceivable means to make himself stand out from the mob. Wooed the unusual, cultivated artificiality, defied all conventions of dress and conduct."[104] Paul's life suggests that if one pushes hard enough against the social fabric, one may bring about a rip. The potential for bringing about openings in race-speak in *Infants,* to actually bring forth a "new" Negro, seem finalized as the reader's sights are trained on Paul's "final stanza," his last-ditch effort at being endowed with queer voice. Thus, Raymond recognizes the suicide as it is, as a *manner of speaking* and is "not so much interested in the fact that Paul was dead as he was in wanting to know how death had been accomplished."[105]

Paul has staged his death to produce "delightful publicity" for the novel he has written; his self-murder acting as the trump card in a game of body politics pushing him farther out in the middle of nowhere. Posthumously published, his work would presumably be acknowledged; it would also be fueled by fascination sparked by the death scene: Paul locked himself in the bathroom, scattered the pages of his novel about the floor so that it could be immediately recognized in all of its glory; he lit incense and hung his art on the walls; he ran bath water and dressed in a "crimson mandarin robe" and scarf, and slashed his wrists; "Paul lay crumpled at the bottom, a colorful, inanimate corpse in a crimson streaked tub."[106] *Infants* contemplates the conditions of queer voice and voicelessness; Paul's novel is in need of acknowledgment for the endowment of his voice. But he has written it in pencil and the tub has overflowed, rendering the novel illegible, save for the title page. On the title page of Paul's never-to-be-read novel is a sketch he made in black ink of the Niggeratti Manor collapsing because of a crumbling foundation. Raymond recognizes the irony: Paul's suicide "speech" drowns out his voice. His self-mutilation becomes his last word on the subject of how Harlem body politics affect black queer life. And so, Paul's voice is not as he wished it to be; what we finally hear is not the articulate soul of a queer life, for it is forever erased by the flood caused by the inanimate corpse; rather, we hear *finally* the inarticulate exhalation made by Paul's bodily surrender.

Infants of the Spring is not a story that ends with the death of Paul Arbian; it testifies still to Wallace Thurman's attempts at cultivating his queer voice during the New Negro movement. In the novel, Thurman mocked both Harlem's literary establishment and its would-be saviors. Although Thurman has trouble maintaining any sort of stable footing in his staging of *Infants,* he dramatized the limitations inscribed onto the black body as it was both claimed and consumed by racial and sexual politics. As Harlem responded to being in vogue, some New Negro aesthetic and artistic practices were strengthened by the promise of racial advancement. Meanwhile, the tourism industry that shifted into high gear by 1926 happily traded in those same black bodies. Thurman and friends discovered that their bodies were overvalued because their queerness was perceived as exceptional.

The Niggeratti Manor was the setting for the testing of these pressures; it was constitutive of a queer ethos and was the crucible for queer voices. I have argued that for queer voice to be actualized, its ethical and affective dimensions must be acknowledged. *Infants* offered an ethical challenge to the New Negro's answer to the humanistic question "how shall I live?" Thurman's artistic practices in *Infants* offered a refutation of the aesthetic practices that brought the Niggeratti Manor into prominence. The novel considered the very terms in which queer life was experienced and valued as vivacious. It opened up for us the development of aesthetic understandings of queer sensibilities and dramatized how their "excess" was subject to New Negro discipline and how the emancipation of those excesses imparted tendencies at once regulated as "preferences" and experienced by Thurman as "prejudices." It is as though Thurman is constantly involved in an attempt to disrupt through the production of an aesthetic experience the very practices making him a New Negro subject. I have attempted to clarify how Thurman's activities interrupted New Negro orthodoxy by positing alternative living arrangements. The production of *Fire!!* and *Harlem* were attempts to transform the aesthetic practices amplifying and muting queer voice. Zora Neale Hurston was in full agreement with Thurman's motives for inventing *Fire!!,* quipping to Locke in a letter in the fall of 1927, "I suppose that 'Fire' has gone to ashes quite, but I still think the idea is good. We needed better management that's all. Don't *you* think there ought to be a purely literary magazine in our group. . . . Why can't our triangle-Locke-Hughes-Hurston do something with you at the apex?"[107] Thurman realized that the failure of these efforts to remain or become viable threatened voice. Perhaps Thurman was caught up deep inside as he wrote *Infants,* a chilly notice to those who dare dream—or dance, or laugh, or cry—of warm embraces of home. Friends of Thurman like Langston Hughes and Augustas Granville Dill testify to the way that Thurman seemed to cover over his emotions in much of his writing.[108] The narrator of *Infants* favors the distant observation of the journalist to the sensual lyricism of the poet. And so, the reader is *told of* emotions, not immersed in them. This detachment is most glaring when the reader is told of Paul's suicide. The reader has little sense of how Raymond feels about what he sees; indeed, we are told that he does not feel, that he is mechanical.[109] Thurman turned Raymond into a robot, a move that frayed and weakened the artistic imperative for Thurman to disclose his feelings through Raymond.

In addition to the sense that *Infants* has a numbing effect, the reader is made to ponder its voice and voicelessness. As a reader I was called by it. Thurman wrote after its publication that "the characters and their problems *cried out* for release. They intruded themselves into [my] every alien thought. And assumed an importance which blinded [me] to their true value."[110] Thurman was very disappointed with his writing of *Infants* and might have been embarrassed by its mixed reception and criticism.[111] This tepid acknowledgment by Harlem literati in general disconfirms its voice and might be linked to its "unspeakable . . . true value."[112] *Infants* cries out still, but its voice has difficulty reaching us because of the dissipative energies also inscribed within it. Racial politics overwhelm same-sexualities in the novel as Thurman's own racial anxieties disquiet Raymond's social world.

Although Dorothy West and Langston Hughes understood the novel to be an autobiographical statement about Thurman's preoccupation with race, the Niggeratti Manor also signifies a problematic of queer containment and shelter.[113] The "closet" has been discussed as a space where queer living can be sustained precisely because it is hidden from view.[114] But in terms of the United States' racial history, such spaces for black folk are constitutive of racist systems in which the body can be disciplined.[115] Thurman registers disgust for the Manor because, despite intermingling with white folk, his body was subjected to a form of segregation; that is, the Manor's value as a queer harbor was directly related to the determination of his identity as a *black* queer. More than anything else, Thurman wanted to be a writer, but the Manor disperses *his* desire in favor of the longing that others have for his black "deviance." This sort of excessive appetite for the livelier queer Harlem is predicated upon passing over a racial boundary. As such, the boundary is delineated as a thing to be crossed after hours and under cover. The allure of these transgressions cannot be maintained if Thurman gets his wish. Queer Harlem must be peculiar even to gay New York.

Patriarchal heteronormativity, the novel suggests, is what's left standing as the Manor's walls come crumbling down. Put down in ink, Paul's drawing of the fall of the Manor survives the bloodbath. The death scene, too, speaks. Paul's novel would have served as strings of affective conduction, as signs that can transmit but cannot hold onto the resonance that orbit it. We could have opened ourselves up to the emotions constitutive of the novel and its characters. We could have listened for that un-remarkable sound of voice that gets audiblized when we acknowledge the affective and ethical dimensions of the work's speech, asking us to make a choice regarding the injunction of voice. But, what we do get from *Infants* is the sound of Paul's erasure. Like the sound of a stylus being yanked off a record, we hear the rip. These are the queer sounds of *Infants* and of Thurman; drifting to us over time and space, from the edges of no place, we hear "rip-rumble," a tear and a fall. *Infants* can always produce these queer sounds and that is an important accomplishment. Thurman did not believe so; after its publication he wrote that there was "no excuse for having allowed [*Infants*] to be published."[116] Thurman's disavowal might be linked to his disclaimers to his wife that he was ever a participant in queer Harlem's sexual experimentations.[117]

Despite their motivations, such attempts to shape-shift are evident with other "queer" artists. For example, Arnold Rampersad has been accused of exerting "Herculean efforts" to show that Hughes was not gay in the biography *Life of Langston Hughes.* The persistent mission for black intellectuals to show racial figures and black history in general in their best light provokes the reinvention of African American ethos and, thus far, the suppression of queer voices.[118] Black history is in dire need of cultural reclamation because the development of black nationality has aided in the negation of black gay and lesbian narratives.[119] The character of rhetorical voice is uniquely suited for this task because it requires the critic to attend to the affective and ethical dimensions of public discourse. Let us here and now acknowledge the intensity with which Countee Cullen wanted to meet New Negro expectations *and* the elation of a late night visit from a new friend that must be kept from New Negro ears: "we quite conclusively understand one another. . . . There is so invigorating a relief in being happy!"[120] Voice issues a "call of conscience" where we must attempt to feel the joy and pain of our fellows. These are not only calls for that very important human gift, empathy; the endowment of voice informs the rediscovery of the speech that first carried it. We are newly attuned to how much of Cullen's lovesickness was generative of his own deeply felt commitment to New Negro ideals, particularly those that seemed to suggest a transcendence of race as a by-product of social equality. Thurman seemed to intervene in his subjection by clarifying the affective registers associated with experiencing race as a queered strait(straight) jacket. *Infants* may be anesthetizing in the end, but Thurman's voice is arousing to this day. If this assessment is viable, then Thurman must be mistaken about having "no excuse" for *Infants.* For if black queer voices are to continue to be moved out of the recesses of the imaginary in black rhetorical and cultural studies, our social body must not cease to hear such cries. As exasperating as this queer predicament seemed to Thurman, Cullen, and others, when we trace its coordinates through race, sex, class, and gender, however, we arrive at the paradox offered by the undecidability of murder/suicide.

8
"You Mean You Don't Want Me, 'Rene?"
Anxiety, Desire, and Madness in Nella Larsen's *Passing*

By spring of 1929, Alfred Knopf Publishing required little encouragement to distribute new literary works produced by younger members of the New Negro movement. Having already published Langston Hughes's first two collections of poems, *The Weary Blues* and *Fine Clothes to the Jew,* Nella Larsen's first novel, *Quicksand,* and re-released the now author-identified *Autobiography of an Ex-Colored Man* by James Weldon Johnson, the New York City publishing house had become one of the chief outlets for black writers. Emerging black talent also had the support of a tremendous in-house ally in Carl Van Vechten.[1] A prized thoroughbred in the Knopf stables that enjoyed fast tracks to Harlem's socialites, Van Vechten was eager to convince Alfred Knopf that Larsen's second novel deserved the sort of marketing blitz usually reserved for mainstream bestsellers like his own. He was successful. The novel was placed in prime locations in bookstores and advertised as the thriller of the season. One observer noted: "Since most potential readers would never pick up a black-authored novel in a bookstore, they would learn that *Passing* was a 'Negro novel' only after being drawn in by the tantalizing hoopla surrounding it."[2]

It was an intriguing coincidence that Larsen's artistic practices dramatizing the social phenomenon of "passing" converged with Knopf's aesthetic practices regarding the visibility of the novel. Each set of practices concerned tactical transgressions of the color line. And yet, the significance of this conjuncture is not undermined by its "accidental" appearance. From the beginning of the movement, the artistic practices of the New Negro were constitutive of aesthetic practices of regimes responsible for their emergence and circulation.[3] The marketing of *Passing* certainly drew inspiration from the exhilaration of New Negro literary works, and the increasingly ardent consumption of the works helped propel Larsen's literary aspirations. I am hardly making a radical observation here, but as in other chapters in this book, I will shift the accent mark that often rests on the "content" of New Negro literary production or on the biographies of its agents, to highlight the interstices among the aesthetic regimes mapping New Negro ventures, the aesthetic practices guiding the emergence of artworks, and the artistic practices being supported or undermined. A brief case in point will be illustrative.

As a "black" novel initially passing for a work of general (non-black) interest, *Passing* garnered a number of high-profile, mainstream reviews. Let us momentarily dwell on a review that appeared in the *New York Herald Tribune Books* on Sunday, April 28, 1929. The review is noteworthy because it ruminated on the tastes of white readers, and as it did so it exposed the difficulty this writer experienced while rendering an aesthetic judgment of Larsen's artistic practice: "Among white people there seem to be two common attitudes toward Negroes, one that they are a different order of beings with utterly foreign feelings and thoughts, the other that they are, in a sad, luscious way, entirely romantic."[4] These "common attitudes" were not mutually exclusive, but the former notion suggested absolute otherness while the latter idea tethered black living to a single primitive instinct. To this reviewer, however, Larsen's writing registered a different difference. "Nothing startles the white man so surely as the discovery of a simple, dignified routine in the life of educated Negroes" like Larsen's protagonists. The reviewer noted that black authors have displayed this dignity previously;[5] "but not, I think, in the unselfconscious, taken-for-granted" manner of Larsen. Larsen naturalized black dignity with such "effectiveness that she throws all the emphasis of her story onto those spectacular phases of the race problem which are more commonly supposed to be interesting." And it is here where the review turned odd, queer even. Larsen's artistic practice was perceived as catapulting the white reader into familiar racial territory, "commonly supposed to be interesting," but doing so through a kind of suspense, felt as "one of the most arresting things in her book." Larsen's "taken-for-granted" style was sensed as being at once mundane and astonishing. She drew attention to an inherent lack in common attitudes about blackness through an artistic practice that self-effaced. And as the reviewer sketched Larsen's story about a reunion between two childhood female friends, both of whom have the capacity to pass for white, the suspension neared disorientation:

> Any novel that deals with a public problem can be judged either for the sharpness of its point in controversy or for distinction of style. As a piece of writing, *Passing* can only be deemed adequate. Perhaps the romanticism that associates the Negro with powerful rhythms and broad good humor is false as far as this newer generation is concerned. It is doubtless well that we be pricked to consciousness of growing sobriety and

> responsibility among them. But the flat, unimpassioned sentences are a disappointment to an expectancy of beauty. However, that strange excitement arising from the mere mention of race, as from the word sex, holds one's interest to the end.[6]

How could a "taken-for-granted" and "unselfconscious" style startle and catch-up white readers? How could common racial themes expressed in "flat, unimpassioned sentences" evoke a "strange excitement"? And why must a "growing sobriety and responsibility" in the work violate "an expectancy of beauty"? The answer to this last question may lie in the fact that Larsen may have simply been unable to pull the whole thing off and deserved the refusal by this critic to judge the work beautiful. But I am not wondering whether this judgment is sound. I am interested in what we might learn from the review about "common" aesthetic understandings of black life and of race that this critic engaged as she was required to write it. We should keep in mind that the *Herald Tribune's* book editor, Irita Van Doren, was a well-known enthusiast regarding the capacity for New Negro artistic practices to revitalize modernity's social body.[7] If we think about the review as productive of desires for New Negro racial difference making up aesthetic practices of New York City's art world and of unstable tropes of race mobilized through Larsen's artistic practices, something significant might be revealed to us. By moving the novel into intimate contact with critics in the habit of commemorating a peculiar racial endowment, the aesthetic practices promoting Larsen's visibility and audibility (and other New Negro artists) set off potent affects regarding her artistic practice. We witness in this review a stark recognition of the "arresting" evacuation of racial fantasies alongside the animation of disappointment over the loss of those common attitudes, lamented as "false *as far as this newer generation* is concerned."[8]

Melancholia over this loss might account for this aesthetic judgment, but it does not explain the review's overall tone. Midway into the review, this critic sought to characterize the work's central emotive energy: Throughout the novel Irene "holds a curious attitude toward Clare—another interesting aspect to the white reader—a mixture of contempt and admiration, envy and disgust." As common attitudes about race were emptied out, something else emerged, "that strange excitement arising from the mere mention of race, *as from the word sex*." Newly falsified "common attitudes" regarding race were transfigured by the reviewer into a "curious attitude" held by a female protagonist toward her antagonist. This curiosity was said to be animated by sensations vaguely described as "another interesting aspect to the white reader." The "curious attitude" and the "strange excitement" registered for this reviewer a similar immanent affect. It was as though the review narrated the experience of the critic who gingerly, and with a "curious attitude," approached an unexpected rupture in the novel, a gap out of which the past haunted and estranged the present; where Larsen's sentences seemed dead, yet the work resonated excitement; where black middle-class life was routinized, but race was sexualized; where Larsen's style was at once arresting and disappointing and mobilized a story that had been "used in Negro fiction before, but not, I think" like this.[9] Larsen's artistic practice disturbed common aesthetic judgments rooted in the very aesthetic practices enabling her visibility and circulation. The conjuncture between New Negro aesthetic and artistic practices invigorated tropes of difference that flashed tempting and tormenting secrets. This reviewer sensed the "passing" of racial fantasies, and the uncertainty that flowered in their place sparked curiosity but also threatened to displease. Experiencing a violation of her "expectancy of beauty" and not knowing exactly what to make of the "strange" (queer) anticipation of a racial and sexual relation between two women in *Passing,* this reviewer judged Larsen's work to be what we might call an acquired taste.

Passing moved Larsen fully into Harlem's spotlight, but she has generally been remembered as a voiceless fugitive of the New Negro movement. Her novel brought to life uncommon senses but was typically faulted, even while being praised, for not satisfying common sense regarding narratives of passing. The very idea that the New Negro movement, a brightly illuminated phenomenon that regularly gave itself up to spectacular modes of publicity, might have birthed a "so-called mystery woman"[10] in plain sight seems paradoxical. We should not approach such an occurrence Platonically, that is, by walking toward the light. Rather, we should ourselves "pass" further into the shadows cast by New Negro shine. Larsen's world was populated by dark places that were harrowing and enticing and always in flux. Passing is, of course, about mobility, but fantasies that assemble objects of desire require fixity. And it is this very tension that we must endure in order to endow Larsen's voice and remark upon her rhetorical imagination. In this chapter, I explore how *Passing* disclosed the fragility of fantasies regarding New Negro racial identity and white supremacy. *Passing* deployed two inter-animating senses of "passing." On the one hand, passing functioned as a way for some black folk to make new social worlds. In this sense, passing did not merely signify racial deception, it was a tactic made available by specific modes of visibility and audibility constitutive of New Negro aesthetic and artistic practices. On the other hand, "passing" named an affect. In the novel, passing is an intense performative act that undermines the law of racial and sexual order, showing identities to be held together by matrices of desire and anxiety. Mobility and undecidability collaborate to open spaces for the emergence of new forms of life, but these forms persistently register the potential for catastrophic failure of sensemaking. This chapter will investigate how *Passing,* as a work of art, is an opening, or, putting the matter more playfully, how the novel is ajar. And we shall also hear what passes out of *Passing* when we acknowledge the ethics and affects of Larsen's speech. This occurrence of voice will not only allow us to better appreciate the production of this very important New Negro violation but also to sense the peculiar stresses bearing down on some black female bodies as they were asked to be fetishized and phantasms in service to social vitality and racial advancement. In order to contemplate this predicament, I contend one must attempt to think the paradox of *Passing*'s murder/suicide.

"Bad mixed blood"[11]

M. M. Bakhtin issued a well-known warning of the dangers that a "national" language poses to freedom, creativity, and criticism. Nationalistic discursive formations seek to universalize a specific lived experience by speaking it aloud (over and over) as essentially shared by all.[12] In a moral sense, it is unfair to assert that resistance movements launching counter-hegemonic offensives sometimes embody the same threat to freedom, but theoretically and historically such movements, when successful, become the new regime. I have argued elsewhere in this book that key movement leaders like W. E. B. Du Bois and Alain Locke sought to cobble together dominant forms of aesthetic practices supported by emergent regimes during this era.[13] New Negro movement leaders often (and sometimes unwittingly) invented rhetorical practices out of universalizing topoi. For example, two years prior to the publication of Larsen's *Quicksand,* Harlem embraced the appearance of two collections of poems that heralded a new phase of the production of the New Negro. Although Countee Cullen's *Color* preceded Langston Hughes's *The Weary Blues* by months, Jessie Fauset reviewed them in tandem in the *Crisis* in March 1926.[14] As the journal's literary editor, Fauset was partly responsible for lifting Cullen and Hughes onto the movement's stage by publishing their works with regularity. She also often ran the journal for months due to the editor's hectic travel schedule.[15] Fauset was not merely a fan of the artworks of the New Negro movement; she was one of the movement's chief architects. In two months' time, she would resign from her post at the *Crisis* to pursue her own important career as a novelist.[16] Her review not only passed judgment on specific artistic practices like Hughes's use of dialect—of which she was "no great lover"[17]—it exhibited the very racial ideology Larsen would soon challenge.

While reviewing Cullen's *Color,* Fauset commented on how the work treated race in three distinct ways: by carefully avoiding it (in some poems "no mention is made of color"), through explicit representation of it, or by allowing a maturing black "consciousness" to manifest it. This final category offered "the most beautifully done" poetry and required careful consideration: "But to pour forth poignantly and sincerely the feelings which make plain to the world the innerness of the life which black men live calls for special understanding." By defending the "special treatment" of blackness in poetry, Fauset was rebuking the call made by some contemporaries that poets ought to strive for universality. It was, therefore, ironic that her defense of Cullen presumed a consummate (universal) New Negro consciousness and "innerness of the life" that could be made "plain to the world."[18] I am not claiming that Fauset believed that this racial consciousness was inherently coherent, only that she was heavily invested in regulating a set of artistic and aesthetic practices important to racial uplift which made use of discourses that posited a unified black subject. Nella Larsen was not.

Born Nellie Walker on April 13, 1891, in Chicago to a white Danish mother (Mary) and a "colored cook" (Peter), Larsen's interracial body signified a peculiar anxiety regarding racial identity that has historically structured a master narrative commonly referred to as the "tragic mulatta."[19] Scholars seeking to understand Larsen have been influenced by the aesthetic practices constitutive of this master narrative. For some reasonable and some questionable motivations, Larsen's life story has been brought into alignment with the tragic mulatta story and, in turn, this alignment has offered key hermeneutic logics that have been applied to her novels. There is no doubt that Larsen contributed to this configuration by being somewhat mysterious; and her obscure post-renaissance life and isolated death seemed to warrant the tragic frame.[20] The association of Larsen with the tragic mulatta narrative did more than shape readings of her life and artistry; it also sustained the drive to solve the mystery, to compose the truth about her existence and, more intensely, her work. After all, frames presuppose the knowledge to be produced. Scholars have approached Larsen like an explosive ordnance in need of defusing; noting that Larsen "is a master of ambiguity,"[21] critics over the years have set about clarifying that her novels are about queer desire,[22] or that they are about female oppression, or that they are about racial identification.[23] I am fully aware that my exploration might be similarly characterized; I hope that my conclusions are felt as adventurous, however, in the sense of always already provoking feelings of risk associated with the unknowable. And this brings us back to that strangely powerful alignment of Larsen's life and fiction with the tragic mulatta narrative. We must first trace the contours of this coalition in order to untangle it.

As a child and a young adult woman, Larsen's body provoked her perpetual motion, slipping her between homes, neighborhoods, and institutions. Her skin signified "mulatta" and her shifting social circumstances registered a kind of racial trauma. Her biological father, Peter Walker, disappeared when she was very young, and when her mother re-married, this time to a white man, Peter Larsen, her fair-skinned blackness triggered an irreparable split within herself: "As she grew older, she would come to recognize that she was a burden to her mother. . . . But it gradually became clear that Nellie would have to live a life apart. Tangled feelings of love and abandonment, anger and self-loathing, empathy, shame, and powerlessness stamped Larsen's emotional development in childhood and shaped the attachment problems that would afflict her until she died." Larsen's blackness barred the family from being able to live as whites; in fact, her presence "darkened" the entire clan as Negroes "passing." Constantly on the move, Larsen's family struggled to find a stable dwelling place; although capable of living among working-class blacks and whites, upward mobility into bourgeois white or black society was stymied by questions regarding Larsen's interracial origins; she was always potentially seen as illegitimate, both racially and morally.[24] Readers familiar with the generic conventions of the tragic mulatta narrative will readily see their patterns in this biographical snapshot. As we continue to explore Larsen's journey, the resemblance sharpens but then fractures.

Larsen was sent to Fisk University in 1907 after her family apparently decided to go "white" without her. The Jim Crow South shocked her sensibilities, but it is entirely possible that she was even more shaken by the prescribed role that black women like the ones admitted to Fisk were determined to play in the advancement of the race. Hutchinson notes in his biography of Larsen that "the girl's and women's housing in Jubilee Hall, the architectural symbol of the university, expressed the sense of their sacred role in the race's progress." Integral to fulfilling this role was "'the *right education* . . . intelligence, frugality, virtue, and noble aspirations.'" The nearly all-white faculty eschewed much-better-paying jobs so they could be missionaries in the Negro cause; thus, they tended to be zealots who sought to bring about born-again transformations in the student body and enforced morality rituals that regulated attire, social events, and thought. In some very important ways, Fisk was at odds with Larsen's "fiercely independent intelligence." Larsen was expelled at the end of the academic year; it was obliquely documented by the university as being due to violations of its moral codes.[25] As the story goes, homelessness haunts the tragic mulatta.

Rather than a life sealed shut by this master narrative, however, Larsen's story leaks. She sailed to Copenhagen and was welcomed by her mother's family. According to the tale, the tragic mulatta must reject black people because of internalized whiteness, but must herself be rejected by white people as non-white. But Larsen's mother did not simply abandon her to Fisk; she loved Nella and cared for her until the stress of racial in-betweenness compelled the Larsens to prioritize the needs of their younger (white) daughter, Anna. Mary's people in Denmark fractured the tragic frame by opening their hearts and homes to their slightly darker-skinned American kin. Larsen's stay was short. Perhaps she missed the United States, or she got fed up with being an "exotic" spectacle for Copenhagen's residents, for after a few months Larsen moved to New York City to become a nurse. After graduating in May 1915, she got a post at John A. Andrews Memorial Hospital at Tuskegee Institute, just in time to experience the aftershock caused by Booker T. Washington's death. A year and a half later, she went back to New York City, where she met and married Elmer Imes. This union stabilized Larsen's social world by promoting her to the status of black middle class, and spun it in new and exciting directions. The years 1919 through 1923 marked the advent of Larsen's "involvement in New York's black bourgeoisie thanks in part to her husband's background and professional status."[26]

During these key years, Larsen caught the literary bug. It was spreading through Harlem like a virus. Unlike influenza, however, folks passing this contagion did so merrily, lustily, and knowingly. Although there were plenty of hot spots, the 135th Street Library in Harlem might be considered ground zero. After working through health care crises as a nurse, Larsen warmed to the idea of being amidst a cultural epidemic; she got to know James Weldon Johnson, Walter White, and the head librarian, Ernestine Potowski Rose. The library was a vital organ of Harlem and its aesthetic practices included lectures by authors like Jean Toomer and famous anthropologist Franz Boas, readings by poets like Countee Cullen, and art exhibits showcasing painters like Henry Tanner. Larsen's lifelong liminality was suspended by the manner in which the library constituted a hospitable intersection of diverse persons and groups. The staff was integrated and its facilities housed forums for the politics of the radical Left, (Booker T.) Washingtonians, NAACP integrationists, and Marcus Garveyites, allowing the library to become "the intellectual crossroads of the community, as well as a meeting point with white downtown."[27] The tragic mulatta finds no respite; but it is difficult to believe that Larsen was not, at least temporarily, at home here. She quit nursing and trained as a librarian, eventually becoming the head of the Children's Reading Room at the 135th Street branch.

Nearly everyone Larsen was to meet during these years encouraged her to write. Indeed, the buoyancy amounted to a conspiracy. Despite a childhood full of economic hard times, Larsen received a pretty strong education and she was worldly. On the face of it at least, she appeared to be a perfect candidate for New Negro womanhood. Some Harlem socialites undoubtedly expected her to behave like Walter White's wife, Gladys, who "immersed herself in the role of wife to the rising race man, standing quietly behind him, hosting, raising their children, maintaining a succession of increasingly expensive apartments, and stifling her own ambitions." Larsen, however, was drawn to the "more racially integrated, sometimes less strait-laced circles" spinning through Greenwich Village and Harlem cabarets.[28] It was while being swept through this whirlwind of parties and teas that she met Carl Van Vechten.[29] Flamboyant and salacious, Van Vechten was a lightning rod for controversy, but his friends were fiercely loyal. By spring of 1925, Larsen was thrilled to be considered one of them and was well on her way to conceiving of *Quicksand*.[30] By the year's end, Larsen had quit her job and was writing full time. It is toward the context of her emergence as an author that we turn now.

"I dream I am a Negro & being pursued."[31]

Popular novels like *Peter Whiffle* and *The Blind Bow-Boy*[32] made Carl Van Vechten famous; *Nigger Heaven*[33] made him infamous. Although he would write *Nigger Heaven* within a brief six-month window, his "intensive study"[34] of Harlem began two years prior to its conception. By the time *Nigger Heaven* was in bookstores, Van Vechten more than fancied himself as having been darkened by his aesthetic experiences above 110th Street in Manhattan; he expected he could be both author and object of his own racial imaginary. His interest in the cultural expressions of Negroes was cultivated by an intense aesthetic sensitivity toward artworks that approached a break from stale convention. Van Vechten felt that, for example, the music of George Gershwin pushed against the grain of what Europe gushed over because "Gershwin's rhythms [found] their roots in the music of the Negro."[35] This artistic communion was accompanied and stimulated in the early 1920s by the aesthetic practices of the Great White Way. The all-black cast of *Shuffle Along*[36] performed blocks from DuBose Heyward's *Porgy*.[37] Critics, editors, and novelists like Van Vechten would meet black singers and composers like Paul Robeson and Rosamond Johnson.[38]

The boundary between white downtown and black uptown virtually disappeared for members of New York City's celebrity culture. James Weldon Johnson and his wife Grace hosted regular interracial parties in Harlem, while Van Vechten's apartment on West 55th Street was considered a lower Westside New Negro hangout. It was at the Johnson's where Van Vechten met NAACP operative Walter White. White had been encouraged by Van Vechten's friend, the journalist and satirist H. L. Mencken, to write a book about "real" middle-class struggle. White reportedly was not satisfied with Clement Wood's sympathetic treatment of racial struggle in his novel called *Nigger.* Van Vechten would soon trumpet White's novel, *The Fire in the Flint,* to influential friends as "written by a Nigger. It is some document & I want you to talk about it & write intriguing letters around the world about it." Van Vechten's casual use of the term "nigger" is explained by his biographer as unremarkable because "most white people" were unaware that it was offensive. Van Vechten's letters and his daybooks provide evidence of Van Vechten's ignorance, to a point. Soon after a full immersion in Harlem's artistic life, described as providing one "thrilling experience" after another, Van Vechten seemed to understand that in everyday parlance, white folks' use of "nigger" was problematic.[39] By 1925, it virtually disappeared as an interpersonal reference from his letters and daybooks.[40] The recognition that "nigger" was a slur, however, did not dampen Van Vechten's previous understanding of the value of the term to aesthetic practices generative of marketing interests. In a letter to white novelist Ronald Firbank in 1923 regarding a draft of Firbank's upcoming book, Van Vechten admitted that "after reading this delightful opus, I suggested that Prancing Nigger would be a better title, and [the editors] all agreed to this. . . . I may say, however, that beyond a doubt the new title would sell at least a thousand more copies."[41]

If we disarticulate this commercial advantage from recognition of "nigger" as slur, we are left pondering as to the source of this "strange excitement" generating white consumption. In August 1925, after a night of partying with Langston Hughes, Eric Walrond, Countee Cullen, Rudolph Fisher, and Richard Bruce Nugent, Van Vechten revealed in his daybooks that the "title of 'Nigger Heaven' comes to me today."[42] Inspired by aesthetic experiences of Harlem's nightlife and New Negro artistic practices, Van Vechten seized upon "nigger" as a trope of visibility for his novel *despite* its racist intonations and *because* of its racial resonance. The evidence for this claim can be gleaned from Van Vechten's strategic execution of the aesthetic practices advertising his novel. It is clear that during 1925, Van Vechten's advocacy of New Negro works was no longer principally about being a talent scout, but was also geared toward warranting his own artistic practices. In a letter to Gertrude

Stein, he reported, "I am reading proofs . . . and when I am finished . . . I shall start on my Negro novel. I have passed practically my whole winter in company with Negroes and have succeeded in getting into most of the important *sets.* This will not be a novel about Negroes in the South or white contacts or lynchings. It will be about NEGROES, as they live now in the new city of Harlem. . . . I hope it will be a good book."[43] Six months later, Van Vechten was pleading with his good friend and publisher, Alfred Knopf, for a very advanced advert because

> this book is *different.* It is necessary to prepare the mind not only of my own public, but of the new public this book may possibly reach, particularly that public which lies outside of New York. *If they see the title,* they will ask questions, or read *The New Negro* or something, so that the kind of life I am writing about will not come as an *actual* shock. To that end, as you know, I have during the past year written countless articles on Negro subjects . . . and I have seen to it that as many outoftowners as possible saw enough of the life themselves so that they would *carry some news* of it back to where they came from.[44]

We should note two specific developments here. First, Van Vechten sensed the need to prepare the palate for a different racial taste; such preparations would both whet an appetite and cultivate a habit. Van Vechten's critical essays on black artistry and culture are thrown into a peculiar light here. Van Vechten authored more than half a dozen essays during his "intensive study" of Harlem. His subjects included folk songs and spirituals, blues songs and singers, the Negro theater, and a caution regarding the "Negro's reluctance" to cultivate a unique artistry by depicting "the squalor and vice of Negro life."[45] Taken as a whole, the essays condensed blackness and "racial gifts" into forms of life and expressions that stimulated primitivist imaginations. They were meant to educate both the white intellect and the body, to provide white readers with a safe aperture through which to experience "enough of the life" to inflame desire, rather than to induce "actual shock." These works also served as evidence to New Negro artists that broad audiences expected them to further immerse themselves in their putatively peculiar raciology. In a letter to Irita Van Doren, Van Vechten happily reported making headway in this regard with Langston Hughes: "These new blues I think will prove to you that Langston is improving along the lines *we spoke about,* i.e. he is getting deeper into a *real racial idiom.*"[46] What we see here is the coordination, among white critics and editors, of specific aesthetic and artistic practices that animated what white tastes craved about race.

Second, we should evaluate Van Vechten's aesthetic understanding of the significance of the work of *Nigger Heaven*. The novel is forgettable in nearly every way, save two. First, it staged an encounter with Van Vechten's sense of blackness—it invited white readers into its intimate spaces where they might "remember" that their aesthetic understandings of race had always been constitutive of the sensorium.[47] In a stern letter to a European publisher translating *Nigger Heaven* into French, Van Vechten spelled out what was at stake if the company edited the work in ways he found objectionable: "My decision remains unchanged. I have no desire to appear before the French public in the mutilated version that you propose. You write that the French public would be unable to understand the conditions about which I write. . . . The book depends for what effect it may make far more on its *background than it does on its plot*."[48] Even if we allow for the possibility that Van Vechten was being hyperbolic, he shed light on the importance of affective resonance. *Nigger Heaven* did not depend upon the teleology of narrative; its work was generative of a vibratory aliveness in excess of plot. It held readers in suspense by moving them into contact with a fantasy of racial joie de vivre made sensible by a white observer authentically passing as a reliable tour guide. Van Vechten's locomotion into the dark helped to generate this resonance as it propelled the movement of the white imaginary through a virtual "jungle."[49] The story of New Negro love, sex, and sadness was beside the point. The crucial work of *Nigger Heaven* was its capacity to register partial enjoyment of New Negro "authentic difference."

Nigger Heaven must also be understood as being the subject of some New Negro nightmares. While Van Vechten dreamed that because of his immersion in blackness his "colour would now be at least seal-brown,"[50] advocates of New Negro artistic uplift were nearly apoplectic. Grace Johnson had warned Van Vechten that the title would "be hated" and Countee Cullen was "white with hurt" over it.[51] Du Bois wrote a scathing review in the *Crisis,* directly undermining an earlier advertisement for the book in the journal;[52] in the review, the editor advised folks "who are impelled by a sense of duty or curiosity to drop the book gently in the grate."[53] Not surprisingly, the controversy boosted sales and dragged Van Vechten's black friends into a spiral of negative commentary from the black press. By the end of 1926, criticism of the so-called cabaret school took the place of sustained engagement with the novel. In particular, black women were blamed for many signs of "depravity" accompanying the white invasion of Harlem indexed by *Nigger Heaven*.[54] To these critics, racial solidarity should have prevented New Negro women like Larsen from playing the role of escort for folks like Van Vechten.

Anxiety over loss of control of the New Negro movement seized much of the black middle class and conditioned the reception of nearly every work to appear thereafter. When Claude McKay's *Home to Harlem* was published in 1928, it became a bestseller; it was also scorched by the black press for allegedly reveling in the "squalor and vice" championed by Van Vechten. In a letter to Alain Locke, Langston Hughes chirped that he was "wild about [it]. It ought to be named *Nigger Hell*, but I guess the colored papers will have even greater spasms than before anyhow. It's the best low-life novel I've ever read. . . . Up till [sic] now, it strikes me, that *Home to Harlem,* must be the flower of the Negro Renaissance,—even if it is no lovely lily."[55] The popularity of *Home to Harlem* among downtowners convinced many "old school" observers that white tastes were fully steering the movement into the gutter. And so, when Larsen's inaugural novel was published a few weeks after McKay's, it was read as an entrant in the contest between racial uplift and racial exploitation: "Larsen's *Quicksand* . . . would seem to them [McKay's detractors] just the antidote they were looking for. The reaction against McKay so conditioned responses to *Quicksand* that it blinded most readers to Larsen's main concerns [female restraint and moral policing], that she would go down to posterity, paired with Jessie Fauset, as an apologist for the light-skinned black elite."[56] It is ironic that Larsen was viewed as being a kindred spirit with Du Bois's sidekick; it was nearly perverse to presume that her work neatly aligned with New Negro racial orthodoxy.

Although *Quicksand* made Larsen a New Negro star, her celebrity was also constitutive of aesthetic practices structuring a neglect of the ethical and affective dimensions of her speech. While fully engaged in loud and luminous New Negro spectacles above and below 110th Street, Larsen was being enveloped by a mysterious voicelessness. Partially muzzled and straitjacketed by competing notions of how race figured in the artistic and aesthetic practices of the New Negro, Larsen sought release from this grip. But she was not necessarily attempting to get away from race, as some critics have surmised. It is more productive and provocative to think her writing as transfusing, rather than escaping race; as pushing "blackness" and "whiteness" through alternating and fluid forms of difference and equivalence and as scarring the subjects who sought to resist the flow. As *Quicksand* sold briskly, her readers increasingly wedged her into convenient cultural binaries offered up by the aesthetic practices circulating through Harlem; she was pitted against artistic practices deemed harmful to the race even while being linked to black folks' dangerous admirers.[57] *Passing* was conceived and entirely written within this stifling and exciting context. One way to begin an encounter with *Passing* is to sense how the work caught its breath and released it through a break in New Negro consciousness.

"Really, 'Rene, I'm not safe."[58]

Sitting in her bedroom sifting through her morning mail, Irene Redfield does not wish to be reminded of unfulfilled desires. The ordinary correspondences occupying her time, helping to secure her forgetfulness, are comforting in the way they ease her into her dawn rituals. But this particular sunrise is different; "the long envelope of thin Italian paper with its almost illegible scrawl seemed out of place and alien."[59] Despite its mysterious character, the letter Irene pinches between anxious fingers registers strong and doubled recollections; memories of a friend's desperate childhood and of a fleeting, disturbing embrace two years ago are stirred. In a sense, the letter appears to come from nowhere—having neither return address nor a name—and Irene knows immediately that Clare Kendry sent it. The opening pages of *Passing* rehearses the novel's intensity and magnetism. Irene recognizes who authored the letter, but is fully aware of the fact that she does not really know Clare at all; she recalls her admiration and incomprehension of her; she feels the "danger . . . [in] the letter's content . . . and she disliked the idea of opening and reading it." Before the reader has turned the first page, one recognizes that Larsen has pushed Irene into Clare's gravitational field, locating her near what Albert Camus has explored as the absurd, the recognition of an "illusory meaning" for existence; sense-making is a habit of mind that comforts the subject. One's world, however, can at any moment become a dazzling fragmentation. "From the moment absurdity is recognized," Camus writes, "it becomes a passion, the most harrowing of all."[60] To Irene, Clare seems to always somehow illuminate this illusion; she withholds the unity of time and place by dancing on their outer limits: "This, she reflected, was of a piece with all that she knew of Clare Kendry. Stepping always on the edge of danger. Always aware, but not drawing back or turning aside. Certainly not because of any alarms or feeling of outrage on the part of others."[61] Using three case studies to explore Lacanian anxiety, Joan Copjec draws this relevant conclusion: "All three [studies, Charlie Chaplin, a voyeur, and a mental patient], concentrated in some activity, are caught off-guard by a disturbance . . . that thwarts their willed concentration, seems to come from outside, from some other place, but actually comes from the very core of their being. In each case the disturbance functions as a counterweight, an unexpected resistance that causes a swerve in the main flow of activity." Still fingering the slim envelope, Irene wants to run away from Clare—to be rid of her. But she, too, is "riveted."[62] Filled with dreadful anticipation, Irene Redfield slowly opens the letter.

Clare's letter provokes three occurrences: it sets in motion Irene's desires, it dramatizes "passing" as creative and chaotic, and it unsettles powerful racial fantasies. The letter gushes forth Clare's "terrible, wild desire" to see Irene again. It confesses that Clare endures "an ache, a pain that never ceases." Although Irene is alarmed by the appearance of even a trace of Clare's body in purple ink, she wades through page after page of Clare's emotional torrent. And these feverish waters sweep her mind back two years to a sweltering August day spent shopping in Chicago, and to her escape from the heat into a cool rooftop restaurant where she became the object of a penetrating gaze from across the room. Irene wondered nervously to herself: "Did that woman, could that woman, somehow know that here before her very eyes on the roof of the Drayton sat a Negro?" Irene had "passed" into the white space of the restaurant and now feared an outing. Recall the aesthetic practices placing *Passing* in "white" space for consumption. The reader is moved from an encounter with a work of allegedly conventional interest, through an excruciating (queer) yearning, and into intimate contact with a challenge to the aesthetic understanding that race can be determined through the senses. Having been perceived as white while shopping in "white" Chicago, Irene considered and then dismissed the possibility of her blackness being disclosed by this white spectator: "Absurd! Impossible! White people were so stupid about such things for all that they usually asserted that they were able to tell; and by the most ridiculous means, finger-nails, palms of hands, shapes of ears, teeth, and other equally silly rot. . . . No, the woman sitting there staring at her couldn't possibly know." Clare approached, intensifying Irene's feeling of danger, and marking it with a sense of the erotic. "Irene studied the lovely creature standing beside her for some clue to her identity. . . . Her lips, painted a brilliant geranium-red, were sweet and sensitive and a little obstinate. A tempting mouth. . . . And the eyes were magnificent! dark, sometimes absolutely black, always luminous, and set in long, black lashes. Arresting eyes, slow and mesmeric, and with, for all their warmth, something withdrawn and secret about them."[63]

Irene's appreciation for Clare's beauty shapes their reunion and reminiscences and charges a dialectical tension between them that becomes tauter throughout the novel. Clare tells Irene that she has "thought of [Irene] often and often," whereas, after Clare left the old neighborhood, Irene has "never given [Clare] a thought." Clare explained that she decided to "pass" because she "wanted things," but Irene rebuffed her, saying, "You see, Clare, I've everything I want. Except, perhaps, a little more money." Clare's existence as "white" was fraught with the danger of an outing; Irene's life as a New Negro was a "smooth routine." The novel exercises this tension, expanding and contracting it like a tendon. Importantly, much of this movement is dramatized by Larsen as occurring between Irene's conscious and unconscious states; she attributes an uncommon beauty to Clare—"she's almost too good-looking"—but her body "wholly rebel[s]" at the idea of passing. She considers passing an "abhorrent thing," and yet "the truth was she was curious. . . . She wished to find out about this hazardous business of 'passing,' this breaking away from all that was familiar and friendly to take one's chances in another environment, not entirely strange, perhaps, but certainly not entirely friendly." Clare's "having way" is productive of a troubling convergence of beauty and whiteness.[64] Irene's interest in passing cannot be disarticulated from her admiration of Clare's good looks, and thus it is also sutured to whiteness as an aesthetic value. Here, whiteness, beauty, mobility, and consumption make up a discursive formation responsible for a mode of attraction that is palpable to Irene. Her body "wholly rebels," but not from passing; Irene's body revolts against her repressive mastery over it. As a phenomenon associated with movement, "passing" brings to life dimensions of Irene's motivations that are asleep, and aggravates her loyalty to blackness by bonding them to beautiful whiteness. Irene is being drawn from the social space of comfort and familiarity and toward the space of alluring terror.

We should take a moment to consider a set of contradictions in *Passing* that clarify the significance of the tropological alignment noted above and mark its distinction from narratives of passing occupying Larsen's historical era. During this initial get-together, Irene expresses disgust at the notion of passing, but since she was passing when she met Clare, the animus is partial, not whole: "her reason partly agreed."[65] Irene understands that passing could reasonably be a tactic for material acquisition—like a cool drink in an exclusive restaurant. Irene's recollection of their childhood reveals that Clare was the only child of a drunken father who labored as a janitor. In a community of wannabe bourgeoisie, Clare was an outcast as the bastard child of a poor, sullen bum. Clare's inevitable departure from blackness is not simply about getting things, it is the logical extension of being denied the consumptive authority legitimized by the black community into which she was born. Clare's passing is not mobilized simply for "having," it is invigorated as a way of "making." Following the death of her father, Clare is completely destitute; passing is a way to constitute new social spaces that are, in turn, altered by her being there.

And we should mull over the significance of Irene's dismissal of white senses "knowing" blackness; she herself did not have a "clue to [Clare's] identity." Her black sensitivity for spotting Negroes failed her. The important point is not that Irene is simply mistaken about her assumption that Clare is white; neither can this failure be adequately accounted for by saying that in this "white" space atop the Drayton Hotel, Irene does not expect to come across another passing black person and, thus, is not attuned for sensing blackness. The ontology of race is utterly called into question. Irene is not the only observer drawn toward the "tempting mouth" of the absurd. The reader, too, might experience vertigo due to a dizzying affect emerging from the opening where certitude used to pose. Race is, of course, never skin deep, but common aesthetic understandings of it coerce its signature onto the surface of our bodies. *Passing* contemplates an awe-full erasure—no signature and nothing to notarize. Swinging like a pendulum between feeling "petted and caressed" by Clare and being "through with Clare," Irene resists the realization that Clare "had for her a fascination, strange and compelling."[66] Larsen's biographer describes Clare as "the nearly perfect human embodiment of a fetish";[67] and Judith Butler notes that what remains unspoken by either woman, the narrator articulates as " 'queer' or as 'queering.' "[68] Clare is deeply disruptive and she marks her friend as an open-ended subject by breaking off a part of her name and calling her "'Rene." I wish to extend this last observation: that Clare, as the object-cause of Irene's desire, opens a gap in Irene's world that is experienced as lovely and horrific; that she tears the fabric of the order of identity; that she emanates an electrical charge that short-circuits attempts at restoration, reconciliation, or remediation. As such, the work of *Passing* is always already doubly dissembling. I shall return to these annotations later, but for the present we must follow Irene's anxious path toward that gap.

Clare invites Irene to tea at her home later in the week. She might have wanted Irene to get close to the "hazardous business" central to her life; she might have been lonely, as her later letter professed. Irene agrees to attend the gathering but feels as if she is watching someone else caught in a trance, like a spectator bemused by a stranger on puppet strings. "Clare met her in the hall with a kiss," awakening her from her dream-like state. Irene immediately begins to warm to the idea of spending the afternoon there. Much to Irene's chagrin, however, the tea is a threesome. Sitting in the parlor is Gertrude Martin, another childhood friend from the old neighborhood, also now "passing." The scene strains to maintain credulity as it stages a conversation among three "black" (white) women regarding the constraints that race imposed on their bodies. Gertrude zeroes in on the crux of the matter, the always-lurking bad seed. The historical imperative here is tremendous; the female body is the site of racial regeneration and degeneration; it is viewed with suspicion precisely because birthing is a doubled phenomenon. It begets radical possibility—a break from what was—and as a trope birth emits "aliveness." Hence, racial (dis)continuity is immanent as an essential capacity. Moreover, as race is destabilized, it re-groups its "authenticity" through rhetoric of biological reproduction. Even though each woman has white-like skin, one may be betrayed by maternity: "But, of course, nobody wants a dark child,"[69] Gertrude puts it flatly. As the mother of darker children, Irene's ire verges on the explosive. But just then, Clare's husband, Jack Bellew, arrives. What ensues is a full blown racial farce verging on the precipice of the outlandish. The scene provides the reader's first and only look into Clare's world, a space of material comfort and leisure, but also where the illusions of race have sharp and gnawing edges. In the presence of Jack, the air is sucked out of the room, leaving a vacuum and near voicelessness.

"Hello Nig," Jack pleasantly greets his wife. Irene and Gertrude glance at each other and then at Clare. Irene briefly wonders if Jack knows Clare was a "Negro." Clare asks him to explain the reference: "'Well, you see, it's like this,' Jack started. 'When we were first married, she was as white as—as—well as white as a lily. But I declare she's gettin' darker and darker. I tell her if she don't look out, she'll wake up one of these days and find she's turned into a nigger.'" Both senses of "passing" operating in *Passing* converged here. Clare has successfully created a life-as-white with Bellew; so much so that her darkening skin no longer signifies race, but merely an innocent change in complexion. Indeed, his interpretive logic is a form of self-preservation, indexing the fragility of a world composed of racial doctrine. What if, Clare asks, after years of marital bliss, "you were to find out that I was 1 or 2 percent coloured?" Jack's reply is at once clear and dense: "You can get as black as you please as far as I'm concerned, since I know you're no nigger. I draw the line at that. No niggers in my family. Never have been and never will be."[70]

Clinging desperately to the (illusive) idea of his family's white "racial" purity, Jack rejects a single drop of "coloured" blood in the body of his (darkening) wife. Clare, thus, lives a partially voiceless existence. She can never speak of her father or of her "black" communal relations before Bellew. Her memories are severed from her speech in her own "home," making it impossible for the affective and ethical dimensions of her (former) life to be acknowledged. It is not so much that "passing" forces Clare to forget family and friends—she recalls them vividly, but they have already forgotten her—it brings about a life-threatening condition. As Audre Lorde has maintained, silence is a form of social death;[71] perhaps this void is the source of that "ache" and "terrible, wild desire" to be with Irene, to be in the company of a person who can endow her voice. In this way, voice enables one's "fuller" being by providing expectations and imaginations regarding one's futurity. Clare seems to need Irene for the sake of her tomorrow. Irene, however, is free-falling. Having been forced to "pass" along with Gertrude and Clare, Irene is deeply offended by Jack's racism and the predicament introduced by Clare. But, she too may not speak of her "blackness" since she is now outside the law. Passing is structured around rules and rituals well-known by the three women and the absurdity of having tea with a racist while attending to his (overturned) superiority and (undermined) racial purity provokes uncontrollable laughter, especially in Irene, who "laughed and laughed and laughed. Tears ran down her cheeks. Her sides ached. Her throat hurt. She laughed on and on and on, long after the others had subsided."[72] Resonating through and around her laughter is the "utterly ambiguous" voice, the "transgressive" sound of affect.[73] Unable to speak of her black indignation, Irene is taken over by the vocal objection of the voice to being silenced. Clare and Gertrude acknowledge its presence. Passing makes this "expression event" possible and conditions its utter ambiguity.[74] The structure of common sense about race falls away, taking Irene on an exhilarating plunge toward the absurd. Her laughter announces her proximity to a terrifying and amazing opening that hurts with enjoyment. Irene's descent is broken, however, by "catching sight of Clare's face, the need for . . . caution, struck her. At once she stopped."[75] Clare's nonverbal communication warns Irene of the danger of allowing the voice to "talk back" to racism for too long. Finally composed, Irene seeks refuge on the street. *Passing* rapidly returns us to the present and to Irene's Harlem home in October and to Clare's letter.

Bellew and Irene share the muting force of fantasy bonded to racial orthodoxy. Her home exhibits trappings of the cult of New Negro womanhood. She employs a dark-skinned maid named Zulenga. She has two sons who are expected to grow to lead the race. She volunteers with all the right charities and organizations. And her husband, Brian, anchors her world as a well-respected physician. *Passing* dramatizes the analogy between Bellew's racist fantasies and Irene's New Negro fantasies. Each of their worlds is hinged by strict racial doctrine structuring social life. The terrorizing excitement of "passing" can be momentarily tolerated by Irene because its affect destabilizes public white spaces and Clare's private white space. Passing could never be endured in her neat, ordered New Negro world. In fact, the rhythm of Irene's daily rituals need masterful orchestration. As such, Brian's discontent with his profession and with the hypocrisy of the United States as the home of the "free," threaten her world. Irene has grown accustomed during their marriage to distracting him from disquieting desires and to imposing a form of voicelessness on him. When sensing his restlessness is peaking, primarily through a rise in her own anxiety over wrinkles in the fabric of her seamless life, Irene devises diversions. One in particular is helpful here. One evening Irene concocts a crisis with "Junior" regarding him getting from schoolmates "some queer ideas about things." Although the reference is oblique, Brian sutures it to his own deep-seated sexual dissatisfaction: "The sooner and the more he learns about sex, the better for him. And most certainly if he learns that it's a grand joke, the greatest in the world. It'll keep him from lots of disappointments later on." Brian does not share Irene's bed.[76] Not only is sexual repression staged as a constitutive feature of Irene's fantasies in order to maintain her world, Irene cannot acknowledge the ethical and affective dimensions of Brian's outburst. His speech is like a roadblock that she must veer around to stay on course. In Irene Redfield's home, the production of voicelessness is a New Negro strategy.

Evasion was another strategy Irene executed. She ignores Clare's "wild, terrible desires." Ignores them, that is, until Clare enunciates them in person during an uninvited visit to Harlem. Voice and voicelessness index for us the resonation of anxiety and the dampening operations working through it. Clare arrives unannounced and, without knocking, barges into Irene's bedroom. In her most intimate space, passing sets off tremors throughout Irene's body and clang alarms in her head. Clare, however, seems still in need of a sincere addressee: "But I did think you'd understand, 'Rene. It was that [Jack's racism] partly, that has made me want to see other people. It just swooped down and changed everything. If it hadn't been for that, I'd have gone on to the end, never seeing any of you. But that did something to me, and I've been so lonely since! You can't know. Not close to a single soul. Never anyone to *really* talk to." Irene feels snagged in a catch-22; on the one hand, the acknowledgment of the affective and ethical aspects of Clare's speech endowing her voice might cause Irene's world to fall apart. On the other hand, Clare is "black" and New Negro orthodoxy encourages her to mend "race" relations among "black" people in the name of solidarity: "She was caught between two allegiances, different, yet the same. Herself. Her race. Race! The thing that bound and suffocated her. Whatever steps she took, or if she took none at all, something would be crushed. A person or the race. Clare, herself, or the race. Or, it might be all three. Nothing, she imagined, was ever more completely sardonic."[77]

Irene's central motive for the remainder of the novel involves managing the tension between her fantasies formalized by New Negro racial beliefs and the disruptive forces of passing. Clare's beautiful black (white) body functions as a capacitor for these upsetting forces—drawing them together, accelerating them, and unleashing their potential. Clare is experienced by everyone in Irene's social circles as a dynamo. She insists on attending the "Negro Welfare League Dance" being organized by Irene and her friends. At the shindig, she galvanizes attention as a racially ambiguous object of beauty. But the uncertainty is deeper than folks' confusion over whether she is black or white. As a black woman passing as a white woman passing (back) into the black community, she is both a foreigner—a tourist—and a prodigal daughter. She de-familiarizes the familiar; she intrigues Brian; and she terrorizes Irene. Convinced that Clare wants Brian (and may have already "had" him), Irene obsessed over darning the frayed edges of her life. She seems willing to ignore the possibility that Brian and Clare are having an affair: "It hurt. It hurt like hell. But it didn't matter, if no one knew. If everything could go on like before. If the boys were safe." It is tempting to say that Irene is neurotic, disturbed enough to self-impose voicelessness for the sake of a fantasy providing her sanctuary. She will not (cannot) acknowledge to herself the full depth and range of the affective and ethical character of Clare's passing: "Security. Was it just a word? If not, then was it only by the sacrifice of other things, happiness, love, or some wild ecstasy that she had never known, that it could be obtained?"[78] Neurosis privatizes the ailment. *Passing,* however, stages a psychosis emanating throughout the social body.

As fate would have it, a chance encounter downtown begins a series of events that unravels Irene's predicament and everything else. Irene is shopping with a Harlem friend, Felise Freeland, when she literally bumps into Bellew. Initially, Jack is happy to once again make Irene's acquaintance, but then he spied Felise who is "golden, with curly black Negro hair." Irene, feeling "that instinctive loyalty to a race," feigns non-recognition of Jack and rushes Felise along. The damage has been already done; Bellew knows enough about the sociality of race relations and segregation to surmise that Negroes typically mingle with other Negroes. We learn that he lies to Clare about a business trip to Philadelphia over the weekend, so he can stalk her to Harlem and discover her secret and unearth his horror. At a dinner party at Felise's home, Bellew barges into the parlor: "'So,'" he screams, "'you're a nigger, a damned dirty nigger!'" His intrusion and frothed anger provoke a stir among the partygoers; some men restrain Bellew, but all eyes are on Clare: "Clare stood at the window, as composed as if everyone were not staring at her in curiosity and wonder. . . . There was even a faint smile on her full, red lips, and in her shining eyes." During the melee, Irene has moved to her side and "laid a hand on Clare's bare arm." And Clare goes out the window.[79]

The question that haunts readers of *Passing* is: how does Clare die? The novel suggests that Irene murders her in a panic; if Clare were "outed," she would be free to stay in Harlem, forever challenging Irene's sanity. At the window, Irene advances upon Clare for the first time in the novel, initiating her only touch. Larsen narrates a meltdown metastasized through denial; Irene is consumed by a negative critique that continuously attacks the ground of any conviction about what happened to Clare. In a sense, we see the operations of a guilty conscience. But guilty of what? Of feeling relieved that Clare is gone? Guilty of shoving her out of the window? At the point in the work when the narrator usually speaks what Irene cannot bring herself to say, the narrator's voice drifts into the fog enveloping Irene's psyche. And what did that "faint smile" on Clare's lips mean just before going out the window? *Passing* never allows the reader access to Clare's thoughts, only her speech. Clare speaks of the sting of being forgotten; we can reasonably conjecture that she wants to be remembered and she wants her memories to be public. And one suspects while reading the work that Clare is always "acting," shape-shifting for her private amusement. Hence, she may have seized upon the moment at the Freeland's (at free-land) to stage her greatest performance. Her suicide would be a form of escape that would never be forgotten. To ponder such possibilities engages one in thinking a murder/suicide.

It is in this peculiarity that *Passing* is doubly dissembling. The work seems to conceal the "truth" of Clare's demise within Irene's damaged mind. Her trauma forms a scab under which the key is hidden. This perspective encourages the reader to put Irene on the "couch," to become her analyst. But Larsen has employed psychoanalysis itself as a metaphor throughout the work. Larsen's artistic practices invent a discourse of the perpetual motion of the signifier—*it* is passing. We may pick at the scab all that we want—indeed, the work encourages it so as to regenerate the wound—but there will be no key, no code. What we unearth is the indivisible difference of murder/suicide. In thinking this difference, we sense the affect of passing. This sensation regards the intensity of resonance over and against signification, its excess and overabundance. When associated with race, we at once can appreciate the intensity of the trope of race and its gap. The love (and hate) for the (New) Negro makes sense when one remembers that human beings were bonded (and divorced) by tropes of race in a struggle for freedom and power. We also see that the laws and orders race makes are illusory. The work of *Passing* calls attention to the unclosable gap at the heart of race. Thinking race in this manner highlights the perpetual participation of the virtual in the actual, the "not-yet" in the "is," making the point of contact between the two a space of no-thingness, and, of everythingness; a paradox. But Larsen did provide an image of this paradox—the window. Its frame was the arbitrary boundary through which one sees the world. Clare momentarily stood in that gap and then disappeared. Passing from black to white and passing from life to death, Clare haunts the opening and our contemplation of it. *Passing* moves us to think our identities and social places—race, sex, gender, and class—as constitutive of anxious tropes that can only be partially suffered by being grafted onto a beautiful specter. As we sense that Clare is a ghost, we can no longer lay claim to her phantasmic body. And, since Larsen did not replace her, we are left (forever) thinking of an open window.

Pragmatically speaking, *Passing* was utilized by New Negro leaders like Du Bois as a stopgap measure. Since Larsen did not take white readers on a tour of Harlem's seedy underground and back alleys, she received high praise from the editor for changing direction from the course of the "cabaret writers" and the typical passing narrative: "Nella Larsen attempts quite a different thing," he wrote. "She explains just what 'passing' is." But we should wonder what Du Bois thought Larsen explained. He applauded *Passing*'s "simplicity and charm" and ordered readers of the *Crisis* to buy the book.[80] Such a command to purchase and consume, although certainly what Larsen would have wanted financially, seems evasive. Du Bois was fond of giving marching orders, but is that what passing is? The aesthetic practice of mobilizing the race used by regimes like the *Crisis* and *Opportunity* was at odds with Larsen's sense of passing. One of the tricks of passing resembles the work of the escape artist who looks for openings through which to act "out." In dire circumstances, this performance may scar the audience while making onlookers complicit in forms of violent death—particularly of women. For example, Booker T. Washington's death was marked by "a terrific scandal" at Tuskegee. Adella Hunt Logan, wife of the "Acting Principle," had been committed to a sanitarium in Michigan for "female hysteria." Mr. Logan, it was widely rumored, was having an affair, and Mrs. Logan might have endured the public humiliation associated with this alleged indiscretion for some time before Washington made the arrangements personally to have her shipped off. She was allowed to return to campus "hours before Booker T. Washington's death." Larsen was a nurse at the hospital, where "on Friday, December 10, while the famous trustees were gathering on campus, she [Logan] walked to a fourth-floor window of the academic building, in which her sister and daughter were teaching, and jumped, breaking her body on the pavement below."[81]

Masculine (im)morality indexed the space of feminine incarceration and escape through a suddenly available opening. Thinking murder/suicide, we can recall how Larsen, after being accused of plagiarizing a short story called "Sanctuary," published in *Forum* in 1930, was beginning to be pushed aside in Harlem. Some of the histories of the 135th Street Library barely register her involvement beyond a footnote. Like Clare, Larsen's passing haunts the spaces among the aesthetic practices of New Negro regimes. She was made hyper-visible and semi-voiceless; she was briefly celebrated then dismissed; her work has been theorized and conceived as brilliant and confounding. By acknowledging the affective and ethical aspects of her speech, we can become sensitive to the manner in which *Passing* evokes misgivings. The issue is not simply that the New Negro rhetorical culture was both beautiful and ugly; we must not settle on conclusions that parade clairvoyance and insight, for these spectacles take place through shimmering rituals of omission. We can, however, find solace (if not joy) in the fleeting (and recurring) notion that New Negro aesthetic and artistic practices were underwritten by rhetorical phenomena gesturing, sometimes under extreme duress, toward openings and gaps—toward the new.

Postscript

The New Negro movement was pronounced dead by 1935. This obituary in part reflected the economic catastrophe that impelled some formerly wealthy persons to fling themselves out of office windows. The death notice was true in the sense that the declaration followed a terse alteration in the quality and intensity of interest in black art. Many people simply could no longer afford to be so indulgent; other folks were gripped by the kind of depression that made a quest for art's pleasures seem like an absurdly moot adventure. The putative demise of the New Negro movement, however, was predicated upon a conceptual error that separated—and then killed—the energetic sociality that emerged through the "work" of the work of art.[1] Pronouncements regarding the failure of the New Negro movement to invent a viable black aesthetics paralleled the logic organizing its funeral; that is, the production of a revelatory aesthetic state of blackness was thought to have come to an end with no lasting effects—and that was that. My work regarding tropes of the New Negro is supported by a theoretical orientation that does not precisely allow us to bring the dead to life so much as it unearths the warm bodies thought to have turned to dust in the early stages of the last century. The New Negro movement should be appreciated as a phenomenal *movement* of tropes of race that set up relations and opened up places for becoming black (and white) and for valuing blackness (and whiteness) that resonated well beyond the spatiotemporal dimensions of 1920s Harlem. We should spend a little time considering two qualities of "movement" that usually get bracketed when the topic of the New Negro movement is broached: first, the New Negro movement was dynamic, involving displacement, dispersal, and motion. Second, such action emulsified commonplaces, inclusions, and exclusions in social life; and, thus, New Negro aesthetic practices established the basic requirements for rethinking racial identifications and politics.

Aesthetic experience is potentially achieved through sensation and motion. We have contemplated how tropes of race provided an intense sensory experience that could at once hold one's attention and launch one's imagination. One could be caught in a suspenseful force and be flung out of oneself. Tropes of the New Negro were carefully calibrated to pulse through complex energy circuits, bonding with alignments and configurations that provided pathways for resonance and radiation, or for blunt grounding and termination. The significance of the New Negro movement must be thought of in terms of the polemical character of the operations of tropological coalitions and annulments, rather than solely in terms of the specific judgments of its art objects. The distinction is enormous. On the one hand, the manufacture of taste remains steeped in motives regarding hierarchies of beauty that are often posited as residing outside of the forces that produced them. The artist becomes a "genius" and the work of art a "masterpiece," and the operations that bonded these tropes into a form fit for the canon are obscured by the presumption that the beautiful is "real" and "true" and somehow not historically derived. Indeed, a key task for modernity has been to unify and universalize these operations, hiding their politics through a careful and necessary production of the modern subject implicated in individualism and privacy.[2]

On the other hand, the importance of the circulation of tropes of the New Negro can be appreciated in terms of the emergence and coherence of values promoting and disposing of forms of social life.[3] We must reflect on the modes of thought that clashed as the New Negro movement distributed black sensibility, audibility, and consumption. We should figure the ways in which "new" forms of aesthetic and artistic practices opened up modes of speech and how these practices were always already being "raced"; how these speech acts put ways of being on notice as outdated or overdue; and how these discursive formations can be attended to so as to bring ourselves into productive relation with the radically contingent material conditions people inhabited as they fought to improve their lives. This last implication marks the point of my project's departure. Interested in the rhetorical significance of voice, I began my inquiry into the New Negro movement with a consideration of the problem of bringing forth the affective and ethical dimensions of speech. I sensed that a neglected aspect of rhetorical studies involved thinking the intervention of the speaking subject into the circulatory system of culture and value, but without giving oneself over to the mastery of the speaker or the privileging of isolated speech texts. By focusing on the character and motion of the trope of the New Negro, I am positing it as the sort of "object" needed in Rhetorical Studies and in American Studies—one that requires the researcher to be sensitive to multiple spaces and complex temporalities.[4] Thomas B. Farrell, in *Norms of Rhetorical Culture,* attempted to situate a productive humanism into the interstices of sociality and politics.[5] Michael McGee rearticulated the "text" as a fragment where one could "read" the complicity of a Marxist materialism through a Burkean discursivity.[6] The value of these works cannot be underestimated. Farrell, for instance, labored mightily for poiesis to implicate the affective and ethical as well as the creative, so much so that he left the reader of *Norms* contemplating the eternal connotations of the term by positing "life" as his last (and lingering) word on the subject.[7]

Life takes shape and moves in vectors that can be traced and charted. It is a vibratory energy that holds, binds, and disintegrates. Signifiers radiate (are alive) with the affective capacity for discourses to move us. Of course, when speaking of signification I am not referencing affect per se; in communicative contexts our sensations of this primal life force is mediated. Part of the task of rhetoric, then, is to map and assess how discourses cohere, dissolve, or explode in social and political life in rhythm with the currents of affect. Complementing studies of persuasion, we need to theorize how we may become magnetized to forms of speech or performances of bodies, and how we may be repelled and disgusted. Our responses are intricately social and so we develop habits of relations to these practices and occurrences and learn to think of them as "true" and "good," "bad" and "obscene" because we prefer to do so, because they satisfy us in significant ways. Furthermore, we invent modes of speech that mold and constitute these feelings, and coordinate and coax their development in others. In this way, affect is a bonding force of the social. This overview, however, is thin and weak because it does not account for the first person, the "I" precariously holding the place of an emotional moment along the wavelengths of affect. And why is this inscription important? Not due to a claim regarding the autonomy of "I" and its agency; rather, because the power marking a moment of rhetorical efficacy is, in part, conceivable as an alteration in intensity of affect—a dampening, a strengthening, a redirecting. "I" may be able to see the frustration in the face of a friend when "I" object to a proposition she sets forth. But if we emphasize the capacity of the optical too much, we give away key facets of what we ironically call "insight." As subjects we feel toward objects in our social worlds, thus, our unseen, sensed, and habituated relations to what we claim to know about our behaviors, values, and attitudes are imbricated in this "insight."

Rhetoric is peculiarly capable of providing an account of the discursive activity and of the contexts in which we make this sense. Although we have the ability to "see" some of the work of sense-making, we can also listen for its harmonics and frequencies, drawing us toward—or driving us away—from the "I" (or "them" or "us") holding the place of an affective spike or vocalizing a shriek. Ranciere gestures in the direction of the art of rhetoric when he notes: "Whatever might be the specific type of economic circuits they lie within, artistic practices are not 'exceptions' to other practices. They represent and reconfigure the distribution of these activities."[8] Aristotle understood the potential to represent and reconfigure the social order in terms of persons being able to discern in any given situation and at any given time the accessible modes of making and performing speech. The capacity of discernment is critical to rhetorical invention, and discernment should not be reduced to the sense of sight. I have been saying throughout this work that in US sociality, tropes of race have always been particularly sonorous. Rather than treat the sounds of affect as ambient noises, as distractions from the real work of rhetoric, I have tried to show in this work the richness that is acquired when voice is endowed in an acknowledgment of the affective and ethical dimensions of speech. US politics and sociality have been doggedly haunted by the affects of "race" and some scholars have struggled with equal intensity to move beyond race, or "against" it. Paul Gilroy describes the task of accounting for the movement of tropes of race in this way: "As actively depoliticized consumer culture has taken hold, the world of racialized appearances has become invested with another magic. . . . Layer upon layer of easily commodified exotica have culminated in a racialized glamour and contributed an extra cachet to some degree of nonspecific, somatic difference. . . . The stimulating pattern of this hyper-visibility supplies the signature of a corporate multiculturalism in which some degree of visible difference from an implicit white norm may be highly prized as a sign of timeliness, vitality, inclusivity, and global reach."[9] The Harlem Renaissance is the popular name that has be assigned to this potent example of the emergence and configuration of the racialized circuitry concerning black cultural studies. I have outlined elsewhere the complicated troubles of efforts to address race and to better our understanding of it.[10] The New Negro movement offered a unique environment in which to figure the alterations and habituation of ideas, moods, desires, and fears cultivated and generated through the flows of tropes of race.

We have also been concerned in this work with the struggles among cultural institutions to determine (or overdetermine) these movements and currents. At its heart, aesthetics concerns "the specific mode of being of whatever falls within the domain of art, to the mode of being of the objects of art."[11] The New Negro movement enveloped much more than books, essays, poems, and the theater; it seized within its circumference the actual bodies of writers—their histories and dreams. It also marked a peculiar moment where modernity could bear witness to its own disclosure as a paradigm manufacturing consensus regarding the kind of regimes "proper" to its authority.

Ranciere discusses three sorts of regimes satisfying different political agendas: the ethical, the representative, and the aesthetic. Platonic idealism shaped the ethical regime of the arts, where all productive activities were judged by their relation to the Truth. Within an ethical regime, forms of leisure for the ruling classes were secured by the mode of thought that held a person in a space of work for which one was "authentically" fit. Moreover, a worker only had the time to do one thing for society. And so, one's occupation kept one from producing democratic governance since one's work was private. This is why the poetic threatened this order: the "work" of the poet ruptured this allocation of time and space by producing "objects" specifically for public display, and by producing a "worker" no longer confined to a single place and time; the poet's work, then, doubled spaces and times and constituted a form of citizenship.[12]

Mimesis is the hallmark of the representative regime of the arts. Promoted in part by an Aristotelian revolt against the ethical regime, representation does not name an essential characteristic of the arts, it labels a strategy for "freeing" signifiers to roam indifferently among communities and locations, times and places. It also asserts a structure for organizing artistic practices and objects into genres and norms. It establishes a logic for narration and action that indicates, if perceived critically, a governing "law" of social determinations. To practice an art of making resemblances is not simply to enter into a specific kind of craft dedicated to depicting the world as the artist sees it; rather, representation "organizes . . . ways of doing, making, seeing and judging" that can be linked to complementary and contradictory powerful interests.[13] Whereas ethical regimes privilege a form of epistemic certitude, representative regimes promote dynamic and fluid relations among forms of "subjectivity" and "objectivity," institutions and communities. Each regime, however, produces a blueprint for the design of community. And so, it should not sound odd to hear that US slavery was upheld, in part, by modes of thought associated with an ethical regime.

The very idea of "race" and of a racial hierarchy emerged in Western thought as a way of organizing a permanent forced labor class and was distributed throughout networks obeying convoluted rules of a representative regime. We have seen how the circulation of tropes of blackness produced forms of violent white supremacy and how artistic practices of black folk masked tactics of resistance. Although Ranciere associates the domination of the ethical regime with Plato, modernity harnesses the affects of such idealism within the same action that authorizes the judgment of images of race as authentic or false, as beautiful or ugly, as valuable or worthless. This project resides in the fold alluded to above, in the crevice where the residue of the ethical regime gets pasted to the deployment of energetic tropes of race legitimized and organized by the author function of the representative regime.[14] In a sense, the New Negro was a doubled trope; it drew upon some powerful sentiments associated with the aesthetic values of an ethical regime—a distribution of sensibility ordered on the idea that "Negroes" occupy singular spatiotemporal coordinates articulated as one's "proper place." New Negro artistic practices, however, disturbed the memories of racial singularity by asserting black artists and art, by refusing to be silent and transparent. The New Negro constituted aesthetic practices of representative regimes marked by drives for social justice and structured by civil rights institutions and New York City's art world. Understood in this way, Du Bois's insistence upon "agitation" as an artistic practice of the New Negro not only extended a protest tradition, it posited black activists as indexing the avant-garde.

The trope of the New Negro was doubled by the twin senses of avant-garde. On the one hand, black intellectuals like Du Bois and Alain Locke sought to consign an army. This "military notion" specified a massive force advancing the goals of civil rights through unified, coordinated efforts.[15] From this perspective, the training of the youth took on a fierce urgency and constituted forms of control through stiff alignments of the images and sounds of blackness. Du Bois's *Darkwater,* then, was a kind of field manual laying bare the relations between the key fronts in a war—between the aesthetic values of whiteness and the operations of a vast circuitry of discourses materializing a hierarchy of race. *The New Negro: An Interpretation* was more than a sacred text, it articulated a sophisticated strategy for realigning the aesthetic practices of New York City's representative regimes. Importantly, tropes of the New Negro provided the vigor and the vehicle for provoking debates, disagreements, and for bonding temporary alliances regarding techne for black aesthetics. We should keep in mind that the sort of debate sponsored by the *Crisis* in 1926, "The Negro in Art: How Shall He Be Portrayed? A Symposium," signified much more than a failed consensus; it more properly registered a "dissensus"; an activity that ripped across former "stable" identities and political practices to make visible and audible "new" objects and subjects.[16] It marked the volatility that allowed black artists to have a say in the ongoing production of prevailing taste. The New Negro movement should be credited with this breakthrough.

The military function of the avant-garde could be considered militant, but not radical. New Negroes were ordered in line and issued marching orders. But one cannot seal off affect and one cannot police poiesis. And so, it should not be considered a shortcoming of the movement when folks like Langston Hughes, Wallace Thurman, and Nella Larsen refused to close ranks. Indeed, the very possibility for the emergence of black art depended in part on such insubordination. We should not expect art to behave. Thus, the avant-garde also suggests an "aesthetic anticipation of the future," the horizon where one can bring to oneself a radical openness, a denial of limits and a disruption of the spatiotemporal order. By contemplating the two senses of avant-garde, we have come upon Ranciere's third kind of regime—the aesthetic: "The aesthetic state is a *pure instance of suspension,* a moment when form is experienced for itself. Moreover, it is the moment of the formation and education of a specific type of humanity."[17] The aesthetic regime seeks to unleash the power of affect in artistic practices; it seeks to breathe life into human action and thought.

The New Negro brought together new coalition forces and roused their alignments; this "internal" tension seized civil rights dreams and the fantasies of the primitivist. When Carl Van Vechten went gaga over the New Negro, his desires were fused with the hopes of James Weldon Johnson. The representative regime promised each of these men a picture of social life where race would hold out revivalist sensations, where Harlem would actually become a sign of black modernity and peasantry. Each vision, however, relied upon the concept of verisimilitude ensconced in the representative regime. This mimetic principle bonded tropes of the primitive and the "ultra modern" as "authentic." But tropes of race are always heating up, transfiguring into combustible formations that suddenly break apart, fracture, or crack up. These moments of "fire" paralleled the emergencies that registered as a kind of estrangement indexed by aesthetic regimes: "The idea of modernity would like there to be only one meaning and direction in history, whereas the temporality specific to the aesthetic regime of the arts is a co-presence of heterogeneous temporalities."[18] It is in this vital respect that the hope for an energetic black aesthetics was not hampered by disputes between folks like Du Bois and Booker T. Washington, Langston Hughes and George Schuyler. The infighting signaled the active production of the very political subjectivities required to imagine the radical possibilities of black aesthetics.

And finally, these possibilities demand that we be sensitive to the moments when the objects of artistic and aesthetic practices place before us our own humanity for inspection, interrogation, and transformation. Each of the chapters in this work offers such a moment, when a call for agitation revealed the tremendous affects of race hate and redemption; when the manufacture of black publicity required the recognition of neglected intellectual commonplaces; when the politics of the Radical Left were bracketed and excluded from the movements of the New Negro; when the faith of the true believer in racial essences might be shaken by savage satire; when the work of black art was asserted as the systematic development of black self-interest under the banner of propaganda; when Harlem's sexual tourism was shown to be a potent elixir and poison; and when the body under extreme pressure dissolved before one's eyes in the absurd space-time of murder/suicide. In one sense this particular project is here coming to an "end"; but, if it is possible to enact a strategy that inaugurates the aesthetic state propelled through aesthetic regimes, then this project is also just beginning. It looks forward (and backward) toward the idealism associated with the election of the first African American US president. It sets forth a way to appreciate the sustenance made available by such a momentous rupture in political convention. It presents a mode of thinking the "zombie" culture that many "news" outlets have produced—a culture of fear and panic and hysterics that also threaten to infect the Left and the Right.[19] We must acknowledge these affects and act accordingly, endowing voice. This act is neither a panacea nor a remedy to racism or fear; voice is the sound of affect, and so it puts in front of us a choice. It is not a choice between a racial world and a postracial one. In fact, such a binary is no choice at all. Voice announces a way out, an opening through which a future—our future—is very much alive.

Notes

Introduction

1. W. E. B. Du Bois, *Black Reconstruction in America, 1860–1880* (1935; repr., New York: The Free Press, 1992), 725.

2. Du Bois, *Black Reconstruction in America, 1860–1880,* 713.

3. Toni Morrison, *Playing in the Dark: Whiteness and the Literary Imagination* (Cambridge, MA: Harvard University Press, 1992).

4. For slightly different perspectives on who New Negroes were, see Theodore Kornweibel Jr., "*Seeing Red": Federal Campaigns Against Black Militancy, 1919–1925* (Bloomington, IN: Indiana University Press, 1998); Eric King Watts, "African American Ethos and Hermeneutical Rhetoric: An Exploration of Alain Locke's *The New Negro,*" *Quarterly Journal of Speech* 88 (2002): 19–32; Barbara Foley, *Spectres of 1919: Class and Nation in the Making of The New Negro* (Urbana, IL; University of Illinois Press, 2003).

5. See, for example, Nathan Irvin Huggins, *Harlem Renaissance* (New York: Oxford University Press, 1971); J. Martin Favor, *Authentic Blackness: The Folk in the New Negro Renaissance* (Durham, NC: Duke University Press, 1999); Cary Wintz, *The Politics and Aesthetics of "New Negro Literature"* (New York: Garland Press, 1996); James de Jongh, *Vicious Modernism: Black Harlem and the Literary Imagination* (Cambridge, UK: Cambridge University Press, 1990); Houston Baker Jr., *Afro-American Poetics: Revisions of Harlem and the Black Aesthetic* (Madison, WI: University of Wisconsin Press, 1988).

6. See Martha Jane Nadell, *Enter the New Negro: Images of Race in American Culture* (Cambridge: Harvard University Press, 2004); Anne Elizabeth Carroll, *Word, Image, and the New Negro: Representation and Identity in the Harlem Renaissance* (Bloomington, IN: Indiana University Press, 2005); Cherene Sherrard-Johnson, *Portraits of the New Negro Woman: Visual and Literary Culture in the Harlem Renaissance* (New Brunswick, NJ: Rutgers University Press, 2007); and Daphne Lamothe, *Inventing the New Negro: Narrative, Culture, Ethnography* (Philadelphia: University of Pennsylvania Press, 2008).

7. Henry Louis Gates Jr., "The Trope of a New Negro and the Image of the Black," *Representations* 24 (Autumn 1988): 133.

8. See, for example, Arna Bontemps, *Harlem Renaissance Remembered* (New York: Dodd, Mead & Co., 1972); David Levering Lewis, *When Harlem Was in Vogue* (New

York: Oxford University Press, 1979); Nathan Huggins, *Harlem Renaissance* (New York: Oxford University Press, 1971).

9. Foley, *Spectres of 1919.*

10. Lewis, *When Harlem was in Vogue.*

11. Kenneth Burke, "Four Master Tropes," in *A Grammar of Motives* (Berkeley, CA: University of California Press, 1969), 503–17.

12. Burke, "Four Master Tropes," 509, see in particular Burke's discussion of the emotive bonds made possible by synecdoche.

13. See Christopher Bracken, *Magical Criticism: The Recourse of Savage Philosophy* (Chicago: University of Chicago Press, 2007).

14. I am referring to a scale registering quality of exposure to "real" blackness; Zora Neale Hurston often "sold" her findings—churches, geological artifacts, or unknown artists—as old, natural, earthy, and real, thus, "authentically" Negro. See Zora Neale Hurston, letters to Alain Locke, May 1, 1928, and March 24, 1934; Alain Locke, letter to Zora Neale Hurston, October 30, 1934, box 164, folder 22 and 38, in which Locke hoped that her work would be a "credit to real Negro things," Alain Locke Collection, Moorland-Spingarn Research Center, Howard University.

15. Carla Kaplan, *Zora Neale Hurston: A Life in Letters* (New York: Anchor Books, 2003), 35.

Chapter 1

1. W. E. B. Du Bois, *Darkwater: Voices from within the Veil* (1920; repr., NY: Kraus-Thomson, 1975), 9.

2. David Levering Lewis, *W. E. B. Du Bois: Biography of a Race, 1868–1919* (New York: Henry Holt and Co., 1993), 73.

3. Booker T. Washington, *A New Negro for a New Century: An Accurate and Up to Date Record of the Upward Struggles of the Negro Race* (1900; repr., New York: Arno Press, 1969), 92 (emphasis added).

4. See Louis R. Harlan, ed., *The Booker T. Washington papers,* vol. 3 (Urbana, IL: University of Illinois Press, 1974), 583–87.

5. Washington's biographer offers a corrective regarding these differences, arguing that they were based in part on different geographic perspectives; Du Bois was a New Englander who habituated norms related to higher education, while Washington was a Southerner acutely aware of the stresses of working the land. See Robert J. Norrell, *Up from History: The Life of Booker T. Washington* (Cambridge, MA: Harvard University Press, 2009), 1–16.

6. Indeed, Washington's goal for Tuskegee included building the apparatus for black collective industrial farming; also see W. E. B. Du Bois, "An Institute of Negro Literature and Art," *Crisis* 24 (June 1922): 58–59.

7. Norrell, *Up from History,* 117.

8. William E. Wiethoff, *The Insolent Slave* (Columbia, SC: University of South Carolina Press, 2002).

9. See August Meier, *Along the Color Line: Explorations in the Black Experience* (Urbana, IL: University of Illinois Press, 2002); Meier, *Negro Thought in America, 1880–1915: Racial Ideologies in the Age of Booker T. Washington* (Ann Arbor, MI: University of Michigan Press, 1988).

10. Norrell, *Up from History,* 117–18.

11. Grace Elizabeth Hale, *Making Whiteness: The Culture of Segregation in the South, 1890–1940* (New York: Pantheon Books, 1998).

12. Hale, *Making Whiteness,* 118–19.

13. Mark Smith, *How Race Is Made: Slavery, Segregation, and the Senses* (Chapel Hill, NC: University of North Carolina Press, 2006), 24–66.

14. Norrell, *Up from History,* 92–114.

15. Ibid., 120, 120–21.

16. Ibid., 123–24.

17. Ibid., 127.

18. Ibid., 140.

19. Many scholars have noted how Washington's autobiography, *Up From Slavery,* dramatized old-time black and white relations in which whites felt fondness for some slaves. See Meier, *Negro Thought in America.*

20. Robert Norrell argues that Washington really had no choice but to cut this sort of contract with segregation, living as he was among violent southern racists (*Up from History,* 238–62).

21. Norrell, *Up from History,* 128; "Du Bois had seen clearly Washington's goal in the Atlanta speech."

22. It is undeniable that Washington and Du Bois's relation appears from our twenty-first-century point of view to have been toxic; I am contending that the eventual hostility Du Bois expressed toward him, and the vicious attacks Washington sustained at the hands of activists like Monroe Trotter, has overdetermined our assessment of the overall character of their encounters; see Stephen R. Fox, *The Guardian of Boston: William Monroe Trotter* (New York: Antheneum, 1970).

23. See W. E. B. Du Bois, *The Souls of Black Folk* (1903; repr., New York: Oxford University Press, 2007).

24. See for example, W. E. B. Du Bois, "The Conservation of the Races," *The American Negro Academy Occasional Papers,* no. 2 (1897).

25. Norrell, *Up from History,* 214.

26. I do not use this term in the "scientific" sense of carrying "information"; rather, I mean the capacity for the trope to transfer sensation. See Teresa Brennan, *The Transmission of Affect* (Ithica, NY: Cornell University Press, 2004), 117–26.

27. Eric King Watts, "The Problem of Race in Public Address Research: W.E.B. Du Bois and the Conflicted Aesthetics of Race," in *Handbook on Rhetoric and Public Address,* ed. Shawn Parry-Giles and J. Michael Hogan (Malden, MA: Wiley-Blackwell, 2010), 373–97.

28. See Catherine Chaput, "Rhetorical Circulation in Late Capitalism: Neoliberalism and the Overdetermination of Affective Energy," *Philosophy and Rhetoric* 43

(2010): 1–25. In this essay, Chaput argues that rhetoric's critical protocols need to be refashioned to keep up with neoliberalism's athletic circuitry that is speeding tropes through time and space and provoking "transsituational" sensitivity.

29. See *The Matrix* (Warner Bros. Pictures, 1999).

30. Martin Heidegger, *Being and Time,* trans. John Macquarrie and Edward Robinson (New York: Harper, 1962).

31. Darwinists might object here and say that evolution itself would have been arrested by such "monotony" long before the dawn of human being.

32. Don Ihde, *Listening and Voice: Phenomenologies of Sound,* 2nd ed. (Albany, NY: State University of New York Press, 2007), 204–5.

33. Brian Massumi, *Parables for the Virtual: Movement, Affect, Sensation* (Durham, NC: Duke University Press, 2002), 26–28.

34. See Audre Lorde's discussion of the sensation of eroticism, "Uses of the Erotic: The Erotic as Power," *Sister/Outsider: Essays and Speeches by Audre Lorde* (1984; repr., Berkeley, CA: Crossings Press, 2007), 53–59.

35. Massumi, *Parables for the Virtual,* 25.

36. Ihde, *Listening and Voice,* 190.

37. Massumi, *Parables for the Virtual,* 28.

38. Richard M. Weaver, *The Ethics of Rhetoric* (1953; repr., Davis, CA: Hermagoras Press, 1984).

39. Massumi, *Parables for the Virtual,* 27, 35, 26.

40. Gilles Deleuze and Felix Guattari, *A Thousand Plateaus: Capitalism and Schizophrenia,* trans. Brian Massumi (Minneapolis: University of Minnesota Press, 1987), 111–148.

41. Massumi, *Parables for the Virtual,* 26–27.

42. Christian Lundberg puts this point sharply in "Enjoying God's Death: *The Passion of the Christ* and the Practices of an Evangelical Public," *Quarterly Journal of Speech* 95 (2009): 387–411.

43. Massumi, *Parables for the Virtual,* 42–43.

44. Anatole Broyard, *Intoxicated By My Illness: And Other Writings on Life and Death* (NY: Fawcett Columbine Books, 1992), 6.

45. See Jurgen Habermas, *The Theory of Communicative Action,* vol. 2, *Lifeworld and System: A Critique of Functionalist Reason,* trans. Thomas McCarthy (Boston: Beacon Press, 1987).

46. Massumi, *Parables for the Virtual,* 36.

47. Ihde, *Listening and Voice,* 190.

48. M. M. Bakhtin, *Toward a Philosophy of the Act,* ed. Michael Holquist and Vadim Liapunov, trans. Vadim Liapunov (Austin, TX: University of Texas Press, 1993), 7.

49. David Appelbaum, *Voice* (Albany, NY: State University of New York Press, 1990), 8.

50. Mladen Dolar, *A Voice and Nothing More* (Cambridge, Mass: MIT Press, 2006), 13.

51. Dolar, *A Voice and Nothing More,* 16.

52. Louis Althusser, *Essays on Ideology* (1975; repr., London: Verso, 1984); Michael

J. Hyde, *The Call of Conscience: Heidegger and Levinas: Rhetoric and the Euthanasia Debate* (Columbia, SC: University of South Carolina Press, 2001); Appelbaum, *Voice,* 8.

53. Dolar, *A Voice and Nothing More,* 23.

54. Bakhtin, *Toward a Philosophy of the Act,* xi.

55. Dolar, *A Voice and Nothing More,* 96–97.

56. Eric King Watts, "Voice and Voicelessness in Rhetorical Studies," *Quarterly Journal of Speech* 87 (2001): 179–96.

57. Dolar, *A Voice and Nothing More,* 98–99.

58. Mel Brooks directed this masterpiece (Warner Bros., 1974); among the co-writers was Richard Pryor.

59. Dolar, *A Voice and Nothing More,* 103–7; Dolar is discussing how voice can authorize the law as well as undermine it. For a fuller examination of "bare life," see Giorgio Agamben, *Homo Sacer: Sovereign Power and Bare Life,* trans. Daniel Heller-Roazen (Stanford: Stanford University Press, 1988).

60. Wiethoff, *The Insolent Slave,* see in particular, "Part Four: The Moral Perspective," 133–60.

61. Dolar, *A Voice and Nothing More,* 120.

62. Jacques Ranciere, *The Politics of Aesthetics,* trans. Gabriel Rockhill (New York: Continuum, 2004), 12, 24–41.

63. Terry Eagleton, *The Ideology of the Aesthetic* (Malden, MA: Blackwell Publishing, 1990), 24.

64. Roger Scruton, *The Aesthetic Understanding: Essays in the Philosophy of Art and Culture* (Manchester: Carcanet Press, 1983), 139–42.

65. For a nice discussion of innovative aesthetic practices of displaying the New Negro, see Anne Elizabeth Carroll, *Word, Image, and the New Negro: Representation and Identity in the Harlem Renaissance* (Bloomington, IN: Indiana University Press, 2005).

66. W. E. B. Du Bois, "Easter," *Crisis* 1 (April 1911): 20.

67. W. E. B. Du Bois, "Credo," *Darkwater: Voices from within the Veil* (1920; repr., New York: Kraus-Thomson, 1975), 3.

68. W. E. B. Du Bois, "Writers," *Crisis* 1 (April 1911): 20–21.

69. Lewis, *W. E. B Du Bois: Biography of a Race, 1868–1919,* 485.

70. W. E. B. Du Bois, "Writers," *Crisis* 1 (April 1911): 20–21.

71. Michael J. Hyde, *The Call of Conscience: Heidegger and Levinas; Rhetoric and the Euthanasia Debate* (Columbia, SC: University of South Carolina Press, 2001). Du Bois and the *Crisis* would eventually become household names in many middle-class black enclaves. See Lewis, *Biography of a Race,* 471–505.

72. Responding to criticism from readers and from the NAACP's board of directors about the journal's sharp tone, Du Bois intoned, "We are in earnest. This is a *newspaper.* It tries to tell the Truth" (*Crisis* 4 [February 1912]: 153). Interestingly, despite the claim of objectivity, Du Bois refused a suggestion by NAACP Chairman Oswald Villard to publish stories about black criminality. See Lewis, *W. E. B. Du Bois: Biography of a Race, 1868–1919,* 471; W. E. B. Du Bois, *Crisis* 1 (December 1910): 16.

73. Letter to Joel Spingarn, October 28, 1914, in *The Correspondence of W. E. B.*

Du Bois, Vol. 1 *Selections, 1877–1934*, ed. Herbert Aptheker (Amherst, MA: University of Massachusetts Press, 1973), 204.

74. W. E. B. Du Bois, *Crisis* 2 (June 1911): 63.

75. W. E. B. Du Bois, *Crisis* 11 (December 1915): 82.

76. See "Niagara's Declaration of Principles, 1905," the Gilda Lehrman Center for the Study of Slavery, Resistance, and Abolition, MacMillan Center, Yale University, http://www.yale.edu/glc/archive/1152.htm (accessed March 15, 2010).

77. W. E. B. Du Bois, "The Crisis," *Crisis* 1 (November, 1910): 10.

78. W. E. B. Du Bois, "The Value of Agitation," *Voice* 4 (March 1907): 109–10.

79. W. E. B. Du Bois, "Agitation," *Crisis* 1 (November 1910): 11. Indeed, the letters to members of the NAACP board like Spingarn and Mary White Ovington testify to the fact that many of these "friends" were directing the civil rights organization. See the Letter to Joel Spingarn, October 28, 1914, in *The Correspondence of W. E. B. Du Bois*, Vol. 1 *Selections, 1877–1934*, 203–5.

80. W. E. B. Du Bois, *The Souls of Black Folk*, 7.

81. Elaine Scarry, *The Body in Pain: The Making and Unmaking of the World* (New York: Oxford University Press, 1985), 161–80.

82. Du Bois, "The Crisis," 11.

83. Broyard, *Intoxicated By My Illness*, 20.

84. Ibid., 36.

85. Kenneth Burke, "Four Master Tropes," in *A Grammar of Motives* (Berkeley, CA: University of California Press, 1969), 503–17.

86. W. E. B. Du Bois, *Crisis* 1 (December 1910): 17 (emphasis added).

87. Broyard, *Intoxicated By My Illness*, 102–3.

88. Dolar, *A Voice and Nothing More*, 98.

Chapter 2

1. David Levering Lewis, *W. E. B. Du Bois: Fight for Equality and the American Century, 1919–1963* (New York: Henry Holt & Co., 2000), 13.

2. W. E. B. Du Bois, "Triumph," *Crisis* 2 (September 1911): 194.

3. Orlando Patterson, *Rituals of Blood: Consequences of Slavery in Two American Centuries* (Washington, DC: Civitas/Counterpoint, 1998).

4. Claude McKay was a Jamaican-born writer who indulged Communist ideals. In addition to poetry, he authored novels such as *Banjo* and the controversial and best-selling work, *Home to Harlem*. "If We Must Die" appeared in his collection of poems, *Harlem Shadows*, in 1922.

5. Du Bois, "Triumph," 194.

6. Lewis, *W. E. B. Du Bois: Fight for Equality and the American Century*, 2, 4.

7. W. E. B. Du Bois, "The Manufacture of Prejudice: Three American Fairy Tales from the Associated Press," *Crisis* 2 (May 1911): 35–37.

8. W.E.B. Du Bois, "Promotion of Prejudice," *Crisis* 2 (September 1911): 196.

9. Lewis, *W. E. B. Du Bois: Fight for Equality and the American Century*, 2.

10. Hazel Carby, *Race Men* (Cambridge, MA: Harvard University Press, 1989).

11. David Levering Lewis, *W. E. B. Du Bois, Biography of a Race, 1868–1919* (New York: Henry Holt and Co., 1993), 277.

12. George Santayana, *The Sense of Beauty: Being the Outline of Aesthetic Theory* (New York: Dover Publications, 1955), 6, 7, 8, 10.

13. Santayana, *The Sense of Beauty,* 15, 14.

14. Ibid., 16, 17.

15. W.E.B. Du Bois, *Darkwater: Voice from within the Veil* (1920; repr., New York: Kraus-Thomson, 1975), 176.

16. Santayana, *The Sense of Beauty,* 17.

17. Du Bois, *Darkwater,* 174 (emphasis added).

18. Santayana, *The Sense of Beauty,* 31.

19. Du Bois, *Darkwater,* 176–77, 177–78.

20. Santayana, *The Sense of Beauty,* 21.

21. I am deferring here to Du Bois's intellectual agenda, not my personal understanding of the nature of beauty; concerned with producing the conditions of black beauty, Du Bois cuts right to the chase—the intersection of race and beauty. I would rephrase this point to signal the understanding that beauty is at its core an ideological conception and, therefore, is not "corruptible" per se. It is always emerging among contested interests in complicated contexts.

22. Du Bois, *Darkwater,* 22.

23. Santayana, *The Sense of Beauty,* 21.

24. Du Bois, *Darkwater,* 22, 25.

25. Santayana, *The Sense of Beauty,* 22.

26. Du Bois, *Darkwater,* 25, 46–54, 46.

27. See Jacques Ranciere, *The Politics of Aesthetics: The Distribution of the Sensible* (New York: Continuum, 2004); Ranciere, *Dissensus: On Politics and Aesthetics,* ed. and trans. Steve Corcoran (New York: Continuum, 2010); Terry Eagleton, *The Ideology of the Aesthetic* (Malden, MA: Blackwell Publishing, 1990).

28. Du Bois, *Darkwater,* 30.

29. Lewis, *W. E. B. Du Bois, Biography of a Race,* 469.

30. Letter to Ovington, April 19, 1914, in *The Correspondence of W. E. B. Du Bois,* Vol. 1 *Selections, 1877–1934,* ed. Herbert Aptheker (Amherst: University of Massachusetts Press, 1973), 188–91.

31. Du Bois, *Darkwater,* 171–72.

32. Letter to Spingarn, October 24, 1914, in *The Correspondence of W. E. B. Du Bois,* 203–7.

33. Du Bois, *Darkwater,* 172.

34. Ibid., 173.

35. W. E. B. Du Bois, *The Souls of Black Folk* (1904; repr., New York: Vintage Books, 1990).

36. William M. Banks, *Black Intellectuals: Race and Responsibility in American Life* (New York: W.W. Norton & Co., 1996), 88–89.

37. Du Bois, *Darkwater,* 48, 54, 23 (emphasis added).

38. Lewis, *W. E. B. Du Bois: Biography of a Race,* 506.

39. Ibid., 509.

40. W. E. B. Du Bois, *Crisis* 13 (November 1916): 10.

41. W. E. B. Du Bois, *Crisis* 11 (January 1916): 139–40.

42. Du Bois, *Darkwater,* 23–24, 22–24 (emphasis added).

43. W. E. B. Du Bois, "The Gall of Bitterness," *The Crisis* 4 (February 1912): 153.

44. A. C. Grayling, *Life, Sex, and Ideas: The Good Life Without God* (Oxford: Oxford University Press, 2003), 121.

45. E. M. Cioran, *The Trouble with Being Born* (New York: Arcade Publishing, 1973), 7.

46. For an extended and vigorous examination of "perfection," see Michael J. Hyde, *Perfection: Coming to Terms with Being Human* (Waco, Texas: Baylor University Press, 2010).

47. Du Bois, *Darkwater,* 31.

48. Grayling, *Life, Sex, and Ideas,* 106.

49. Du Bois, *Darkwater,* 37.

50. Ibid., 190.

51. Ibid., 64.

52. Du Bois, "The Woman," *Crisis* 1 (May 1911): 19.

53. This number is significant for several religions; it references the marked ones who will help fulfill God's mission upon the second coming of the Lord. See, for example, the Book of Revelations 7:4, King James Version.

54. Du Bois, *Darkwater,* 126.

55. Elaine Scarry, *On Beauty and Being Just* (Princeton, NJ: Princeton University Press, 1999), 16–20.

56. Scarry, *On Beauty and Being Just,* 18, 24–25, 28, 30, 31, 81.

57. Ibid., 20.

58. Du Bois, *Darkwater,* 81, 82–83.

59. Santayana, *The Sense of Beauty,* 8.

60. Shamoon Zamir, *Dark Voices: W.E.B. Du Bois and American Thought, 1888–1903* (Chicago: University of Chicago Press, 1995), 160–167, 136.

61. Du Bois, *Darkwater,* 83.

62. Ibid., 97.

63. Ibid., 103.

64. Santayana, 147, 148, 149, 150.

65. Du Bois, *Darkwater,* 191–194.

66. Ibid.

67. Ibid., 192.

68. Ibid.

69. Ibid.

70. Ibid., 193.

71. See Arnold Rampersad, *The Art and Imagination of W. E. B. Du Bois* (Cambridge, MA: Harvard University Press, 1976).

72. Scarry, *On Beauty and Being Just,* 25.

73. Du Bois, *Darkwater,* 193.

74. Ibid., 193.

75. Ibid., 194.

76. Ibid.

77. Rampersad, *The Art and Imagination of W. E. B. Du Bois,* 105.

78. Zamir, *Dark Voices,* 142.

79. Lothrop Stoddard, *The Rising Tide of Color Against White World Supremacy* (New York: Charles Scribner's Sons, 1920); in this work, Stoddard seems terrified by the lack of white solidarity implicated in the First World War.

80. Scarry, *On Beauty and Being Just,* 31–40.

81. Lewis, *W. E. B. Du Bois: Fight for Equality and the American Century,* 20–21.

Chapter 3

1. Arnold Rampersad, *The Art and Imagination of W. E. B. Du Bois* (Cambridge, MA: Harvard University Press, 1976), 190.

2. David Levering Lewis, *W.E.B. Du Bois: The Fight for Equality and The American Century, 1919–1963* (New York: Henry Holt and Company, 2000), 155.

3. *The Correspondence of W. E. B. Du Bois,* vol. 1 *Selections, 1877–1934.* ed. Herbert Aptheker (Boston, MA: University of Massachusetts Press, 1973), 316.

4. Rampersad, *The Art and Imagination of W. E. B. Du Bois,* 186.

5. Immanuel Kant, *The Critique of Judgment,* trans. by J. H. Bernard (Amherst, NY: Prometheus Books, 2000), 45–53, 67–72.

6. John Dewey, *Art as Experience* (New York: Minton, Balch & Co., 1934), 6–10.

7. Dewey, *Art as Experience,* 6.

8. Richard Shusterman, *Pragmatist Aesthetics: Living Beauty, Re-thinking Art,* 2nd ed. (New York: Rowman & Littlefield Publishers, Inc., 2000), 6.

9. Dewey, *Art as Experience,* 14, 67.

10. Ibid., 9, 6.

11. Shusterman, *Pragmatist Aesthetics,* 20, 19.

12. Dewey, *Art as Experience,* 58.

13. Alan Goldman, *Aesthetic Value* (Boulder, Co.: Westview Press, 1995).

14. Dewey, *Art as Experience,* 17.

15. Shusterman, *Pragmatist Aesthetics,* 9, 15.

16. Dewey, *Art as Experience,* 65, 58, 67–68.

17. Shusterman, *Pragmatist Aesthetics,* 28, 20.

18. John Dewey, *The Public and Its Problems* (New York: Henry Holt & Co., 1927), 17, 18, 27, 35.

19. Dewey, *The Public and Its Problems,* 208, 194, 184.

20. Ibid., 115.

21. David Roediger, *Working toward Whiteness: How America's Immigrants Became White* (New York: Basic Books, 2005), 3–34; also see Gary Gerstle, *American Crucible: Race and Nation in the Twentieth Century* (Princeton, NJ: Princeton University Press, 2001), 14–43.

22. Dewey, *The Public and Its Problems,* 137, 184.

23. Ibid., 145–46, 184, 213.

24. Dewey made more than one research trip to Harlem during the movement; in May 1927, he served as master of ceremonies for the *Opportunity*'s literary contest award dinner. See George Hutchinson, *In Search of Nella Larsen: A Biography of the Color Line* (Cambridge, MA: Harvard University Press, 2006), 248.

25. I also discuss this important event in chapter 4 in terms of its setting for the publication of the *Survey Graphic*'s special issue on Harlem; this number set in motion the production of Alain Locke's *The New Negro: An Interpretation* (1925; repr., New York: Arno Press, 1968).

26. Lewis, *W. E. B. Du Bois: Biography of a Race, 1868–1919* (New York: Henry Holt & Co., 1993), 156.

27. Ibid., 153, 156, 158.

28. Sterling A. Brown, "Negro Characters as Seen by White Authors," *Journal of Negro Education* 2 (1933): 179–203.

29. Amy Helene Kirschke, *Art in Crisis: W. E. B. Du Bois and the Struggle for African American Identity and Memory* (Bloomington, IN: Indiana University Press, 2007).

30. Lewis, *W. E. B. Du Bois: Biography of a Race,* 512.

31. W. E. B. Du Bois, "The Social Origins of American Negro Art," *Modern Quarterly* 3 (October–December 1925): 53–56.

32. W. E. B. Du Bois, "The Contribution of the Negro to American Life," *Pacific Review* (June 1921); University of Massachusetts W. E. B. Du Bois Collection.

33. Du Bois, "Social Origins," 53.

34. W. E. B. Du Bois, "The Ethiopian Art Theatre," *Theatre Magazine* 38 (July 1923); University of Massachusetts W. E. B. Du Bois Collection.

35. W. E. B. Du Bois, "Culture through Literature in Terms of Sociological Foundations" (n.d.); University of Massachusetts W. E. B. Du Bois Collection.

36. Du Bois, "Social Origins," 53.

37. See, for example, William E. Wiethoff, *The Insolent Slave* (Columbia, SC: University of South Carolina Press, 2002).

38. Grace Elizabeth Hale, *Making Whiteness: The Culture of Segregation in the South, 1890–1940* (New York: Vintage Books, 1998), 204.

39. Du Bois, "Social Origins," 54.

40. Hale argues that post-Reconstruction stress on Southern power fragmented white classes and exacerbated growing tensions between white men and women. The grand and awful spectacle of lynching and the consumption of black bodies helped heal these fractures because they reestablished white paternalism as necessary to safeguard white "purity" and minimized class conflict through the shared "tasting" of black flesh and white power.

41. Dewey, *Art as Experience,* 19 (emphasis added).

42. Du Bois, "Social Origins," 54.

43. W. E. B. Du Bois, "What is Civilization: Africa's Answer," *Forum* (February 1925); University of Massachusetts W. E. B. Du Bois Collection.

44. Du Bois, "What is Civilization."

45. Ibid.

46. Shamoon Zamir, *Dark Voices: W. E. B. Du Bois and American Thought, 1888–1903* (Chicago: University of Chicago Press, 1995), 150, 151.

47. Adolph Reed Jr., *W. E. B. Du Bois and American Political Thought: Fabianism and the Color Line* (New York: Oxford University Press, 1997), 46.

48. Shusterman, *Pragmatist Aesthetics,* 59.

49. Dewey, *The Public and Its Problems,* 159, 160.

50. Shusterman, *Pragmatist Aesthetics,* 124.

51. Dewey, *The Public and Its Problems,* 162.

52. W. E. B. Du Bois, *Darkwater: Voices from within the Veil* (1921; repr., New York: Washington Square Press, 2004), 55.

53. Shusterman, *Pragmatist Aesthetics,* 126.

54. Du Bois, "What is Civilization."

55. W. E. B. Du Bois, "Negro Culture" (n.d.); University of Massachusettes W. E. B. Du Bois Collection.

56. Du Bois, "What is Civilization."

57. W. E. B. Du Bois, "The Primitive Black Man," *Nation* (December 17, 1924): 675–76.

58. Dewey, *The Public and Its Problems,* 160–61, 142.

59. Du Bois, "What is Civilization."

60. Dewey, *The Public and Its Problems,* 155.

61. Du Bois, "Social Origins," 55.

62. Shusterman, *Pragmatist Aesthetics,* 61.

63. Dewey, *The Public and Its Problems,* 167, 184.

64. Du Bois, "Social Origins," 56

65. W. E. B. Du Bois, "The Segregated Negro World," *World Tomorrow* (May 1923): 136–37.

66. Du Bois, "Social Origins," 56.

67. Sarah N. Cleghorn, "But of Course No Social Equality!" *World Tomorrow* (March 1922): 84.

68. Dewey, *The Public and Its Problems,* 202.

69. See Elizabeth Povinelli, "Settler Modernity and the Quest for an Indigenous Tradition" in *Alternative Modernities,* ed. Dilip Gaonkar (Durham, NC: Duke University Press), 24–57.

70. I am respecting Richard Rorty's resistance to the term "method" because it contains the residue of scientism. See "Pragmatism Without Method," *Objectivity, Relativism, and Truth: Philosophical Papers,* Vol. 1 (New York: Cambridge University Press, 1991), 63–77.

Chapter 4

1. Leonard Harris and Charles Molesworth, *Alain L. Locke: Biography of a Philosopher* (Chicago: University of Chicago Press, 2008), 204.

2. Harris and Molesworth, *Alain L. Locke,* 16 (emphasis added).

3. Zora Neale Hurston, "How It Feels to Be Colored Me," *World Tomorrow* 11 (May 1928).

4. Alain L. Locke, letter dated 2 June 1928, box 164, folder 38, Alain Locke Collection, Moorland-Spingarn Library, Howard University (emphasis added).

5. Zora Neale Hurston, letter dated 14 June 1928, box 164, folder 38, Alain Locke Collection, Moorland-Spingarn Library, Howard University.

6. *Fire!! Devoted to Younger Negro Artists* 1 (November 1926). This venture was put together by Wallace Thurman and featured a "Board of Editors," including Langston Hughes, Zora Neale Hurston, Aaron Douglas, Gwendolyn Bennett, John Davis, and Richard Bruce Nugent. Hurston and others felt that Thurman had badly mismanaged the enterprise, leaving behind a sizeable bill owed to the printer. See chapter 7 for an elaboration on this project and the relationships that brought it into being.

7. Harris and Molesworth, *Alain L. Locke,* 247–48.

8. Carla Kaplan, *Zora Neale Hurston: A Life in Letters* (New York: Anchor Books, 2003), 48.

9. Harris and Molesworth, *Alain L. Locke,* 237: "[Mason] dispensed money to them, but also advice, and exercised stringent control over their artistic endeavors and demanded a close accounting of how they spent their funds."

10. Hurston, "How It Feels to Be Colored Me."

11. Ibid. This sentiment represents another point of agreement between Hurston and Locke; see Ernest Mason, "Alain Locke's Philosophy of Value," in *Alain Locke: Reflections on a Modern Renaissance Man,* ed. Russell J. Linnemann (Baton Rouge, LA: Louisiana State University Press, 1982), 1–16.

12. Hurston, "How It Feels to Be Colored Me," (original emphasis).

13. Alain Locke, "Beauty Instead of Ashes," *Nation* 126 (18 April 1928): 432–34.

14. Alain Locke, "The Negro's Contribution to American Art and Literature," *Annals of American Academy of Political and Social Science* 140 (November 1928): 234.

15. Hurston, "How It Feels to Be Colored Me."

16. Steven Watson, *The Harlem Renaissance: Hub of African American Culture* (New York: Pantheon, 1995), 24.

17. I am specifically using and altering "strategy" and "tactic" as described by Michel de Certeau, where "strategy" is associated with the mapping of a terrain by hegemonic forces and "tactics" are employed as resistive acts by the "weak." See *The Practice of Everyday Life* (Berkeley, CA: University of California Press, 1984), especially 29–42.

18. Bruce Tyler, *From Harlem to Hollywood: The Struggle for Racial and Cultural Democracy, 1920–1943* (New York: Garland Press, 1992), 13; Alain Locke, *The New Negro: An Interpretation* (1925; repr., New York: Arno Press, 1968).

19. In particular, Jessie Fauset's new novel, *There Is Confusion,* was advertised.

20. Alain Locke, ed., "Harlem: Mecca of the New Negro," special issue, *Survey Graphic* VI, no. 6 (March 1925).

21. Arnold Rampersad, "Introduction," in *The New Negro: Voices of the Harlem Re-*

naissance, ed. Alain Locke (New York: Touchstone, 1997), xvii. This more recent edition marks two alterations from the edition published in 1925; it changes the subtitle from "An Interpretation," to "Voices of the Harlem Renaissance," which erases the hermeneutics of the original and subtracts Winhold Reiss's drawings of W. E. B. Du Bois and Alain Locke.

22. Charles W. Scruggs, "Alain Locke and Walter White: Their Struggle for Control of the Harlem Renaissance," *Black American Literature Forum* 14 (1980): 93, 91.

23. Harris and Molesworth, *Alain L. Locke,* 175. In academic notes that are undated, Locke railed against "the ultra-conservative tradition of these institutions, a paternalism inherited from their missionary founders that has outlived its usefulness and force." See box 164, folder 141, Alain Locke Collection, Moorland-Spingarn Research Center, Howard University.

24. Locke's correspondences with the Harlem-born poet Countee Cullen depict a very private man who desires to fully experience homosexual affection but often deprives himself due to propriety; his letters speak of intense highs and lows. See Alain Locke Collection, especially letters to and from Cullen and Langston Hughes, Moorland-Spingarn Library, Howard University. For a fuller discussion of these letters see chapter 7.

25. Harris and Molesworth, *Alain L. Locke,* 179, 185.

26. Jessie Fauset, "The Gift of Laughter," in *The New Negro: An Interpretation,* 162.

27. Letter n.d., but clearly written during the editing of the anthology. Alain Locke Collection, Moorland-Spingarn Research Center, Howard University. Also the Reiss drawings and his German heritage provoked consternation among some black scholars, provoking the removal of his drawings from some later editions; see *The New Negro: Voices of the Harlem Renaissance* (New York: Touchstone, 1997).

28. See Locke, "Beauty Instead of Ashes," 432, where he argues that "Negro life is an artistic province free to everyone."

29. Harris and Molesworth, *Alain L. Locke,* 221.

30. Locke's dismissal from Howard University had the unanticipated benefit of freeing him up to temporarily live in Harlem as he worked on the anthology.

31. Alain Locke, "Values and Imperatives," in *American Philosophy, Today and Tomorrow,* ed. Horace M. Kallen and Sidney Hook (New York: Lee Furman, Inc., 1935), 313, 319.

32. Locke, "Values and Imperatives," 316.

33. Locke took a course on aesthetics from Santayana that involved a teaching assistant named Horace Kallen; Locke and Kallen shared a friendship that lasted for decades. Indeed, at least one scholar claims that it was Kallen who coined the phrase "cultural pluralism," a notion that was integral to Locke's theory of values. See Rutledge M. Dennis, "Relativism and Pluralism in the Social Thought of Alain Locke," in *Alain Locke: Reflections on a Modern Renaissance Man,* ed. Russell J. Linnemann (Baton Rouge, LA: Louisiana State University, 1982), 31. For a deeper discussion of Santayana's aesthetic theory, see chapter 2.

34. Locke, "Values and Imperatives," 316.

35. Alain Locke, "A Functional View of Value Ultimates," in *The Philosophy of Alain Locke: Harlem Renaissance and Beyond,* ed. Leonard Harris (Philadelphia: Temple University Press, 1989), 79–93.

36. Mason, "Alain Locke's Philosophy of Value," 6.

37. Locke, "Values and Imperatives," 320.

38. Georg-Hans Gadamer, *Philosophical Hermeneutics,* ed. and trans. David E. Linge (Berkeley, CA: University of California Press, 1976), 315.

39. Ernesto Laclau, "Identity and Hegemony: The Role of Universality in the Constitution of Political Logics," in *Contingency, Universality, Hegemony: Contemporary Dialogues on the Left,* ed. Judith Butler, Ernesto Laclau, and Slavoj Žižek (New York: Verso Books, 2000).

40. Locke, "Values and Imperatives," 315–16.

41. Ibid., 329.

42. For a slightly more robust discussion of aesthetic experiences, see chapter 3.

43. Alain Locke, "Unity Through Diversity," in *The Philosophy of Alain Locke,* 135.

44. Locke, "Values and Imperatives," 329.

45. Locke, "Harlem," *Survey Graphic* VI (March 1925): 629; *Survey Graphic* VI, 635–57.

46. Albert C. Barnes, "Negro Art and America," in *The New Negro: An Interpretation,* 19–25.

47. Barnes's piece was the second essay the anthology offered its readers, following Locke's staging of the evolution of the movement in "The New Negro."

48. Barnes, "Negro Art and America," 19, 21, 23–24, 24, 23.

49. Rampersad, "Introduction," xxi.

50. Barnes, "Negro Art and America," 22, 24.

51. Alain Locke, "The New Negro," in *The New Negro: An Interpetation,* 3. African American intellectuals during this time were very skeptical of the abuses of statistics in measuring the advancement of black communities. In just a few years, Locke will call statistics "that most inhuman of sociological instruments" ("This Year of Grace," *Opportunity* 9 [February 1931]: 51).

52. Houston Baker Jr., *The Long Black Song: Essays in Black American Literature and Culture* (Charlottesville, VA: University of Virginia Press, 1972).

53. Locke, "The New Negro," 3.

54. Locke, "A Functional View of Value Ultimates," in *The Philosophy of Alain Locke,* 84.

55. Locke, "The New Negro," 6, 4.

56. Locke, "A Functional View of Value Ultimates,"90 (emphasis added).

57. Locke, "The New Negro," 3.

58. Locke, "Negro Youth Speaks," 47, 48, 50, 48.

59. Ibid., 48, 50 (emphasis added), 51.

60. Locke, "The New Negro," 5.

61. Alain Locke, undated notes, box 164, folder 141, Alain Locke Collection, Manuscript Department, Moorland-Spingarn Research Center, Howard University (emphasis added).

62. Locke, "Beauty Instead of Ashes," 433.

63. Locke, "The New Negro," 8.

64. Locke, "Negro Youth Speaks," 50.

65. Locke, "Beauty Instead of Ashes," 432.

66. Locke, "Unity Through Diversity," in *The Philosophy of Alain Locke,* 133–38.

67. Locke, "Negro Youth Speaks," 51.

68. Locke, "The Negro Spirituals," in *The New Negro: An Interpetation,* 199.

69. Alain Locke, "Pluralism and Intellectual Democracy," in *The Philosophy of Alain Locke,* 56.

70. Locke, "The Negro Spirituals," 199, 202–3.

71. Ross Posnock, *Color and Culture: Black Writers and the Making of the Modern Intellectual* (Cambridge: Harvard University Press, 1998), 27.

72. Locke, "The Negro Spirituals," 199, 200–201, 202, 207–8.

73. Alain Locke, "Roland Hayes: An Appreciation," *Opportunity: Journal of Negro Life* 1 (December 1923): 356 (emphasis added).

74. Harris and Molesworth, *Alain L. Locke,* 241.

75. Locke, "The Negro Spirituals," 200, 205.

76. Locke, "Unity Through Diversity," in *The Philosophy of Alain Locke,* 135.

77. Locke, "Pluralism and Intellectual Democracy," in *The Philosophy of Alain Locke,* 57.

78. Locke, "The Negro Spirituals," 205, 208.

79. Carl Van Vechten, Letter to Alain Locke dated 13 October 1925, Alain Locke Collection, Box 164, Manuscript Department, Moorland-Spingarn Research Center, Howard University. At the end of the letter, Van Vechten happily anticipated a hearty argument with Locke on his next visit to New York.

80. Locke, "The Negro Spirituals," 204.

81. Locke, "Values and Imperatives," in *American Philosophy, Today and Tomorrow,* 319, 328.

82. Locke, "The Negro Spirituals," 210.

83. Locke, The Legacy of the Ancestral Arts," in *The New Negro: An Interpetation,* 254, 258–60, 255.

84. Ibid., 256, 266.

85. Locke had argued that New Negro poetry was unbridled due to tremendous affects enjoyed by an increasing white audience. Indeed, he claimed that black poets were as yet incapable of the kind of "objectivity" necessary for growth in other artistic practices like the novel. Hence, African artistry helped produce New Negro progressivism. See, "Beauty Instead of Ashes," 432–33.

86. Locke, "The Legacy of Ancestral Arts," 266.

87. Harris and Molesworth, *Alain L. Locke,* 210–17.

88. Alain Locke, "The Colonial Literature of France," *Opportunity* 1 (November 1923): 331 (emphasis added).

89. Locke, "The Colonial Literature of France," 334 (emphasis added).

90. See Christopher Buck, "Alain Locke: Race Leader, Social Philosopher, Bahá'í Pluralist," *World Order* 36 (2005): 7–48.

91. Alain Locke, *Four Negro Poets: The Pamphlet Poets* (New York: Simon & Schuster Publishers, 1927).

Chapter 5

1. Sara Alpern, *Freda Kirchwey: A Woman of "The Nation"* (Cambridge, MA: Harvard University Press, 1987). Kirchwey was among several white editors, critics, and publishers invited to attend a reception organized by Charles S. Johnson, editor of *Opportunity,* in honor of Jessie Fauset's new novel, *There Is Confusion.* The event, held in March of 1924 at New York City's Civic Club, is widely viewed as the formal introduction of the New Negro to Manhattan's high society.

2. Sieglinde Lemke, *Primitivist Modernism: Black Culture and the Origins of Transatlantic Modernism* (New York: Oxford University Press, 1998), 118–34.

3. Alpern, *Freda Kirchwey,* 61.

4. For narratives of this occurrence, see Arnold Rampersad, *The Life of Langston Hughes,* Vol. 1 *1902–1941, I, Too, Sing America* (New York: Oxford University Press, 2002); Michael Peplow, *George S. Schuyler* (Boston: Twayne Publishers, 1980).

5. George S. Schuyler, *Black and Conservative: The Autobiography of George S. Schuyler* (New Rochelle, NY: Arlington House Publishers, 1966), 153.

6. Alpern, *Freda Kirchwey,* 53–57.

7. Rampersad, *Life of Langston Hughes,* 56, 130.

8. Ibid., 130.

9. Toni Morrison, *The Bluest Eye* (New York: Holt, Rinehart, and Winston, 1970).

10. Rampersad, *Life of Langston Hughes,* 121.

11. Langston Hughes, letter to Carl Van Vechten, May 17, 1925, in *Remember Me to Harlem: The Letters of Langston Hughes and Carl Van Vechten, 1925–1964,* ed. Emily Bernard (New York: Alfred A. Knopf, 2001), 12. Hughes and Van Vechten enjoyed a long friendship that was sparked by a shared interest in the vitality and beauty of black folk culture. Van Vechten, however, is considered by many Harlem Renaissance scholars as responsible for "white exploitation of black culture" (*Remember Me to Harlem,* xv).

12. Arnold Rampersad, "Hughes' *Fine Clothes to the Jew,*" in *Langston Hughes: Critical Perspectives Past and Present,* ed. Henry Louis Gates Jr. and K. A. Appiah (New York: Amistad Press, 1993), 59.

13. George S. Schuyler, "The Negro-Art Hokum," *Nation* 122 (June 16, 1926): 662–63.

14. Langston Hughes, "The Negro Artist and the Racial Mountain," *Nation* 122 (June 23, 1926): 692–94.

15. Langston Hughes, *The Big Sea: An Autobiography* (New York: Hill and Wang, 1940), 228.

16. Carl Van Vechten, letter dated 17 May 1925, in *Remember Me to Harlem,* 10–14.

17. Yun Lee Too, "Epideictic Genre," in *The Encyclopedia of Rhetoric* (New York: Oxford University Press, 2001), 253.

18. Lawrence W. Rosenfield, "The Practical Celebration of Epideictic," in *Rhetoric in Transition: Studies in the Nature and Uses of Rhetoric,* ed. Eugene E. White (College Park, PA: Pennsylvania State University Press, 1980), 133, 136.

19. Eric King Watts, "African American Ethos and Hermeneutical Rhetoric: An Exploration of Alain Locke's *The New Negro,*" *Quarterly Journal of Speech* 88 (2002): 19–32. See chapters 1 and 4 to comprehend how values and emotions are implicated in the production of "taste."

20. Rosenfield, "The Practical Celebration of Epideictic," 141, 139, 138.

21. For an elaborate examination of aesthetic experience in terms of how John Dewey and W. E. B. Du Bois imagined it, see chapter 3.

22. See Charles I. Nero, "Re/Membering Langston: Homophobic Textuality and Arnold Rampersad's *Life of Langston Hughes*" in *Queer Representations: Reading Lives, Reading Cultures,* ed. Martin Duberman (New York: New York University Press, 1997), 194–95.

23. R. Baxter Miller, *The Art and Imagination of Langston Hughes* (Lexington, KY: University Press of Kentucky, 2006), 47–57.

24. Rampersad, *Life of Langston Hughes,* 58, 65–66 (emphasis added).

25. Ibid., 77–78.

26. Langston Hughes, "The Weary Blues," in *The Weary Blues* (New York: Alfred A. Knopf, 1926), 23.

27. Rampersad, *Life of Langston Hughes,* 100, 102, 105.

28. Hughes, letter to Van Vechten, April 2, 1927, in *Remember Me to Harlem,* 47; in the letter Hughes elaborates on a party he attended in Maryland where "between dances most of the conversation consisted of the merits of different kinds of pistols and razors and there was a great rivalry as to who could show the largest and most beautiful weapons."

29. Rampersad, *Life of Langston Hughes,* 103, 146.

30. Harriett Monroe, "Introduction," in Vachel Lindsay's *The Congo and Other Poems* (New York: The MacMillan Co., 1916), vi, ix.

31. Robin Hackett, *Sapphic Primitivism: Productions of Race, Class, and Sexuality in Key Works of Modern Fiction* (New Brunswick, NJ: Rutgers University Press, 2004), 10.

32. John R. Cooley, *Savages and Naturals: Black Portraits by White Writers in Modern American Literature* (Newark, NJ: Associated University Presses, Inc., 1982), 11–19.

33. See George Hutchinson, *In Search of Nella Larsen: A Biography of the Color Line* (Cambridge, MA: Harvard University Press, 2006), 208–220, 262–272.

34. Marianna Torgovnick, *Gone Primitive: Savage Intellects, Modern Lives* (Chicago: University of Chicago Press, 1990), 7.

35. Sieglinde Lemke, *Primitivist Modernism: Black Culture and the Origins of Transatlantic Modernism* (New York: Oxford University Press, 1998), 5–6.

36. Cooley, *Savages and Naturals,* 11.

37. Torgovnick, *Gone Primitive,* 21, 23, 61.

38. See Tracy McCabe, "The Multifaceted Politics of Primitivism in Harlem Renaissance Writing," *Soundings* 80, no. 4 (Winter 1997): 475–97; Amelia DeFalco,

"Jungle Creatures and Dancing Apes: Modern Primitivism and Nella Larsen's *Quicksand,*" *Mosaic: A Journal for the Interdisciplinary Study of Literature* 38 (June 2005): 19–35.

39. Jeffrey B. Leak, *Rac[e]ing to the Right: Selected Essays of George S. Schuyler* (Knoxville, TN: University of Tennessee Press, 2001), xix.

40. Michael Peplow, *George S. Schuyler* (Boston: Twayne Publishers, 1980), 31, 19.

41. George S. Schuyler, *Black and Conservative: The Autobiography of George S. Schuyler* (New Rochelle, NY: Arlington House Publishers, 1966), 17, 25, 29, 157.

42. Brian A. Connery and Kirk Combe, ed., *Theorizing Satire: Essays in Literary Criticism* (New York: St. Martin's Press, 1995), 1.

43. Dustin Griffin, *Satire: A Critical Reintroduction* (Lexington, KY: University Press of Kentucky, 1994), 29.

44. Edward Bloom and Lillian Bloom, *Satire's Persuasive Voice* (Ithaca, NY: Cornell University Press, 1979), 19.

45. John R. Clark, "Vapid Voices and Sleazy Styles," in *Theorizing Satire,* 21.

46. Griffin, *Satire,* 29.

47. Connery and Combe, *Theorizing Satire,* 2.

48. Peplow, *George S. Schuyler,* 22.

49. Schuyler, "The Negro-Art Hokum," 662.

50. Ibid.

51. Ibid., 662–63.

52. Schuyler often lamented the advantages that white skin afforded recent European immigrants over native-born black folk. See Leake, *Rac[e]ing to the Right,* xviii.

53. Schuyler, "The Negro-Art Hokum," 662.

54. George S. Schuyler, "At the Darktown Charity Ball," *Messenger* 6 (December 1924): 377–78.

55. "Kleagle" is a term referring to a member and sometimes recruiter for the Ku Klux Klan.

56. Griffin, *Satire,* 52.

57. George S. Schuyler, "Our White Folks," in *Speech and Power: The African American Essay and its Cultural Content from Polemics to Pulpit,* ed. Gerald Early (New York: Ecco Press, 1993), 289.

58. Schuyler, "Our White Folks," 292, 294. For an outrageous and ingenious parody of race, see Schuyler's important novel *Black No More,* published in 1931.

59. Clark, "Vapid Voices and Sleazy Styles," 22.

60. George S. Schuyler, "Blessed Are the Sons of Ham," *Nation* 124 (March 1927): 313, 314.

61. Countee Cullen, "The Weary Blues," in *Langston Hughes: Critical Perspectives Past and Present,* 3.

62. Cullen, "The Weary Blues," 3–4.

63. Ibid., 4, 5.

64. For an example of how Schuyler satirizes the "civilizing" influence of "Nordic" culture, see George S. Schuyler, "The Negro and Nordic Civilization," originally published in the *Messenger* in 1925; in Leake, *Rac[e]ing to the Right,* 3–12.

65. Hughes, "The Negro Artist and the Racial Mountain," 693.

66. Ibid., 692, 693, 694.

67. Schuyler, "The Negro-Art Hokum," 662.

68. Hughes, "The Negro Artist and the Racial Mountain," 694.

69. Hughes, *Big Sea,* 238.

70. Elsewhere I take up the issue that Zora Neale Hurston discusses in "Characteristics of Negro Expression" that troubles the notion of "simplicity."

71. Hughes, "The Negro Artist and the Racial Mountain," 694.

72. Alain LeRoy Locke, *The New Negro: An Interpretation* (1925; repr., New York: Arno Press, 1968). For an exploration of the significance of this anthology, see chapter 4.

73. For example, several members of this "black bohemian" group started the magazines *Fire!!* (1927) and *Harlem* (1928); see chapters 4 and 7.

74. Hughes, *Big Sea,* 268.

75. George S. Schuyler, "At the Coffee House," *Messenger* 7 (June 1925): 236–37.

76. Peplow, *George S. Schuyler,* 35.

77. Henry Louis Gates Jr. and Nellie Y. McKay, ed., *The Norton Anthology of African American Literature* (New York: W. W. Norton & Co., 1997), 1171.

78. Peplow, *George S. Schuyler,* 34.

79. Leak, *Rac[e]ing to the Right,* xv.

80. Schuyler, "Our White Folks," 296.

81. Bloom and Bloom, *Satire's Persuasive Voice,* 20.

82. Clark, "Vapid Voices and Sleazy Styles," 25.

83. Schuyler, *Black and Conservative,* 32.

Chapter 6

1. Langston Hughes, *The Big Sea: An Autobiography* (New York: Hill and Wang, 1940), 223.

2. Arnold Rampersad, *The Art and Imagination of W.E.B. Du Bois* (Cambridge, MA: Harvard University Press, 1976), 190.

3. David Levering Lewis, *When Harlem Was in Vogue* (New York: Oxford University Press, 1979), 90, 93.

4. W. E. B. Du Bois, "Our Book Shelf," *Crisis* 31 (January 1926): 141. For discussions of the Civic Club dinner, see chapters 3 and 4.

5. Du Bois, "Our Book Shelf," 141.

6. Ibid.

7. Du Bois and Locke shared enough opinion and intellectual heritage to warrant their collaboration on an essay called "The Younger Literary Movement," published in *Crisis* 27 (February 1924): 161–163; and following Locke's dismissal from Howard University, Du Bois wrote to Jesse Moorland, a prominent black minister in Washington, D.C., imploring him to reinstate Locke. Letter dated 5 May, 1927, Alain Locke Collection, Moorland-Spingarn Research Center, Howard University.

8. Alain Locke, "Enter The New Negro," *Survey Graphic* IV (March 1925): 633.

9. W. E. B. Du Bois, *The Souls of Black Folk* (1904; repr., New York: Vintage Books, 1990), 3.

10. W. E. B. Du Bois, "The Negro Mind Reaches Out," in *The New Negro: An Interpretation,* ed. Alain Locke (1925; repr., New York: Arno Press, 1940), 385, 386, 407, 414.

11. Bruce Tyler, *From Harlem to Hollywood: The Struggle for Racial and Cultural Democracy, 1920–1943* (New York: Garland Press, 1992), 13.

12. For a discussion of Locke's philosophy of value, see chapter 4.

13. John E. Bassett, *Harlem in Review: Critical Reactions to Black American Writers, 1917–1939* (Cranbury, NJ: Association of University Presses, 1992), 48.

14. Emmett J. Scott, "Our Book Shelf," *Crisis* 31 (November 1925): 32–33.

15. For a discussion of Carl Van Vechten's participation in New Negro culture, see chapter 8.

16. Carl Van Vechten, letter dated October 29, 1925, in *The Correspondence of W. E. B. Du Bois,* Vol. 1 *Selections, 1877–1934,* ed. Herbert Aptheker (Amherst: University of Massachusetts Press, 1973), 324.

17. Du Bois, *Souls,* 7.

18. "A Questionnaire," *Crisis* 31 (February 1926): 165.

19. Carl Van Vechten, "The Negro in Art: How Shall He Be Portrayed? A Symposium," *Crisis* 31 (March 1926): 219.

20. Mary White Ovington, "The Negro in Art: How Shall He Be Portrayed? A Symposium," *Crisis* 31 (March 1926): 220 (emphasis added).

21. H. L. Mencken, "The Negro in Art: How Shall He Be Portrayed? A Symposium," *Crisis* 31 (March 1926): 219 (emphasis added).

22. Heyward Du Bose, "The Negro in Art: How Shall He Be Portrayed? A Symposium," *Crisis* 31 (March 1926): 220 (original emphasis).

23. Alfred A. Knopf, "The Negro in Art," *The Crisis* 31 (April 1926): 280.

24. Mencken, "The Negro in Art," 219.

25. John Farrar, "The Negro in Art: How Shall He Be Portrayed? A Symposium," *Crisis* 31 (March 1926): 280.

26. Mencken, "The Negro in Art," 219.

27. Julia Peterkin, "The Negro in Art: How Shall He Be Portrayed? A Symposium," *Crisis* 32 (September 1926): 239.

28. Countee Cullen, "The Negro in Art: How Shall He Be Portrayed? A Symposium," *Crisis* 32 (August 1926): 194.

29. Langston Hughes, "The Negro in Art: How Shall He Be Portrayed? A Symposium," *Crisis* 31 (April 1926): 278.

30. Locke, *The New Negro,* ix.

31. Joel Spingarn, "The Negro in Art: How Shall He Be Portrayed? A Symposium," *Crisis* 31 (April 1926): 279.

32. W. E. B. Du Bois, *Dusk of Dawn: An Essay Toward an Autobiography of a Race Concept* (New York: Harcourt, Brace, & Co., 1945), 99 (emphasis added).

33. Some scholars have pointed to Du Bois's wavering definitions of pure art and propaganda as evidence of weak theorizing. See Bernard Bell, "W. E. B. Du Bois's Struggle to Reconcile Folk and High Art," in *Critical Essays on W. E. B. Du Bois,* ed. William L. Andrews (Boston: G. K. Hall & Co., 1985), 106–22; Darwin Turner, "W. E. B. Du Bois and the Theory of a Black Aesthetic," in *Critical Essays on W. E. B. Du Bois,* 73–92. In 1924, Du Bois argued against propaganda when he defended Paul Robeson's portrayal of an African dictator in the stage performance of Eugene O'Neil's *Emperor Jones.* In this instance, Du Bois believed that such attacks were constitutive of a motive to forget African history. See *Crisis* 28 (1924): 56–57. In my work, I argue that Du Bois was involved in rhetorical practices maximizing the New Negro's service to civil rights.

34. W. E. B. Du Bois, "Criteria of Negro Art," *Crisis* 32 (October 1926): 290.

35. By "progressivism" I refer to a general belief in the early twentieth century in the ability to "perfect" society perpetuated in part by the rise in political economic "expertise." See Adolph L. Reed Jr., "Du Bois's 'Double Consciousness': Race and Gender in Progressive Era American Thought," *Studies in American Political Development* 6 (Spring 1992): 93–139.

36. Du Bois, "Criteria," 290.

37. Ibid.

38. W. E. B. Du Bois, "Parting of the Ways," in *W. E. B. Du Bois: A Reader,* ed. David Levering Lewis (New York: Henry Holt & Co., 1995), 330.

39. Du Bois, "Criteria," 292.

40. W. E. B. Du Bois, *The Souls of Black Folk* (1903; repr., New York: First Vintage Books, 1986), 56.

41. See W. E. B. Du Bois, "Jefferson Davis as a Representative of Civilization," in *W. E. B. Du Bois: A Reader,* 17; *Crisis* 12 (1916): 165; *Darkwater: Voices from within the Veil* (1921; repr., New York: Kraus-Thornson, 1975), 39–41.

42. Arnold Rampersad, *The Art and Imagination of W. E. B. Du Bois* (Cambridge, MA: Harvard University Press, 1976), 6.

43. Du Bois, "Criteria," 292.

44. Terry Eagleton, *The Ideology of the Aesthetic* (Malden, MA: Blackwell Publishing, 1990).

45. Du Bois, "Criteria," 292.

46. W. E. B. Du Bois, "The Essence of African Culture," *Forum* (February 1925): 7–9, in W. E. B. Du Bois Collection, University of Massachusetts. See chapter 3 for a full account of Du Bois's appropriations of African culture.

47. See Marianna Torgovnick, *Gone Primitive: Savage Intellects, Modern Lives* (Chicago: University of Chicago Press, 1990).

48. Du Bois, "Criteria," 292. For a fuller exploration of Du Bois's rhetorical invention of "primitivism," see chapter 3.

49. Ibid., 292.

50. Ibid. (emphasis added).

51. Ibid., 290 (emphasis added).

52. For a discussion of how Alain Locke assaulted this presumption, see chapter 4.

53. Herbert Aptheker, ed., *The Correspondence of W. E. B. Du Bois,* Vol. 1, *Selections, 1877–1934* (Amherst: University of Massachusetts Press, 1973), 316.

54. Michael Osborne, "Archetypal Metaphor in Rhetoric: The Light-Dark Family," *Quarterly Journal of Speech* 53 (1967): 115–26.

55. Du Bois reinvented Plato's cave allegory at least in two famous writings. See "Of the Coming of John," in *The Souls of Black Folk;* and "The Concept of Race," in *Dusk of Dawn.*

56. Du Bois, "Criteria," 292 (emphasis added).

57. See Plato, "Ion," in *Great Dialogues of Plato,* trans. W. H. D. Rouse (New York: Penguin Books, 1956); also, Stephen Halliwell, *Republic 10: Plato; With Translation and Commentary* (Warminster: Aris & Phillips, 1988).

58. Du Bois, "Criteria," 292 (emphasis added).

59. Ibid.

60. Ibid., 294.

61. Du Bois, *Darkwater,* 34.

62. Du Bois, *Dusk of Dawn,* 172.

63. Du Bois, "Criteria," 292.

64. See James Darsey, "'The Voice of Exile': W. E. B. Du Bois and the Quest for Culture," in *Rhetoric and Community: Studies in Unity and Fragmentation,* ed. J. Michael Hogan (Columbia: University of South Carolina Press, 1998), 93–110.

65. Halliwell, *Republic 10,* 7–9.

66. Du Bois, "Criteria," 292.

67. See W. E. B. Du Bois, "Social Origins of American Negro Art," *Modern Quarterly* 3 (1925): 53–56.

68. See Du Bois, "Sorrow Songs," in *Souls of Black Folk.*

69. Du Bois, "Criteria," 292.

70. Stephen Toulmin, *Cosmopolis: The Hidden Agenda of Modernity* (Chicago: University of Chicago Press, 1990), 92.

71. Zamir, *Dark Voices,* 143.

72. Du Bois, "Criteria," 294.

73. Ibid., 294–96.

74. Ibid., 296.

75. Ibid., 296.

76. Ibid., 297 (emphasis added).

77. For a discussion of the importance of the back-to-back essays by Hughes and the black journalist and satirist Schuyler, see chapter 5.

78. See *Crisis* 32 (October 1926): 325.

79. For a discussion of Van Vechten's influence on the New Negro movement and the impact of *Nigger Heaven,* see chapter 7.

80. For a discussion of homosexual and hyper-sexual display in the New Negro movement, see chapter 7.

Chapter 7

1. Alain LeRoy Locke, letter to Scholley Pace Alexander, October 8, 1928. James Weldon Johnson Collection, Box 1, Folder 28. Beinecke Library, Yale University.

2. Jennifer DeVere Brody and Dwight A. McBride, "Part 2: Plum Nelly: New Essays in Black Queer Studies," *Callaloo* 23 (2000): 329.

3. Locke to Alexander, October 8, 1928, James Weldon Johnson Collection.

4. Alain LeRoy Locke, *The New Negro: An Interpretation* (1925; repr., New York: Arno Press, 1968).

5. Richard Bruce Nugent, letter dated November 28, 1928, Alain Locke Collection, Moorland-Spingarn Research Center, Howard University. On 16 November, Locke was asked by the Guggenheim Memorial Foundation to provide a confidential appraisal of Nugent. In his note, Locke aligned his aesthetic strategies with Nugent's artistry. "A Negro Art Theatre will be one of the real focal centres of Negro art, and to stimulate its development some one of great originality and versatility should be singled out. Mr. Nugent has talent and versatility." Moorland-Spingarn Research Center, Howard University.

6. Locke to Guggenheim, Alain Locke Collection, Moorland-Spingarn Research Center, Howard University.

7. George Chauncey, *Gay New York: Gender, Urban Culture, and the Making of the Gay Male World, 1890–1940* (New York: Basic Books, 1994); see also Seth Clark Silberman, "Looking for Richard Bruce Nugent and Wallace Thurman: Reclaiming Black Male Same-Sexualities in the New Negro Movement," *In Process: A Graduate Student Journal of African American and African Diasporan Literature and Culture* 1 (1996): 53–73.

8. Michael L. Cobb, "Insolent Racing, Rough Narrative: The Harlem Renaissance's Impolite Queers," *Callaloo* 23 (2000): 335.

9. Nugent, letter dated November 28, 1928, Alain Locke Collection, Moorland-Spingarn Research Center, Howard University.

10. Richard Bruce Nugent, letter to Locke dated January 24, 1929. Alain Locke Collection, Moorland-Spingarn Research Center, Howard University. For a lengthy exploration of this symposium, see chapter 6.

11. "The Negro in Art: How Shall He Be Portrayed? A Symposium," *Crisis* 31–32 (1926).

12. Ironically, Locke's private homosexual ambitions often led him to "aggressively pursue his favorites" among the "New Negro." See Eric Garber, "A Spectacle in Color: The Lesbian and Gay Subculture of Jazz Age Harlem" in *Hidden From History: Reclaiming the Gay and Lesbian Past,* ed. Martin Bauml Duberman, Martha Vicinus, and George Chauncey Jr. (New York: New American Library, 1989), 327.

13. Leonard Harris and Charles Molesworth, *Alain L. Locke: The Biography of a Philosopher* (Chicago: University of Chicago Press, 2008), 17.

14. Countee Cullen, letter to Locke, January 12, 1923, Alain Locke Collection, Moorland-Spingarn Research Center, Howard University.

15. Harris and Molesworth, *Alain L. Locke,* 17.

16. Cullen, letter dated January 12, 1923, Alain Locke Collection, Moorland-Spingarn Research Center, Howard University.

17. For example, Rudolph Fisher in a review charged that *Infants* was burdened by "so much expositional and argumentative prattle on race prejudice and communism that one can not be sure at the end just what the book started out to say." *New York Herald Tribune Books* 24 (February 21, 1932): 16.

18. Countee Cullen, letter to Alain Locke, September 20, 1924, Alain Locke Collection, Moorland-Spingarn Research Center, Howard University.

19. Cullen, letter to Locke, January 29, 1923, Alain Locke Collection, Moorland-Spingarn Research Center, Howard University.

20. Cullen, letter to Locke, March 3, 1923, Alain Locke Collection, Moorland-Spingarn Research Center, Howard University.

21. Ibid.

22. See Edward Carpenter, *Iolaus: An Anthology of Friendship* (London: Swan Sonnenschein, 1902), 26.

23. Cullen, letter to Locke, March 3, 1923, Alain Locke Collection, Moorland-Spingarn Research Center, Howard University.

24. Cullen to Locke, June 17, 1923, Alain Locke Collection, Moorland-Spingarn Research Center, Howard University.

25. Cullen to Locke, September 30, 1923, Alain Locke Collection, Moorland-Spingarn Research Center, Howard University.

26. Cullen to Locke, August 26, 1923, Alain Locke Collection, Moorland-Spingarn Research Center, Howard University.

27. Cullen to Locke, November 24, 1923, Alain Locke Collection, Moorland-Spingarn Research Center, Howard University.

28. Cullen to Locke, August 26, 1923, Alain Locke Collection, Moorland-Spingarn Research Center, Howard University.

29. Cullen to Locke, November 24, 1923, Alain Locke Collection, Moorland-Spingarn Research Center, Howard University.

30. Alain Locke, letter to Langston Hughes, February 5, 1924. Alain Locke Collection, Moorland-Spingarn Research Center, Howard University.

31. Cullen to Locke, September 30, 1923, Alain Locke Collection, Moorland-Spingarn Research Center, Howard University.

32. Cullen to Locke, August 26, 1923, Alain Locke Collection, Moorland-Spingarn Research Center, Howard University.

33. Cullen to Locke, September 20, 1924, Alain Locke Collection, Moorland-Spingarn Research Center, Howard University.

34. Ibid. Cullen was certainly good as his word regarding his cautious approach to the editor's daughter. It would not be until 1928 that Countee and Yolande would wed in what amounted to a spectacular Harlem coronation of Cullen as New Negro royalty. The marriage was beset by rumor from its inception. Cullen almost immedi-

ately set sail to Paris with his friend and almost certainly part-time lover, Harold Jackman. The sham matrimony survived less than two years; they were divorced in 1930.

35. Cullen to Locke, September 30, 1923, Alain Locke Collection, Moorland-Spingarn Research Center, Howard University.

36. Martin Heidegger, "The Question Concerning Technology," in *Basic Writings,* ed. David Farrell Krell (New York: HarperCollins, 2008), 311–41.

37. Langston Hughes, *The Big Sea: An Autobiography* (New York: Hill and Wang, 1940), 226–27.

38. Chauncey, *Gay New York,* 233.

39. Ibid., 236 (emphasis added).

40. Ibid., 233.

41. Ibid., 233, 244.

42. Charles W. Chesnutt to James Weldon Johnson, January 18, 1913, James Weldon Johnson Collection, Box 1, Folder 90, Beinecke Library, Yale University.

43. James Weldon Johnson to Heywood Broun, May 2, 1924, James Weldon Johnson Collection, Box 1, Folder 62, Beinecke Library, Yale University.

44. W. E. B. Du Bois, "Our Policy," *Crisis* 11 (1916): 133.

45. W. E. B. Du Bois, *Crisis* 12 (1916): 69. For an extensive discussion of Du Bois's political efforts while editor of the *Crisis,* see chapters 1 and 2.

46. Steven Watson, *The Harlem Renaissance: Hub of African American Culture* (New York: Pantheon Books, 1995).

47. Bruce M. Tyler, *From Harlem to Hollywood: The Struggle for Racial and Cultural Democracy, 1920–1943* (New York: Garland Publishing, 1992), 13.

48. For an examination of this anthology, see chapter 4.

49. Eleonore van Notten, *Wallace Thurman's Harlem Renaissance* (Amsterdam, Netherlands: Costerus New Series 93, 1994), 93–130.

50. See chapter 5 for an analysis of Schuyler's significance to the New Negro movement.

51. Van Notten, *Wallace Thurman's Harlem Renaissance,* 94, 119, 109, 119.

52. Hughes, *Big Sea,* 227.

53. W. E. B. Du Bois, "Books," *Crisis* 33 (December 1926): 81–82. For a discussion of the impact of *Nigger Heaven,* see chapter 8.

54. Wallace Thurman, "A Stranger at the Gates: A Review of *Nigger Heaven,* by Carl Van Vechten," in *The Collected Writings of Wallace Thurman,* ed. Amritjit Singh and Daniel M. Scott III (New Brunswick, NJ: Rutgers University Press, 2003), 192; review originally appeared in the *Messenger* (September 1926).

55. Van Notten, *Wallace Thurman's Harlem Renaissance,* 127.

56. Carl Van Vechten, letter dated September 7, 1926, James Weldon Johnson Collection, Box 1, Folder 497, Beinecke Rare Books and Manuscript Library, Yale University.

57. Garber, "A Spectacle in Color," 328.

58. Hughes, *Big Sea,* 235.

59. See chapter 1 for a sustained discussion of the relations among voice, affect, and aesthetics. See also Eric King Watts, "'Voice' and 'Voicelessness' in Rhetorical Studies," *Quarterly Journal of Speech* 87 (2001): 179–96.

60. Michael J. Hyde and Kenneth Rufo, "The Call of Conscience, Rhetorical Interruptions, and the Euthanasia Controversy," *Journal of Applied Communication Research* 28 (2000): 1–23.

61. Wallace Thurman, *Infants of the Spring* (1932; repr., Carbondale: Southern Illinois University Press, 1979), 11.

62. Watson, *The Harlem Renaissance.*

63. Thurman, *Infants,* 12.

64. Garber, "The Spectacle in Color," 329.

65. Thurman, *Infants,* 14.

66. Ibid., 12.

67. Cobb, "Insolent Racing, Rough Narrative," 330.

68. Van Notten, *Wallace Thurman's Harlem Renaissance*, 143.

69. Ibid., 179.

70. Thurman, *Infants,* 107.

71. Nugent's signature aids here. He often signed documents "RBNugent," where "ugent" is an illegible, miniscule scrawl. See Richard Bruce Nugent, letter to Alain Locke, October 28, 1926, Alain Locke Collection, Moorland-Spingarn Research Center, Howard University.

72. Silberman, "Looking for Richard Bruce Nugent and Wallace Thurman," 56.

73. Thurman, *Infants,* 20, 21.

74. Ibid., 23.

75. Brody and McBride, "Part 2," 328.

76. Hughes, *Big Sea,* 237.

77. Silberman, "Looking for Richard Bruce Nugent and Wallace Thurman," 59.

78. Thurman, *Infants,* 34.

79. Cobb, "Insolent Racing, Rough Narrative," 335.

80. Garber, "A Spectacle in Color," 329.

81. Thurman, *Infants,* 39.

82. Singh and Scott, *The Collected Writings,* 35.

83. Van Notten, *Wallace Thurman's Harlem Renaissance*, 182, 286.

84. Thurman, *Infants,* 59.

85. The younger group of artists thanked Locke for his interest, sought plenty of advice, and suggested new ventures when old ones died out. See Countee Cullen, letters to Locke, January 29, 1923, April 30, 1923, and October 8, 1924; Zora Neale Hurston, letter to Alain Locke, October 11, 1927, Alain Locke Collection, Moorland-Spingarn Research Center, Howard University.

86. Locke, *The New Negro,* 3.

87. Thurman, *Infants,* 229.

88. Ibid., 230.

89. Ibid., 186, 175.

90. Garber, "A Spectacle in Color," 321.

91. Thurman, *Infants,* 183.

92. Locke's correspondence over the years with Cullen and Nugent reveal emotional valleys experienced by each, suddenly rising into peaks of sunny bliss. See Countee Cullen, letter to Locke, November 1, 1924, Alain Locke Collection, Moorland-Spingarn Research Center, Howard University; Richard Bruce Nugent, letter to Locke, n.d., but most likely written in the early 1930s, Alain Locke Collection, Moorland-Spingarn Research Center, Howard University.

93. Thurman, *Infants,* 186.

94. Garber, "A Spectacle in Color," 322.

95. Thurman, *Infants,* 184, 187.

96. Ibid., 198.

97. Ibid., 190–91.

98. Van Notten, *Wallace Thurman's Harlem Renaissance,* 200.

99. Biddy Martin, "Sexualities Without Genders and Other Queer Utopias," *diacritics* 24 (1994): 104–21.

100. Thurman, *Infants,* 266–70, 267.

101. Thurman, *Infants,* 268. This sentiment was quite a reversal of attitudes commonly held by many elites in Harlem. See Countee Cullen, letter to Locke, January 12, 1923, Alain Locke Collection, Moorland-Spingarn Research Center, Howard University. In it, Cullen asserts that "we" [the youth Locke advised] need guidance and interest from the older generation "more than we need money."

102. Ibid., 57.

103. Van Notten, *Wallace Thurman's Harlem Renaissance,* 108.

104. Thurman, *Infants,* 270.

105. Thurman, *Infants,* 280–81.

106. Ibid., 283.

107. Zora Neale Hurston, letter to Alain Locke, October 11, 1927, Alain Locke Collection, Moorland-Spingarn Research Center, Howard University. Hurston was noting the fact that extant copies of *Fire!!* were destroyed in a blaze.

108. Van Notten, *Wallace Thurman's Harlem Renaissance,* 266.

109. Thurman, *Infants,* 280.

110. Van Notten, *Wallace Thurman's Harlem Renaissance,* 263.

111. Zora Neale Hurston had a favorable impression upon reading *Infants;* she told Locke, "You and I are in it in a small way. Not a bad book at all." Letter to Locke, February 28, 1932, Alain Locke Collection, Moorland-Spingarn Research Center, Howard University.

112. Cobb, "Insolent Racing, Rough Narrative," 335.

113. Van Notten, *Wallace Thurman's Harlem Renaissance,* 267.

114. Siobhan Somerville, *Queering the Color Line: Race and the Invention of Homosexuality in American Culture* (Raleigh, NC: Duke University Press, 2000), 92–93.

115. Patricia Hill Collins, *Black Sexual Politics: African Americans, Gender, and the New Racism* (New York: Routledge, 2004), 95.

116. Van Notten, *Wallace Thurman's Harlem Renaissance*, 263.

117. Ibid., 208–9. Thurman's marriage to Louise Thompson seemed sudden to Locke: Thurman apologized for "the startling news of my marriage to Louise on your return [from Europe]. It was not fair to shock you like that was it?" See Wallace Thurman, letter to Alain Locke on stationery, in *Harlem: A Forum of Negro Life* (October 3 1928). One week later, Thurman received a "bachelor's pious wish" that he and Louise will "be happy and successful." Locke, letter to Thurman, October 8, 1928, Alain Locke Collection, Moorland-Spingarn Research Center, Howard University.

118. Charles I. Nero, "Re/Membering Langston: Homophobic Textuality and Arnold Rampersad's *Life of Langston Hughes*" in *Queer Representations: Reading Lives, Reading Cultures,* ed. Martin Duberman (New York: New York University Press, 1997), 194–95.

119. Henry Louis Gates Jr., "Black Man's Burden," in *Fear of a Queer Planet: Queer Politics and Social Theory,* ed. Michael Warner (Minneapolis: University of Minnesota Press, 1993), 234–35.

120. Countee Cullen, letter to Alain Locke, November 1, 1924, box 164, folder 22, Moorland-Spingarn Research Center, Howard University.

Chapter 8

1. If Carl Van Vechten had been able to convince Countee Cullen that Knopf was the place for his first collection of poetry titled *Color,* the publishing house would have virtually cornered the market. See *The Letters of Carl Van Vechten,* ed. Bruce Kellner (New Haven: Yale University Press, 1987), 85–86; letter to Countee Cullen dated December 11, 1925.

2. George Hutchinson, *In Search of Nella Larsen: A Biography of the Color Line* (Cambridge, MA: Harvard University Press, 2006), 319.

3. W. E. B. Du Bois, the editor of the *Crisis*, consciously recruited fiction and poetry so as to advance race relations; Charles S. Johnson, of *Opportunity,* followed suit in 1923; each journal sponsored literary contests and held award banquets. These aesthetic practices were constitutive of "criteria" for the kinds of artistic practices considered to be most valuable for racial uplift and black representation. See chapters 2 and 3.

4. Margaret Cheney Dawson, "The Color Line," *New York Herald Tribune Books* 5 (April 28, 1929): 6.

5. Indeed, such works were often disparaged as propaganda based on the perception that they were motivated by a racial motive determined by social uplift. See chapters 2 and 5.

6. Dawson, "Color Line," 6.

7. The *Herald Tribune* book editor was Irita Van Doren, the wife of famous journalist and editor of *Century Magazine,* Carl Van Doren; the Van Dorens were also good friends with Carl Van Vechten and Fania Marinoff; see Carl Van Vechten, *The Splen-*

did Drunken Twenties: Selections from the Daybooks, 1922–1930, ed. Bruce Kellner (Urbana, Il.: University of Illinois, 2003), 51; also, Hutchinson, *In Search of Nella Larsen,* 329.

8. Dawson, "Color Line," 6 (emphasis added).

9. Ibid. (emphasis added).

10. Hutchinson, *In Search of Nella Larsen,* 1; the assumption that Larsen died a mystery is common. See Thaddeus Davis, *Nella Larsen, Novelist of the Harlem Renaissance: A Woman's Life Unveiled* (Baton Rouge: Louisiana State University, 1994); Charles Larson, *Invisible Darkness: Jean Toomer and Nella Larsen* (Iowa City: University of Iowa Press, 1993).

11. Hutchinson, *In Search of Nella Larsen,* 21.

12. M. M. Bakhtin, *Toward a Philosophy of the Act* (Austin: University of Texas, 1993). Also see Ernesto Laclau, "Identity and Hegemony: The Role of Universality in the Constitution of Political Logics," in *Contingency, Hegemony, Universality: Contemporary Dialogues on the Left,* ed. Judith Butler, Ernesto Laclau, and Slavoj Žižek (New York: Verso, 2000), 44–89.

13. See chapters 1, 2, 3, and 4 for discussions of these efforts.

14. Jessie Fauset, "Our Book Shelf," *Crisis* 31 (March 1926): 238–39.

15. W. E. B. Du Bois edited *Crisis* between 1910 and 1934.

16. *Crisis* 32 (May 1926): 7. Fauset continued to help Du Bois with the journal with "the less exacting duties of Contributing Editor." Fauset published *There Is Confusion* in 1924, and *Plum Bun* in 1929.

17. Fauset, "Our Book Shelf," 239, 238.

18. Ibid., 238.

19. This is a story of the interracial child who suffers from forms of racial pathology and confusion due to being rejected by white society, but spurns black communities due to a sense of racial superiority. This figure "passes" into white society, but experiences a strange loneliness that pushes her back toward the black folk she abandoned. The denouement of this master narrative reifies racial solidarity by affirming that true love and happiness are structured according to the law of the color line. The story is tragic because often the mulatta experiences forms of physical and psychological trauma on her journeys. Despite the fact that there have been "mulattos," many scholars have also noted how this narrative is gendered feminine and, thus, disciplined the black female body. See Deborah E. McDowell, *"The Changing Same": Black Women's Literature, Criticism, and Theory* (Bloomington, IN: The University of Indiana Press, 1995), 78–100.

20. Hutchinson, *In Search of Nella Larsen,* 1–15, 11; Hutchinson notes that she reneged on promises to donate archival material to the James Weldon Johnson Collection at Yale University; her flight from Harlem in her middle years was likely due to stress over the loss of her husband, Elmer Imes, to a white woman.

21. Catherine Rottenberg, "Passing: Race, Identification, and Desire," *Criticism* 45 (Fall 2003): 435.

22. McDowell, *"The Changing Same,"* 78–100; Houston Baker, *Workings of the*

Spirit: The Poetics of Afro-American Women's Writing (Chicago: University of Chicago Press, 1991).

23. Anthony Dawahare, "The Gold Standard of Racial Identity in Nella Larsen's *Quicksand* and *Passing*," *Twentieth Century Literature* 52, no. 1 (Spring 2006): 22–41.

24. Hutchinson, *In Search of Nella Larsen,* 25, 29–50.

25. Ibid., 53, 54, 50, 63 ("On June 13 they [the faculty] voted that the following students be not allowed to return to the university next year . . . Nellie Larsen.").

26. Ibid., 64–74 (scholars who suture Larsen to the tragic mulatta plot are skeptical of Larsen's claims to have traveled to Copenhagen and being cared for by her mother's family since these events undermine the narrative), 96 (Larsen's life at Tuskegee was hard as she was demanded to pledge allegiance to rigid forms of race loyalty and gendered doctrine), 128 (Elmer Imes was a well-respected physicist).

27. Ibid., 136.

28. Ibid., 132, 160.

29. Larsen met Van Vechten at a party hosted by her friend, Dorothy; see Van Vechten, *Splendid Drunken Twenties,* 73; entry dated Friday, 6 February 1925.

30. Published in 1928, *Quicksand* is appropriately read as semi-biographical. It narrates the life of a "mulatta" named Helga Crane. A restless soul, Crane wanders from place to place in search of something that she cannot quite articulate. She constantly fends off attempts by others and by institutions to control her. Patriarchy produces intense anxiety for her because she fears its embrace. Desperate, she marries a southern preacher and becomes stuck in a cycle of pregnancy and sickness, forever sinking in quicksand.

31. Van Vechten, *Splendid Drunken Twenties,* 132. From the entry dated Wednesday, September 8, 1926.

32. *Peter Whiffle: His Life and Work* was published by Knopf in 1922; *The Blind Bow-Boy,* also published by Knopf, appeared in 1923.

33. Carl Van Vechten, *Nigger Heaven* (New York: Knopf Publishing, 1926).

34. In a letter to Fania Marinoff in January of 1927, Van Vechten admitted to contemplating a book on Hollywood, but lamented that the work would require the kind of research he conducted about the New Negro. See *The Letters of Carl Van Vechten,* ed. Bruce Kellner (New Haven: Yale University Press, 1987), 92.

35. Bruce Kellner, *Carl Van Vechten and the Irreverent Decades* (Norman: University of Oklahoma Press, 1968), 194.

36. *Shuffle Along* opened in 1922 and featured an all-black cast of singers, dancers, and musicians.

37. DuBose Heyward's immensely popular musical showcased compositions by George Gershwin.

38. Rosamond Johnson is the brother of James Weldon Johnson; he was a talented pianist who set to music many folk songs and spirituals dug up by his brother James.

39. Kellner, *The Letters,* 70 (in a letter to Mabel Dodge Luhan dated summer 1924), 56 (see fn3), 74 (in a letter to Scott Cunningham, January 1925, Van Vechten was describing his response to "Paul Robeson singing spirituals").

40. A notable exception to the newly formed rule appears in a letter to Langston

Hughes, where Van Vechten mused that he and Hughes were the only people in Manhattan who fully appreciated "niggers." Kellner, *The Letters,* 95.

41. Kellner, *The Letters,* 58; dated October 30, 1923.

42. Van Vechten, *Splendid Drunken Twenties,* 93; entry dated August 14, 1925.

43. Kellner, *The Letters,* 80; dated June 30, 1925.

44. Ibid., 85–86; letter dated December 20, 1925 (emphasis added).

45. Carl Van Vechten, "The Folksongs of the American Negro: The Importance of the Negro Spirituals in the Music of America," *Vanity Fair* 24 (July 1925): 52, 92; Carl Van Vechten, "The Black Blues: Negro Songs of Disappointment in Love:—Their Pathos Hardened with Laughter," *Vanity Fair* 24 (August 1925): 83, 86, 92; "Negro 'Blues' Singers: An Appreciation of Three Coloured Artists Who Excel in an Unusual and Native Medium," *Vanity Fair* 26 (March 1926): 67, 106; Carl Van Vechten, "Prescription for the Negro Theatre: Being a Few Reasons Why the Great Colored Show Has Not Yet Been Achieved," *Vanity Fair* 25 (October 1925): 46, 92, 98; Carl Van Vechten, "'Moanin' Wid A Sword In Ma Han": A Discussion of the Negro's Reluctance to Develop and Exploit His Racial Gifts," *Vanity Fair* 25 (February 1926): 61, 100, 102.

46. Kellner, *The Letters,* 95; dated early 1927 (emphasis added).

47. See Mark M. Smith, *How Race Is Made: Slavery, Segregation, and the Senses* (Chapel Hill: University of North Carolina Press, 2006).

48. Kellner, *The Letters,* 99; Van Vechten refused to have the novel published; letter to Phillippe Soupault, September 1, 1927 (emphasis added).

49. Van Vechten, *Splendid Drunken Twenties,* 120; in an entry dated May 23, 1926, he referred to his aesthetic experiences of a "sanctified church" introduced to him by Hurston as "exactly like the jungle."

50. Kellner, *The Letters,* 80; to Arthur Davison Ficke, August 3, 1925.

51. Van Vechten, *Splendid Drunken Twenties,* 101; entry dated Wednesday, November 25, 1925, and entry dated Friday, November 27, 1925.

52. *Crisis* 32 (October 1926): 325. The ad reads: "Every reader of *The Crisis* must read *Nigger Heaven* and keep it in his library. It is a book you cannot afford to miss."

53. W. E. B. Du Bois, "Books," *Crisis* 33 (December 1926): 81–82.

54. See Hutchinson, *In Search of Nella Larsen,* 208–20.

55. Langston Hughes, letter dated March 1, 1928, box 164, folder 22, Alain Locke Collection, Moorland-Spingarn Research Center, Howard University.

56. Hutchinson, *In Search of Nella Larsen,* 272.

57. Ibid., 262–72.

58. Nella Larsen, *Passing,* ed. Deborah E. M. McDowell (1929; repr., New Brunswick, NJ: Rutgers University Press, 1986), 210.

59. Larsen, *Passing,* 143.

60. Albert Camus, *The Myth of Sisyphus and Other Essays* (1955; repr., New York: Vintage Books, 1991), 14, 22.

61. Larsen, *Passing,* 143.

62. Joan Copjec, "May '68, The Emotional Month," in *Lacan: The Silent Partners,* ed. Slavoj Žižek (New York: Verso, 2006), 102.

63. Larsen, *Passing,* 145, 143, 150, 151, 161.

64. Ibid., 154, 160, 188, 156, 160, 161, 157, 153.

65. Ibid., 161.

66. Ibid., 161, 163, 161, 163.

67. Hutchinson, *In Search of Nella Larsen,* 296.

68. Butler, Laclau, and Žižek, *Contingency, Hegemony, Universality,* 176.

69. Larsen, *Passing,* 165, 168.

70. Ibid., 170, 171.

71. Audre Lorde, *Sister Outsider: Essays and Speeches* (Berkeley, CA: Crossing Press, 2007), 40–44.

72. Larsen, *Passing,* 171.

73. Mladen Dolar, *A Voice and Nothing More* (Cambridge, MA: MIT Press,2006), 99.

74. Brian Massumi, *Parables for the Virtual: Movement, Affect, Sensation* (Durham, NC: Duke University Press, 2002), 27.

75. Larsen, *Passing,* 171.

76. Ibid., 188, 224.

77. Ibid., 196 (emphasis added), 225.

78. Ibid., 199, 222, 235.

79. Ibid., 226, 227, 238, 239.

80. W. E. B. Du Bois, "The Browsing Reader," *Crisis* 36 (July 1929): 248.

81. Hutchinson, *In Search of Nella Larsen,* 97–98. I am not indicating a bright line between this tragic event and Clare's figurative demise; only that the correspondence between the two is provocative.

Postscript

1. Martin Heidegger, "The Origin of the Work of Art," in *Basic Writings,* ed. David Farrell Krell (New York: HarperCollins, 2008), 139–206.

2. Jacques Ranciere, *The Politics of Aesthetics* (NY: Continuum Books, 2004), 42–45.

3. Catherine Chaput, "Rhetorical Circulation in Late Capitalism: Neoliberalism and the Overdetermination of Affective Energy," *Philosophy and Rhetoric* 43 (2010): 1–25.

4. Russ Castronova and Susan Gilman, *States of Emergency: The Object of American Studies* (Chapel Hill: University of North Carolina Press, 2009), 1–16.

5. Thomas B. Farrell, *Norms of Rhetorical Culture* (New Haven: Yale University Press, 1993).

6. Michael Calvin McGee, "The 'Ideograph': A Link Between Rhetoric and Ideology," *Quarterly Journal of Speech* 66 (1980): 1–16.

7. *Norms of Rhetorical Culture* literally ends with the word "life"; Farrell revealed this strategy to me once in a conversation regarding my writing.

8. Ranciere, *The Politics of Aesthetics*, 45.

9. Paul Gilroy, *Against Race: Imagining Political Culture Beyond the Color Line* (Cambridge, MA: Harvard University Press, 2000), 21.

10. Eric King Watts, "The Problem of Race in Public Address Research: W. E. B. Du Bois and the Conflicted Aesthetics of Race," in *Handbook on Rhetoric and Public Address,* ed. Shawn Parry-Giles and J. Michael Hogan (Malden, MA: Wiley-Blackwell, 2010), 373–97.

11. Ranciere, *The Politics of Aesthetics*, 22.

12. Ibid., 12–15, 42–43.

13. Ibid., 22.

14. Michel Foucault, "What Is an Author?" in *The Foucault Reader,* ed. Paul Rabinow (New York: Vintage Books, 2010), 101–20.

15. Ranciere, *The Politics of Aesthetics*, 29.

16. Jacques Ranciere, *Dissensus: On Politics and Aesthetics,* trans. Steve Corcoran (New York: Continuum, 2010), 134–51.

17. Ranciere, *The Politics of Aesthetics,* 24 (emphasis added).

18. Ibid., 26.

19. Eric King Watts, "The (Nearly) Apocalyptic Politics of Post-Racial America: Or, 'This is Now the United States of Zombieland,'" *Journal of Communication Inquiry* 34 (2010): 214–22.

Bibliography

Agamben, Giorgio. *Homo Sacer: Sovereign Power and Bare Life.* Translated by Daniel Heller-Roazen. Stanford: Stanford University Press, 1988.

Alpern, Sara. *Freda Kirchwey: A Woman of "The Nation."* Cambridge, MA: Harvard University Press, 1987.

Althusser, Louis. *Essays on Ideology.* 1975. London: Verso, 1984.

Appelbaum, David. *Voice.* Albany, NY: State University of New York Press, 1990.

Aptheker, Herbert. *The Correspondence of W. E. B. Du Bois,* Vol. 1 *Selections, 1877–1934.* Amherst, MA: University of Massachusetts Press, 1973.

Baker, Houston, Jr. *Afro-American Poetics: Revisions of Harlem and the Black Aesthetic.* Madison, WI: University of Wisconsin Press, 1988.

———. *The Long Black Song: Essays in Black American Literature.* Charlottesville, VA: University of Virginia Press, 1972.

———. *Workings of the Spirit: The Poetics of Afro-American Women's Writing.* Chicago: University of Chicago Press, 1991.

Bakhtin, M. M. *Toward a Philosophy of the Act.* Edited by Michael Holquist and Vadim Liapunov. Translated by Vadim Liapunov. Austin, TX: University of Texas Press, 1993.

Banks, William M. *Black Intellectuals: Race and Responsibility in American Life.* New York: W. W. Norton & Co., 1996.

Barnes, Albert C. "Negro Art and America." In Alain Locke, *The New Negro: An Interpretation,* 19–25.

Bassett, John E. *Harlem in Review: Critical Reactions to Black American Writers.* Cranbury, NJ: Association of University Presses, 1992.

Bell, Barnard. "W. E. B. Du Bois's Struggle to Reconcile Folk and Hight Art." In *Critical Essays on W. E. B. Du Bois,* edited by William L. Andrews, 106–22. Boston: G. K. Hall & Co., 1985.

Bloom, Edward, and Lillian Bloom. *Satire's Persuasive Voice.* Ithaca, NY: Cornell University Press, 1979.

Bontemps, Arna. *Harlem Renaissance Remembered.* New York: Dodd, Mead & Co., 1972.

Bracken, Christopher. *Magical Criticism: The Recourse of Savage Philosophy.* Chicago: University of Chicago Press, 2007.

Brennan, Teresa. *The Transmission of Affect.* Ithica, NY: Cornell University Press, 2004.

Brody, Jennifer DeVere, and Dwight A. McBride. "Introduction: Part 2: Plum Nelly: New Essays in Black Queer Studies." *Callaloo* 23, no. 1 (2000): 286–88.

Brown, Sterling. "Negro Characters as Seen by White Authors." *Journal of Negro Education* 2, no. 2 (1933): 179–203.

Broyard, Anatole. *Intoxicated by My Illness: And Other Writings on Life and Death.* New York: Fawcett Columbine Books, 1992.

Buck, Christopher. "Alain Locke: Race Leader, Social Philosopher, Baha'i Pluralist." *World Order* 36 (2005): 7–48.

Burke, Kenneth. "Four Master Tropes." In *A Grammar of Motives,* 503–517. Berkeley, CA: University of California Press, 1969.

Butler, Judith. *Bodies That Matter: On the Discursive Limits of "Sex."* New York: Routledge, 1993.

Camus, Albert. *The Myth of Sisyphus and Other Essays.* 1955. New York: Vintage Books, 1991.

Carby, Hazel. *Race Men.* Cambridge, MA: Harvard University Press, 1989.

Carpenter, Edward. *Iolaus: An Anthology of Friendship.* London: Swan Sonnenschein, 1902.

Carroll, Anne Elizabeth. *Word, Image, and the New Negro: Representation and Identity in the Harlem Renaissance.* Bloomington, IN: Indiana University Press, 2005.

Castronova, Russ, and Susan Gilman. *States of Emergency: The Object of American Studies.* Chapel Hill, NC: University of North Carolina Press, 2009.

Chaput, Catherine. "Rhetorical Circulation in Late Capitalism: Neoliberalism and the Overdetermination of Affective Energy." *Philosophy and Rhetoric* 43 (2010): 1–25.

Chauncey, George. *Gay New York: Gender, Urban Culture, and the Making of the Gay Male World, 1890–1940.* New York: Basic Books, 1994.

Cioran, E. M. *The Trouble with Being Born.* New York: Arcade Publishing, 1973.

Clark, John R. "Vapid Voices and Sleazy Styles." In Connery and Combe, *Theorizing Satire,* 19–42.

Cleghorn, Sarah N. "But of Course No Social Equality!" *World Tomorrow* (March 1922): 84.

Cobb, Michael L. "Insolent Racing, Rough Narrative: The Harlem Renaissance's Impolite Queers." *Callaloo* 23 (2000): 328–51.

Collins, Patricia Hill. *Black Sexual Politics: African Americans, Gender, and the New Racism.* New York: Routledge, 2004.

Connery, Brian A., and Kirk Combe. *Theorizing Satire: Essays in Literary Criticism.* New York: St. Martin's Press, 1995.

Cooley, John R. *Savages and Naturals: Black Portraits by White Writers in Modern American Literature.* Newark, NJ: Associated University Presses, Inc., 1982.

Copjec, Joan. "May '68, The Emotional Month." In *Lacan: The Silent Partners,* edited by Slavoj Žižek, 90–114. New York: Verso, 2006.

Cullen, Countee. "The Negro in Art: How Shall He Be Portrayed? A Symposium." *Crisis* 32 (August 1926): 194.

Darsey, James. "'The Voice of Exile': W. E. B. Du Bois and the Quest for Culture." In *Rhetoric and Community: Studies in Unity and Fragmentation,* edited by J. Michael Hogan, 93–110. Columbia, SC: University of South Carolina Press, 1988.

Davis, Thaddeus. *Nella Larsen, Novelist of the Harlem Renaissance: A Woman's Life Unveiled.* Baton Rouge: Louisiana State University Press, 1994.

Dawahare, Anthony. "The Gold Standard of Racial Identity in Nella Larsen's Quicksand and Passing." *Twentieth Century Literature* 52, no. 1 (2006): 22–41.

Dawson, Margaret Cheney. "The Color Line." *New York Herald Tribune Books,* April 28, 1929: 6.

de Certeau, Michel. *The Practice of Everyday Life.* Berkeley, CA: University of California Press, 1984.

de Jongh, James. *Vicious Modernism: Black Harlem and the Literary Imagination.* Cambridge: Cambridge University Press, 1990.

DeFalco, Amelia. "Jungle Creatures and Dancing Apes: Modern Primitivism and Nella Larsen's Quicksand." *Mosaic: A Journal for the Interdisciplinary Study of Literature* 38 (June 2005): 19–35.

Deleuze, Gilles, and Felix Guattari. *A Thousand Plateaus: Capitalism and Schizophrenia.* Minneapolis: University of Minnesota Press, 1987.

Dennis, Rutledge M. "Relativism and Pluralism in the Social Thought of Alain Locke." In *Alain Locke: Reflections on a Modern Renaissance Man,* edited by Russell J. Linnemann, 31. Baton Rouge, LA: Louisiana State University, 1982.

Dewey, John. *Art as Experience.* New York: Minton, Balch & Co., 1934.

———. *The Public and its Problems.* New York: Henry Holt & Co., 1927.

Dolar, Mladen. *A Voice and Nothing More.* Cambridge, MA: MIT Press, 2006.

Du Bois, W. E. B. "Agitation." *Crisis* 1 (November 1910): 11.

———. *Black Reconstruction in America, 1860–1880.* 1935. New York: Free Press, 1992.

———. "Books." *Crisis* 33 (December 1926): 81–82.

———. "The Browsing Reader." *Crisis* 36 (July 1929): 248.

———. *The Conservation of the Races.* Occasional Papers, no. 2. The American Negro Academy, 1897.

———. "The Contribution of the Negro to American Life." *Pacific Review* (June 1921).

———. "The Crisis." *Crisis* 1 (November 1910): 10.

———. "Criteria of Negro Art." *Crisis* 32 (October 1926): 290–97.

———. "Culture through Literature in Terms of Sociological Foundations." Amherst, MA: University of Massachusetts, W. E. B. Du Bois Collection, n.d.

———. *Darkwater: Voices from within the Veil.* 1920. New York: Kraus-Thomson, 1975.

———. *Dusk of Dawn: An Essay toward an Autobiography of a Race Concept.* New York: Harcourt, Brace & Co., 1945.

. "Easter." *Crisis* 1 (April 1911): 20.

———. "The Essence of African Culture." *Forum* (February 1925): 7–9.

———. "The Ethiopian Art Theatre." *Theatre Magazine* 38 (July 1923).

———. "The Gall of Bitterness." *Crisis* 4 (February 1912): 153.

———. "An Institute of Negro Literature and Art." *Crisis* 24 (June 1922): 58–59.

——. "Jefferson Davis as Representative of Civilization." In *W. E. B. Du Bois: A Reader,* edited by David Levering Lewis, 17–19.

——. "The Manufacture of Prejudice: Three American Fairy Tales from the Associated Press." *Crisis* May 1911: 35–37.

——. "Negro Culture." Amherst, MA: University of Massachusetts, W.E.B. Du Bois Collection, not dated.

——. "The Negro Mind Reaches Out." In Alain Locke, *The New Negro: An Interpretation,* 385–414.

——. "Our Book Shelf." *Crisis* 31 (January 1926): 141.

——. "Our Policy." *Crisis* 11 (1916): 133.

——. "Parting of the Ways." In *W. E. B. Du Bois: A Reader,* edited by David Levering Lewis, 329–32.

——. "The Primitive Black Man." *Nation,* December 17, 1924: 675–76.

——. "Promotion of Prejudice." *Crisis* 2 (September 1911): 196.

——. "The Segregated Negro World." *World Tomorrow* (May 1923): 136–37.

——. "The Social Origins of American Negro Art." *Modern Quarterly* 3 (October–December 1925): 53–56.

——. *The Souls of Black Folk.* 1903. New York: Oxford Univerity Press, 2007.

——. "Triumph." *Crisis* 2 (September 1911): 194.

——. "The Value of Agitation." *Voice* 4 (March 1907): 109–10.

——. "What is Civilization: Africa's Answer." *Forum* (February 1925).

——. "The Woman." *Crisis* 1 (May 1911): 19.

——. "Writers." *Crisis* 1 (April 1911): 20–21.

Du Bois, W. E. B., and Alain Locke. "The Younger Literary Movement." *Crisis* 27 (February 1924): 161–63.

Du Bose, Heyward. "The Negro in Art: How Shall He Be Portrayed? A Symposium." *Crisis* 31 (March 1926): 220.

Eagleton, Terry. *The Ideology of the Aesthetic.* Malden, MA: Blackwell Publishing, 1990.

Farrar, John. "The Negro in Art: How Shall He Be Portrayed? A Symposium." *Crisis* 31 (April 1926): 280.

Farrell, Thomas B. *Norms of Rhetorical Culture.* New Haven, CT: Yale University Press, 1993.

Fauset, Jessie. "The Gift of Laughter." In Alain Locke, *The New Negro: An Interpretation,* 161–67.

——. "Our Book Shelf." *Crisis* 31 (March 1926): 238–39.

Favor, Martin J. *Authentic Blackness: The Folk in the New Negro Renaissance.* Durham, NC: Duke University Press, 1999.

Fisher, Rudolph. *New York Herald Tribune Books,* February 21, 1932: 16.

Foley, Barbara. *Spectres of 1919: Class and Nation in the Making of the New Negro.* Urbana, IL: University of Illinois Press, 2003.

Foucault, Michel. "What Is an Author?" In *The Foucault Reader,* edited by Paul Rabinow, 101–20. New York: Vintage Books, 2010.

Fox, Stephen R. *The Guardian of Boston: William Monroe Trotter.* New York: Pantheon Books, 1970.

Gadamer, Georg-Hans. *Philosophical Hermeneutics.* Berkeley, CA: University of California Press, 1976.

Garber, Eric. "A Spectacle in Color: The Lesbian and Gay Subculture of Jazz Age Harlem." In *Hidden from History: Reclaiming the Gay and Lesbian Past,* edited by Martin Bauml Duberman, Martha Vicinus, and George Chauncey Jr., 327. New York: New American Library, 1989.

Gates, Henry Louis, Jr. "Black Man's Burden." In *Fear of a Queer Planet: Queer Politics and Social Theory,* edited by Michael Warner, 230–38. Minneapolis: University of Minnesota Press, 1993.

———. "The Trope of a New Negro and the Image of the Black." *Representations* 24 (1988): 129–55.

Gates, Henry Louis, Jr., and Nellie Y. McKay. *The Norton Anthology of African American Literature.* New York: W. W. Norton & Co., 1997.

Gerstle, Gary. *American Crucible: Race and Nation in the Twentieth Century.* Princeton, NJ: Princeton University Press, 2001.

Gilroy, Paul. *Against Race: Imagining Political Culture beyond the Color Line.* Cambridge, MA: Harvard University Press, 2000.

Goldman, Alan. *Aesthetic Value.* Boulder, CO: Westview Press, 1995.

Grayling, A. C. *Life, Sex, and Ideas: The Good Life without God.* Oxford: Oxford University Press, 2003.

Griffin, Dustin. *Satire: A Critical Reintroduction.* Lexington, KY: The University Press of Kentucky, 1994.

Habermas, Jurgen. *The Theory of Communicative Action,* vol. 2, *Lifeworld and System: A Critique of Functionalist Reason.* Translated by Thomas McCarthy. Boston: Beacon Press, 1987.

Hackett, Robin. *Sapphic Primitivism: Productions of Race, Class, and Sexuality in Key Works of Modern Fiction.* New Brunswick, NJ: Rutgers University Press, 2004.

Hale, Grace Elizabeth. *Making Whiteness: The Culture of Segregation in the South, 1890–1940.* New York: Pantheon Books, 1998.

Halliwell, Stephen, trans. *Republic 10: Plato with Translation and Commentary.* Warminster: Aris & Phillips, 1988.

Harlan, Louis R. *The Booker T. Washigton Papers,* vol. 3. Urbana, IL: University of Illinois Press, 1974.

Harris, Leonard, and Charles Molesworth. *Alain L. Locke: Biography of a Philosopher.* Chicago: University of Chicago Press, 2008.

Heidegger, Martin. *Being and Time.* Translated by John Macquarrie and Edward Robinson. New York: Harper, 1962.

———. "The Origin of the Work of Art." In *Basic Writings,* edited by David Farrell Krell, 139–206. New York: Harper Collins, 2008.

———. "The Question Concerning Technology." In *Basic Writings,* edited by David Farrell Krell, 311–341. New York: Harper Collins, 2008.

Huggins, Nathan Irvin. *Harlem Renaissance.* New York: Oxford University Press, 1971.

Hughes, Langston. *The Big Sea: An Autobiography.* New York: Hill and Wang, 1940.

———. "The Negro Artist and the Racial Mountain." *Nation,* June 23, 1926: 692–94.

———. "The Negro in Art: How Shall He Be Portrayed? A Symposium." *Crisis* 31 (April 1926): 278.

———. *The Weary Blues.* New York: Alfred A. Knopf, 1926.

Hughes, Langston, and Carl Van Vechten. *Remember Me to Harlem: The Letters of Langston* Hughes and Carl Van Vechten, 1925–1964. Edited by Emily Bernard. New York: Alfred A. Knopf, 2001.

Hurston, Zora Neale. "How It Feels to Be Colored Me." *World Tomorrow* (May 1928).

Hutchinson, George. *In Search of Nella Larsen: A Biography of the Color Line.* Cambridge, MA: Harvard University Press, 2006.

Hyde, Michael J., *The Call of Conscience: Heidegger and Levinas: Rhetoric and the Euthanasia Debate.* Columbia, SC: University of South Carolina Press, 2001.

———. *Perfection: Coming to Terms with Being Human.* Waco, TX: Baylor University Press, 2010.

Hyde, Michael J., and Kenneth Rufo. "The Call of Conscience, Rhetorical Interruptions, and the Euthanasia Controversy." *Journal of Applied Communication Research* 28 (2000): 1–23.

Ihde, Don. *Listening and Voice: Phenomenologies of Sound.* 2nd ed. Albany, NY: State University of New York, 2007.

Kant, Immanuel. *The Critique of Judgment.* Translated by J. H. Bernard. Amherst, NY: Prometheus Books, 2000.

Kaplan, Carla. *Zora Neale Hurston: A Life in Letters.* New York: Anchor Books, 2003.

Kellner, Bruce. *Carl Van Vechten and the Irreverent Decades.* Norman, OK: University of Oklahoma Press, 1968.

———, ed. *The Letters of Carl Van Vechten.* New Yaven, CT: Yale University Press, 1987.

Kirschke, Amy Helene. *Art in Crisis: W. E. B. Du Bois and the Struggle for American American Identity and Memory.* Bloomington, IN: Indiana University Press, 2007.

Knopf, Alfred A. "The Negro in Art: How Shall He Be Portrayed? A Symposium." *Crisis* 31 (April 1926): 280.

Kornweibel, Theodore, Jr. *"Seeing Red": Federal Campaigns Against Black Militancy, 1919–1925.* Bloomington, IN: Indiana University Press, 1998.

Laclau, Ernesto. "Identity and Hegemony: The Role of Universality in the Constitution of Political Logics." In *Contingency, Universality, Hegemony: Contemporary Dialogues on the Left,* edited by Judith Butler, Ernesto Laclau, and Slavoj Žižek, 44–89. New York: Verso Books, 2000.

Lamothe, Daphne. *Inventing the New Negro: Narrative, Culture, Ethnography.* Philadelphia: University of Pennsylvania Press, 2008.

Larsen, Nella. *Passing.* 1929. New Brunswick, NJ: Rutgers University Press, 1986.

Larson, Charles. *Invisible Darkness: Jean Toomer and Nella Larsen.* Iowa City, IA: University of Iowa Press, 1993.

Leak, Jeffrey B. *Rac[e]ing to the Right: Select Essays of George S. Schuyler.* Knoxville, TN: University of Tennessee Press, 2001.

Lemke, Sieglinde. *Primitivist Modernism: Black Culture and the Origins of Transatlantic Modernism.* New York: Oxford University Press, 1998.

Lewis, David Levering. *W. E. B. Du Bois: Biography of a Race, 1868–1919*. New York: Henry Holt & Co., 1993.

———. *W. E. B. Du Bois: Fight for Equality and the American Century, 1919–1963*. New York: Henry Holt & Co., 2000.

———. *When Harlem Was in Vogue*. New York: Oxford University Press, 1979.

Locke, Alain. "Beauty Instead of Ashes." *Nation*, April 18, 1928: 432–34.

———. "The Colonial Literature of France." *Opportunity: Journal of Negro Life* 1 (November 1923): 331.

———. "Enter the New Negro." *Survey Graphic* IV, no. 6 (March 1925): 631–34.

———. *Four Negro Poets: The Pamphlet Poets*. New York: Simon & Schuster Publishers, 1927.

———. "A Functional View of Value Ultimates." In *The Philosophy of Alain Locke: Harlem Renaissance and Beyond*, edited by Leonard Harris, 79–93. Philadelphia: Temple University Press, 1989.

———, ed. "Harlem: Mecca of the New Negro." Special issue, *Survey Graphic* VI, no. 6 (March 1925).

———. "The Negro's Contribution to American Art and Literature." *Annals of American Academy of Political and Social Science* 140 (1928): 234.

———. *The New Negro: An Interpretation*. 1925. New York: Arno Press, 1968.

———. "Pluralism and Intellectual Democracy." In *The Philosophy of Alain Locke: Harlem and Beyond*, edited by Leonard Harris, 51–66. Philadelphia: Temple University Press, 1989.

———. "Roland Hayes: An Appreciation." *Opportunity: Journal of Negro Life* 1 (December 1923): 356.

———. "This Year of Grace." *Opportunity: Journal of Negro Life* 9 (February 1931): 51.

———. "Unity Through Diversity." In *The Philosophy of Alain Locke: Harlem Renaissance and Beyond*, edited by Leonard Harris, 133–38. Philadelphia: Temple University Press, 1989.

———. "Values and Imperatives." In *American Philosophy, Today and Tomorrow*, edited by Horace M. Kallen and Hook Sidney, 313. New York: Lee Furman, Inc., 1935.

Lorde, Audre. *Sister/Outsider: Essays and Speeches by Audre Lorde*. 1984. Berkeley, CA: Crossings Press, 2007.

Lundberg, Christian. "Enjoying God's Death: The Passion of the Christ and the Practices of an Evangelical Public." *Quarterly Journal of Speech* 95 (2009): 387–411.

Martin, Biddy. "Sexualities Without Gender and Other Queer Utopias." *diacritics* 24 (1994): 104–21.

Mason, Ernest. "Alain Locke's Philosophy of Value." In *Alain Locke: Reflections on a Modern Renaissance Man*, edited by Russell J. Linneman, 1–16. Baton Rouge, LA: Louisiana State University, 1982.

Massumi, Brian. *Parables for the Virtual: Movement, Affect, Sensation*. Durham, NC: Duke University Press, 2002.

McCabe, Tracey. "The Multifaceted Politics of Primitivism in the Harlem Renaissance Writing." *Soundings* 80, no. 4 (1997): 475–97.

McDowell, Deborah E. *"The Changing Same": Black Women's Literature, Criticism, and Theory.* Bloomington, IN: University of Indiana Press, 1995.

McGee, Michael Calvin. "The 'Ideograph': A Link Between Rhetoric and Ideology." *Quarterly Journal of Speech* 66 (1980): 1–16.

Meier, August. *Along the Color Line: Explorations in the Black Experience.* Urbana, IL: University of Illinois Press, 2002.

———. *Negro Thought in America, 1880–1915: Racial Ideologies in the Age of Booker T. Washington.* Ann Arbor, MI: University of Michigan Press, 1988.

Mencken, H. L. "The Negro in Art: How Shall He Be Portrayed? A Symposium." *Crisis* 31 (March 1926): 219.

Miller, R. Baxter. *The Art and Imagination of Langston Hughes.* Lexington, KY: University Press of Kentucky, 2006.

Monroe, Harriett. "Introduction." In *The Congo and Other Poems,* by Vachel Lindsay, vi. New York: The MacMillan Co., 1914.

Morrison, Toni. *The Bluest Eye.* New York: Holt, Rinehart, and Winston, 1970.

———. *Playing in the Dark: Whiteness and the Literary Imagination.* Cambridge, MA: Harvard University Press, 1992.

Nadell, Martha Jane. *Enter the New Negro: Images of Race in American Culture.* Cambridge, MA: Harvard University Press, 2004.

Nero, Charles. "Re/Membering Langston: Homophobic Textuality and Arnold Rampersad's Life of Langston Hughes." In *Queer Representations: Reading Lives, Reading Cultures,* edited by Martin Duberman, 188–96. New York: New York University Press, 1997.

Norrell, Robert J. *Up From History: The Life of Booker T. Washington.* Cambridge, MA: Harvard University Press, 2009.

Osborne, Michael. "Archetypal Metaphor in Rhetoric: The Light-Dark Family." *Quarterly Journal of Speech* 53 (1967): 115–26.

Ovington, Mary White. "The Negro in Art: How Shall He Be Portrayed? A Symposium." *Crisis* 31 (March 1926): 220.

Patterson, Orlando. *Rituals of Blood: Consequences of Slavery in Two American Centuries.* Washington, DC: Civitas/Counterpoint, 1998.

Peplow, Michael. *George S. Schuyler.* Boston: Twayne Publishers, 1980.

Peterkin, Julia. "The Negro in Art: How Shall He Be Portrayed? A Symposium." *Crisis* 32 (September 1926): 239.

Plato. *Great Dialogues of Plato.* Translated by W. H. D. Rouse. New York: Penguin Books, 1956.

Posnock, Ross. *Color and Culture: Black Writers and the Making of the Modern Intellectual.* Cambridge, MA: Harvard University Press, 1998.

Povinelli, Elizabeth. "Settler Modernity and the Quest for an Indigenous Tradition." In *Alternative Modernities*, edited by Dilip Gaonkar, 24–57. Durham, NC: Duke University Press, 2001.

Rampersad, Arnold. *The Art and Imagination of W. E. B. Du Bois.* Cambridge, MA: Harvard University Press, 1976.

———. "Hughes' *Fine Clothes to the Jew.*" In *Langston Hughes: Critical Perspectives Past and Present*, edited by Henry Louis Gates Jr. and K. A. Appiah, 59. New York: Amistad Press, 1993.

———. "Introduction." In *The New Negro: Voices of the Harlem Renaissance*, ix–xxiii. New York: Touchstone, 1997.

———. *The Life of Langston Hughes*, Vol. 1: *1902–1941, I, Too Sing America*. New York: Oxford University Press, 2002.

Ranciere, Jacques. *Dissensus: On Politics and Aesthetics.* Translated by Steve Corcoran. New York: Continuum, 2010.

———. *The Politics of Aesthetics.* Translated by Gabriel Rockhill. New York: Continuum, 2004.

Reed, Adolph L., Jr. "Du Bois's 'Double Consciousness': Race and Gender in Progressive Era American Thought." *Studies in American Political Development* 6 (1992): 93–139.

———. *W. E. B. Du Bois and American Political Thought: Fabianism and the Color Line.* New York: Oxford University Press, 1997.

Roediger, David. *Working toward Whiteness: How America's Immigrants Became White.* New York: Basic Books, 2005.

Rorty, Richard. *Objectivity, Relativism, and Truth: Philosophical Papers*, Vol. 1. New York: Cambridge University Press, 1991.

Rosenfield, Lawrence W. "The Practical Celebration of Epideictic." In *Rhetoric in Transition: Studies in the Nature and Uses of Rhetoric*, edited by Eugene E. White, 131–55. College Park, PA: Pennsylvania State University Press, 1980.

Rottenberg, Catherine. "Passing: Race, Identification, and Desire." *Criticism* 45 (2003): 435–53.

Santayana, George. *The Sense of Beauty: Being the Outline of Aesthetic Theory.* New York: Dover Publications, 1955.

Scarry, Elaine. *The Body in Pain: The Making and Unmaking of the World.* New York: Oxford University Press, 1985.

———. *On Beauty and Being Just.* Princeton, NJ: Princeton University Press, 1999

Schuyler, George S. "At the Coffee House." *Messenger* 7 (June 1925): 236–37.

———. "At the Darktown Charity Ball." *Messenger* 6 (December 1924): 377–78.

———. *Black and Conservative: The Autobiography of George S. Schuyler.* New Rochelle, NY: Arlington House Publishers, 1966.

———. "Blessed Are the Sons of Ham." *Nation*, March 1927: 313–14.

———. "The Negro and Nordic Civilization." In Jeffrey B. Leak, *Rac[e]ing to the Right*, 3–12. Knoxville: University of Tennessee Press, 2001.

———. "The Negro-Art Hokum." *Nation*, June 16, 1926: 662–63.

———. "Our White Folks." In *Speech and Power: The African American Essay and Its Cultural Content From Polemics to Pulpit*, edited by Gerald Early, 289–94. New York: Ecco Press, 1993.

Scott, Emmett J. "Our Book Shelf." *Crisis* 31 (November 1925): 32–33.

Scruggs, Charles W. "Alain Locke and Walter White: Their Struggle for Control of the Harlem Renaissance." *Black American Literature Forum* 14 (1980): 91–99.

Scruton, Roger. *The Aesthetic Understanding: Essays in the Philosophy of Art and Culture.* Manchester: Carcanet Press, 1983.

Sherrard-Johnson, Cherene. *Portraits of the New Negro Woman: Visual and Literary Culture in the Harlem Renaissance.* New Brunswick, NJ: Rutgers University Press, 2007.

Shusterman, Richard. *Pragmatist Aesthetics: Living Beauty, Re-Thinking Art.* 2nd ed. New York: Rowman & Littlefield, 2000.

Silberman, Seth Clark. "Looking for Richard Bruce Nugent and Wallace Thurman: Reclaiming." *In Process: A Graduate Student Journal of African American and African Diasporan Literature and Culture* 1 (1996): 53–73.

Smith, Mark. *How Race Is Made: Slavery, Segregation, and the Senses.* Chapel Hill, NC: University of North Carolina Press, 2006.

Somerville, Siobhan. *Queering the Color Line: Race and the Invention of Homosexuality in American Culture.* Durham, NC: Duke University Press, 2000.

Spingarn, Joel. "The Negro in Art." *Crisis* 31 (April 1926): 279.

Stoddard, Lothrop. *The Rising Tide of Color against White World Supremacy.* New York: Charles Scribner's Sons, 1920.

Thurman, Wallace. *Infants of the Spring.* 1932. Carbondale, IL: Southern Illinois University, 1979.

———. "A Stranger at the Gates: A Review of Nigger Heaven, by Carl Van Vechten." In *The Collected Writings of Wallace Thurman,* edited by Amritjit Singh and Daniel M. Scott III, 192. New Brunswick, NJ: Rutgers University Press, 2003.

Too, Yun Lee. "Epideictic Genre." In *The Encyclopedia of Rhetoric,* 253. New York: Oxford University Press, 2001.

Torgovnick, Marianna. *Gone Primitive: Savage Intellects, Modern Lives.* Chicago: University of Chicago Press, 1990.

Toulmin, Stephen. *Cosmopolis: The Hidden Agenda of Modernity.* Chicago: University of Chicago Press, 1990.

Turner, Darwin. "W. E. B. Du Bois and the Theory of a Black Aesthetic." In *Critical Essays on W. E. B. Du Bois,* edited by William L. Andrews, 73–92. Boston: G. K. Hall & Co., 1985.

Tyler, Bruce. *From Harlem to Hollywood: The Struggle for Racial and Cultural Democracy.* New York: Garland Press, 1992.

van Notten, Eleonore. *Wallace Thurman's Harlem Renaissance.* Amsterdam: Costerus New Series 93, 1994.

Van Vechten, Carl. "The Black Blues: Negro Songs of Disappointment in Love—Their Pathos Hardened with Laughter." *Vanity Fair* 24 (August 1925): 83, 86, 92.

———. "The Folksongs of the American Negro: The Importance of the Negro Spirituals in the Music of America." *Vanity Fair* 24 (July 1925): 52, 92.

———. "'Moanin' Wid a Sword in Ma Han': A Discussion of the Negro's Reluctance to Develop and Exploit his Racial Gifts." *Vanity Fair* 25 (February 1926): 61, 100, 102.

———. "Negro 'Blues' Singers: An Appreciation of Three Coloured Artists Who Excel in an Unusual and Native Medium." *Vanity Fair* 25 (March 1926): 67, 106.

———. "The Negro in Art: How Shall He Be Portrayed? A Symposium." *The Crisis,* March 1926: 219.

———. *Nigger Heaven.* New York: Knopf Publishing, 1926.

———. "Prescription for the Negro Theatre: Being a Few Reasons Why the Great Colored Show Has Yet Been Achieved." *Vanity Fair,* October 1925: 46, 92, 98.

———. *The Splendid Drunken Twenties: Selections from the Daybooks, 1922–1930.* Edited by Bruce Kellner. Urbana, IL: University of Illinois Press, 2003.

Washington, Booker T. *A New Negro for a New Century: An Accurate and Up-to-Date Record of the Upward Struggles of the Negro Race.* 1900. New York: Arno Press, 1969.

Watson, Steven. *The Harlem Renaissance: Hub of African American Culture.* New York: Pantheon, 1995.

Watts, Eric King. "African American Ethos and Hermeneutical Rhetoric: An Exploration of Alain Locke's *The New Negro.*" *Quarterly Journal of Speech* 88 (2002): 19–32.

———. "The (Nearly) Apocalyptic Politics of Post-Racial America: Or, "'This is Now the United States of Zombieland.'" *Journal of Communication Inquiry* 34 (2010): 214–22.

———. "The Problem of Race in Public Address Research: W.E.B. Du Bois and the Conflicted Aesthetics of Race." In *Handbook on Rhetoric and Public Address,* by Shawn Parry-Giles and J. Michael Hogan, 373–97. Malden, MA: Wiley-Blackwell, 2010.

———. "Voice and Voicelessness in Rhetorical Studies." *Quarterly Journal of Speech* 87 (2001): 179–96.

Weaver, Richard. *The Ethics of Rhetoric.* 1953. Davis, CA: Hermagoras Press, 1984.

Wiethoff, William E. *The Insolent Slave.* Columbia, SC: University of South Carolina Press, 2002.

Wintz, Cary. *The Politics and Aesthetics of "New Negro Literature."* New York: Garland Press, 1996.

Zamir, Shamoon. *Dark Voices: W. E. B. Du Bois and American Thought.* Chicago: University of Chicago Press, 1995.

Index